LEXICOGRAPHICA Series Maior

LEXICOGRAPHICA

Series Maior

Supplementary Volumes to the International Annual for Lexicography
Suppléments à la Revue Internationale de Lexicographie
Supplementbände zum Internationalen Jahrbuch für Lexikographie

Edited by
Sture Allén, Pierre Corbin, Reinhard R. K. Hartmann,
Franz Josef Hausmann, Hans-Peder Kromann, Oskar Reichmann,
Ladislav Zgusta

20

Published in cooperation with the Dictionary Society of North America (DSNA) and the European Association for Lexicography (EURALEX)

The DANLEX-Group
Ebba Hjorth, Bodil Nistrup Madsen, Ole Norling-Christensen,
Jane Rosenkilde Jacobsen, Hanne Ruus

Descriptive Tools for Electronic Processing of Dictionary Data

Studies in Computational Lexicography

Mit einer deutschen Zusammenfassung /
Avec un résumé français

Max Niemeyer Verlag
Tübingen 1987

CIP-Kurztitelaufnahme der Deutschen Bibliothek

Descriptive tools for electronic processing of dictionary data : studies in computational lexicography ; mit e. dt. Zusammenfassung ; avec un résumé français / the DANLEX-Group. – Tübingen : Niemeyer, 1987.
(Lexicographica : Series maior ; 20)
NE: Danske Lexikografiske Gruppe; Lexicographica / Series maior

ISBN 3-484-30920-2 ISSN 0175-9264

Printed in Germany. Druck: Weihert-Druck GmbH, Darmstadt.

PREFACE

This book presents the results of several years' cooperation on the description of lexicographical data for the purposes of electronic data processing. In the course of this work the differences in our disciplinary backgrounds have been a great asset. Inspiration and helpful comment have come from many of our fellow lexicographers. Special thanks must go to Birgitte Lau, who took part in the work of the DANLEX group in the initial phases; to Bodil Vestergaard, who experimented in the autumn of 1986 with the storage of our data in database systems; and to Gert Engel, who has constantly followed the work and lent advice and assistance. We would also like to take this opportunity to thank our translator, James Manley, whose linguistic and lexicographical expertise has made a substantial contribution to the presentation of our results. The responsibility for any errors and inconsistencies, however, lies of course with the authors alone. Finally, we thank *Statens Humanistiske Forskningsråd* — the Danish Research Council for the Humanities — whose interest in and economic support for the field of computers and lexicography has been of crucial importance for our project.

April 1987 The DANLEX Group

CONTENTS

1. INTRODUCTION

This book grew out of a wish on the part of the authors to use the power of the computer for lexicographical cooperation: cooperation between lexicographers and publishers, between the editors of individual dictionaries, between authors and users of dictionaries, and between different dictionaries.

The DANLEX group itself is an example of cooperation between five people with expertise in lexicography, computational linguistics, terminology, publishing, Scandinavian philology and modern languages. Its members are Ebba Hjorth, leader of the *Gammeldansk Ordbog* dictionary project of the Danish Society for Language and Literature; Jane Rosenkilde Jacobsen, research assistant at the Lexicographical Centre at the Department of Linguistics of the University of Copenhagen; Bodil Nistrup Madsen, Lecturer at the Department of Computational Linguistics of the Copenhagen School of Economics and Business Administration; Ole Norling-Christensen, Editor-in-Chief at the Dictionary Department of the Gyldendal Publishing House; and Hanne Ruus, Lecturer at the Department of Scandinavian Philology and Head of the Danish EUROTRA research unit. The work was begun at the initiative of the Danish Research Council for the Humanities, which has promoted computational lexicography through the research initiative *Edb for Tekst, Tale og Ordbøger* (ETTO 1983-85) (Computers for Text, Spoken Language and Dictionaries) and *Forskningsprogrammet for Teknologisk Udvikling* (FTU, from 1986) (the Research Programme for Technological Development). The overall rubric for our work is Electronic Processing of Dictionary Data.

After experiments with the general description of a number of Danish dictionaries (Hjorth 1984) it emerged that there is a need for various tools for the description of lexicographical data. We need both a classificatory apparatus, a taxonomy or typology of the many different types of information in dictionaries, and a formal apparatus for the description of structure, a notation capable of registering how the different types of information are interrelated within a given lexicographical work.

The classification of the information in a dictionary into categories for data processing is nothing new (cf Chapter 2). But the present study has both a broader and a deeper aim. We generalize the categories into a taxonomy meant to cover many very different types of dictionary (Chapter 3), and we test the taxonomy as a descriptive apparatus on radically different types of dictionary (Chapter 4). We also attempt to formalize and standardize the format description thoroughly and consistently and detail how the formalized description can be used to process data from a printed dictionary (Chapter 5); and in two chapters (6 and 7) we demonstrate how dictionary data, once described and structured, can be recorded and stored in a computer, and discuss the demands that one must make as a lexicographer on software for the processing of lexicographical data.

If dictionary formats are uniformly described, using a common taxonomy, cooperation among dictionary projects can be made considerably easier. The advantages we gain from this are:

- a unique description of the content of the dictionaries that can form a basis for comparative work;
- the possibility of wholly or partially automatic exchanges of lexical data among different dictionaries;
- that the lexicographer is helped to compile dictionary entries with as much consistency and as little wasted time as possible;
- the potential to produce dictionaries with different types of content on the basis of the same dictionary data;
- that the same dictionary can be presented in various ways in printed or other media;
- that it becomes easier to consult, revise and update dictionary data.

Of course all this requires, besides a standardized taxonomy and format description, dictionary information that is available or can be made available in machine-readable form, and that software suitable for processing dictionary data exists or can be developed.

So far we have seen the issue from the "editorial" angle; but consideration for the users points in the same direction. Teachers in primary and secondary education appear to prefer the dictionaries used in different language subjects to be uniformly structured (Norling-Christensen 1983). Experience suggests that this greatly facilitates the acquisition of dictionary skills. If the format used for editing such dictionaries is as standardized as possible and uniform printing conventions are used to represent it, the desired uniformity will be ensured.

Finally, in our experience taxonomy and format work lead to a fruitful interplay between editorial rules — often only vaguely formulated — and experiments with an exhaustive formal description of the structure of the book or manuscript. A rule which proves difficult or impossible to formulate will often turn out to reflect some vagueness in the text to be described. Editorial awareness of this may lead to new principles of arrangement that will make the dictionary more accessible to its users. Even where rules are clear enough in themselves, a formal description can lead to increased awareness of editorial practice. If the description becomes very complex, the editors must ask themselves whether this reflects a mode of presentation that complicates access to the information for the users. Examples of this ("telescoping", etc.) are dealt with in Chapter 4.

The computerization of lexicographical work primarily involves controlling and ordering processes, while excerpting and editing still build almost exclusively on brainwork. Given precise descriptions of lexicographical data it will gradually become possible to have computer support in excerpting and editing.

Many dictionaries now exist in machine-readable form. But lexicographical cooperation with computerized systems is not yet as smooth as it could be. Quite a few systems and stand-alone programs are already used internationally in dictionary work — publishers and research departments have them, software companies can provide them — but they have usually been developed with a specific dictionary or dictionary type in mind, and the systems used are not compatible with those of other projects. Yet development costs are high, and prohibitive for many projects. A common system will enable many users in the public, semi-public and private spheres to draw on the same resources.

The taxonomy, the tools for the description of structure and lexicographical specifications for computer systems offered here represent knowledge that can be incorporated in the design of a general computer system for lexicographical work. A flexible general system will be a substantial step forward in making the computer a productive tool for lexicography (Ruus 1981).

2. DESCRIPTIVE TOOLS OF METALEXICOGRAPHY

2.1 The general metalexicographical situation

In "A Terminological Note: 'Multiword Lexical Unit'", an appendix to a *DSNA Newsletter* (1983), the Dictionary Society of North America's Committee on Lexicographic Terminology has asked the members of the society how they employ the following lexicographical terms in practice:

> *bound syntagma, complex lexeme, compound lexical unit, compound lexical item, conjunct, fixed phrase, idiom, lexeme, lexeme cluster, lexicalized phrase, locution, MLU, multi-word lexeme, multi-word lexical unit, polylexeme, set collocation, set phrase* and *syntheme*.

Each of these terms has been seen employed in various places in the lexicographical literature — in metalexicography — to refer to what Zgusta in his *Manual of Lexicography* (1971) calls a *multiword lexical unit*; the terms have been seen, for example, in the discussion of the phenomenon that "at least a fifth of all the entry words given in *Webster's Third New International Dictionary* are composed of two or more simple words." In this respect it is mentioned that Kocourek (1979) has stated that lexicographical literature in French uses at least 25 different terms to refer to the concept *multiword lexical unit*.

The object of the terminological questionnaire appended to the newsletter is not to arrive at one preferred term; it is primarily to investigate whether the various lexicographers really mean the same thing by all these terms — some of which (for example, *idiom* and *lexeme*) also have other uses. It is stated, however, that a certain preferential status will be accorded to the term that is chosen as a keyword for the main treatment of the concept, in the event of the results of the survey being used in the compilation of a prospective dictionary or glossary of *well-established* lexicographical terms.

A similar effort to clarify the terminological problems of lexicography is found in the lexicographical handbook project presented in the article "Konzeption zu einem internationalen Handbuch der Lexikographie" (Hausmann/Reichmann/Wiegand/Zgusta 1984). The handbook is planned as a 2000-page work furnished with a *Sachregister*, concerning which the authors (1984: 494) say:

> Das Sachregister wird dreisprachig (deutsches Lemma, englisches und französisches Äquivalent und Verweislemmata in diesen Sprachen) angelegt. Es soll über die Aufschlüsselung der im Handbuch behandelten Sachgebiete einen Beitrag zur Systematisierung, Standardisierung und Internationalisierung der lexikographischen Terminologie liefern.

The object of the handbook is described (1984: 489) as:

> ... die Metalexikographie, genauer: der Metabereich der Sprachlexikographie, also die Gesamtheit all derjenigen wissenschaftlichen Bemühungen, deren Ergebnis nicht selbst ein Wörterbuch ist, sondern die darauf abzielen, alle mit dem Erarbeiten von Wörterbüchern verbundenen theoretischen Fragestellungen und methodischen Verfahrensweisen zu registrieren, zu beschreiben, zu bewerten und dadurch zur Verbesserung der lexikographischen Praxis beizutragen.

The projects described above are indicative of the present metalexicographical situation: almost every time metalexicography is enriched by a new idea, the total inventory of terms used to describe the lexicographical data is also increased. Lexicographical terms multiply, and this situation can easily impede or even prevent communication; for what, quite specifically, is meant by all these terms? And — more important still — how are they interrelated? Is there complete or only partial equivalence between certain of the different terms or sets of terms?

One of the most important reasons for the terminological difficulties in lexicography — apart from scholarly inventiveness in general — is that metalexicography borrows its terms from the other branches of linguistics. But linguistics is not just *one* science of language: language can be and is scientifically described in terms of a voluminous and steady flow of emergent theoretical positions which carries with it an equally steady flow of new terms. Theoretical linguistics and its subdisciplines are constantly affected by new impulses, and this means that lexicography, as an applied linguistic discipline, is also constantly fed by new impulses that are discussed in metalexicographical terms.

One such new impulse comes from the use of computers in various branches of both theoretical and applied linguistics.

2.2 Lexicography and computers

Particularly within the last fifteen years computers have found increasing use internationally in the various phases of lexicographical work: the recording, description and presentation of data for the purpose of dictionary production.[1].

Kipfer (1984: 162 ff) characterizes these three phases as follows:

1. Collection and the transfer of data from its original form to another, including citation retrieval (RECORDING),
2. Sorting and alphabetizing, including lemmatization and homograph separation (DESCRIPTION),
3. Editorial and analysis procedures including definition writing and the composition of entries (PRESENTATION).

---

1. Knowles (1983) has a short overview of computational linguistics, the mechanization of practical lexicographical work processes and machine translation systems. Urdang (1984) gives, on the basis of his rich personal experience, an outline of the history of computers in lexicography since the very first hesitant attempts, which Urdang himself was responsible for. Landau (1984: 272 ff) reviews the history of the computer in lexicography; this survey too bears the imprint of the author's personal experience of using computers to produce dictionaries. Kipfer (1984: 161 ff), in the chapter on "Computer applications in lexicography" gives a brief review of the subject under the subject headings "A. Introduction and a short history"; "B. Processes"; "C. Further and special applications"; "D. The automated dictionary as a teaching tool"; "E. Computer archives" and "F. Conclusion". Kipfer (1983) is a bibliography of "Computer applications in lexicography" whose most important titles are discussed explicitly in Kipfer (1984: 161 ff). Amsler (1984) gives a thorough review of work in English on machine-readable dictionaries; Heß/Brustkern/Lenders (1983) do the same for German machine-readable dictionaries.

Goetschalckx/Rolling (1982); Hartmann (1983, 1984); the forthcoming proceedings of ZüriLEX '86, EURALEX International Congress, 9 — 14 September 1986, Zürich, Switzerland; of the ESF/IAI Conference on "Standardization in Computerized Lexicography", 15 — 17 October 1986, Saarbrücken, Federal Republic of Germany; and those of the workshop "On Automating the Lexicon", 19 — 23 May 1986, Marina di Grosseto, Italy — all provide both overviews and reports from various projects in computer-aided lexicography.

In the first phase texts are recorded in machine-readable form, making the (partially) automatic second phase possible — lemmatization and homograph separation still require human intervention. In the second phase the lexicographical raw material is formed, while the third phase converts this into lexicographical data proper as they appear, for example, in printed dictionaries or term banks.

The presentation phase is the one that requires most brain-work: in this phase the computer is used in the first instance for word-processing purposes, that is for making fair copies of traditionally compiled dictionary entries — either draft entries or finished versions, with the computer as a handy tool for making corrections; but at this stage the computer also offers the possibility of preparing the entry material for storage in and retrieval from a database. To this end the lexicographical data can be ordered in coded *fields*. These fields contain the lexicographical data as distinct information categories, the construction of which must both be appropriate to the product — for example printed dictionaries or on-screen dictionary information — and to the ends the lexicographer wishes to make possible. Such ends may be the data processing of the product in hand, or allowing for later use of the lexicographical data for other purposes, whether other dictionaries or linguistic analysis of a more theoretical nature. In addition, computerized storage or filing permits the exchange of lexicographical data in machine-readable form.

2.3 Metalexicographical descriptive apparatuses with and without computers in mind

It is especially in the third phase of the lexicographical work that the terminological problems of lexicography, in the form of metalexicographical descriptive apparatuses exhibiting varying degrees of congruence, encounter on the one hand the computer's promise of database storage and thus of multi-user access to the lexicographical data; and on the other the demands that data processing makes on the preparation of such data.

For example, if subsets of a lexicographical database are to be retrieved, exchanged or used otherwise than in the immediate product, it is essential that these subsets contain one or more informational categories with unambiguous names for unambiguous data identification. The way one orders lexicographical data in various coded or named information categories, however, is very much determined by the needs one wants to cater for.

With the following examples of some of the variety of metalexicographical descriptive systems we will try not only to show how differently the ordering of the data into information categories can be approached depending on electronic processing needs and the type of lexicographical product required; but also how differently the data can be described depending on the metalexicographical communication purposes of the description. We will cite some systems for the comparative description of a collection of machine-readable dictionaries; for the description of monolingual dictionaries; for that of translation dictionaries; and for onomasiological dictionaries.

2.3.1 Apparatuses for the comparative description of a collection of machine-readable dictionaries: the BONNLEX lexicon system and the MDW draft for lexical microstructure

The BONNLEX lexicon system, presented in Brustkern/Heß (1982) has been built up on the basis of detailed comparative analyses of a number of machine-readable German dictionaries and lexica, only one of which was originally meant to function as a traditional dictionary. The others were intended to function in various ways in automatic question-and-answer systems, dialogue simulation systems, and in indexing, machine translation and other computerized systems.

The intended application of BONNLEX is the production of an integrated, cumulative word database including material from the dictionaries and lexica analysed. For this purpose a so-called lexicon structure has been worked out that can collate the existing lexical data and incorporate new data.

In a rough outline Brustkern/Heß (1982: 36 f) present the microstructure of this dictionary database — that is, the structure of each of the lexical entries that go to make up the macrostructure of the dictionary — as follows.

Each lexical entry consists of a number of units of information from the following lexicologically determined "K" classes:

K_1 : spelling (graphemics) WG
of the lexeme entered in the lexicon
K_2 : phonology P
the phonetic transcription, with information on syllabification and stress
K_3 : lemma L
information on the basic form found in each form of an inflectional paradigm
K_4 : word class WK
classification of word types defined in syntactic, morphological or semantic terms
K_5 : information on the morphology of inflections F
details on the declension of substantive elements, such as case, number, gender and degree of comparison, on the conjugation of verbal elements, such as person, number, mood, tense and voice (active/passive), and on ways of forming the compound past
K_6 : derivation data D
details on the word formation process using derivational morphemes
K_7 : syntactic environment OS
surface structure, valency, rection, surface case
K_8 : deep case TS
the required deep-case frame
K_9 : semantic information SEM
(see below)

In an entry of this kind, which consists of the tuple

$$LE_i = (WG_i, P_i, L_i, WK_i, F_i, D_i, OS_i, TS_i, SEM_i)$$

individual information units can be broken down still further. Thus, the semantic part of the lexicon (SEM) might itself consist of a 6-tuple:

SEM = (DEF, SEMKON, ANW, SEREL, PRIM, FG)

where

DEF	=	semantic definition, explanation of meaning
SEMKON	=	semantically relevant context, semantic environment
ANW	=	examples of use
SEREL	=	semantic relationships
PRIM	=	semantic primitives
FG	=	marking of specialized field

Characteristic of this system is the fact that "alle Angaben prinzipiell als gleichrangig aufgefaßt werden", as it is formulated in Heß/Brustkern/Lenders (1983: 26) in a comment on the formal structure required in word databases. This means that there are access and search facilities in the BONNLEX database that provide a basis for various types of sorting by way of any given unit of information. This way one avoids the traditional classification of dictionaries as either semasiological or onomasiological (1983: 28 f)(cf Chapter 3).

The existing BONNLEX system is a pilot system, specially designed to answer simple questions put to the database, and for the study of screen dialogue techniques, as is evident from Heß/Brustkern/Lenders (1983: 218). Here too (1983: 33 ff) one finds an outline of a somewhat altered structure for this system, the MDW draft for lexical microstructure.[2] The structural alterations affect the following points:

1. Wortlaut WG

> ... die im Lexikon eingetragene Repräsentation der lexikalischen Einheit ... Andere hier synonym gebrauchte Begriffe aus der Literatur sind "Worteintrag", "Suchwortlaut", "Stichwort" bzw. "Identifikationswortlaut". (Diese Informationseinheit kann ... weitere graphische Angaben enthalten, wenn graphische Varianten verzeichnet werden sollen ...)

In contrast to the BONNLEX system, WG in the MDW draft thus also includes orthographic variants.

3. Wortklasse WK

Here it is stressed that the classification into parts of speech found in the WK of the BONNLEX system is dependent on the selected grammatical model.

4. Morphologie M

> ... setzt sich in erster Linie aus den flexionsmorphologischen Angaben und den Derivationsangaben zusammen. Ggf. kann eine "Grundform" hinzutreten, wenn diese nicht algorithmisch abgeleitet werden kann oder soll.

So M in the MDW draft comprises the BONNLEX system's L, F and D.

---

2. The name used, MDW, is an abbreviation of the title of Heß/Brustkern/Lenders (1983), i.e."Maschinenlesbare deutsche Wörterbücher".

5. Syntaktische Angaben (Oberflächen/Tiefenstrukturen) SYN

The SYN of the MDW draft thus combines the OS and TS of the BONN-LEX system.

6. Semantische Angaben SEM

The SEM of the MDW draft takes the form of the BONNLEX SEM minus FG.

7. Pragmatik PRA

> Zum Bereich der pragmatischen Information im Wörterbuch sind Angaben zu zählen, wie sie z.B. von Wiegand (1981) aus "auffälligen Wörterbucheinträgen" als pragmatische Kommentare herausgezogen wurden (S. 146):
>
> - Angaben zur Stilschicht
> - Gebrauchsangaben
> - Kommentare zu Beispielen
> - Belegstellenangaben
>
> Wiegand faßt die pragmatische Information als eine besondere "pragmatische Markierung" lexikalischer Sprachzeichen auf (S. 165 ff), die durch eine pragmatische Kommentarsprache angegeben werden können. Für eine solche pragmatische Kommentarsprache entwirft Wiegand anhand einer Beispielanalyse einige Vorschläge, die in eine systematische Typologie pragmatischer Informationen mündet. Als Beispiele seien aus dieser Typologie die pragmatischen Informationstypen "diakritische Zeichen" [i.e symbols indicating, for example, style register], "Zuordnung zu einem System von Schreibe-/Sprecharten", "wertende Prädikaten" [i.e. evaluative statements], "Verbesserungsvorschläge", "Gebrauchsangaben", "Stilschicht", "Sprachvarietät", "Sprachstadium", "Frequenz", "Illokution", "Situation" und "Textsorte" erwähnt.

The reason the BONNLEX system does not include an independent informational unit for pragmatic information is evident from the following comment in Heß/Brustkern/Lenders (1983: 36):

> In der vorliegenden Arbeit wird der pragmatische Bereich weitgehend außer Betracht gelassen, da derartige Angaben in den untersuchten Lexika nicht berücksichtigt oder in anderen Informationseinheiten untergebracht wurden.

It should be emphasized that neither the BONNLEX nor the MDW version allows for information on equivalence in other languages or etymological information — unless one chooses to regard etymological information as a pragmatic category. But Heß/Brustkern/Lenders (1983: 32) state explicitly that etymological information is not included because it has no function in a lexicon intended for automatic language processing.

What both the BONNLEX system and the MDW draft are aiming at is thus a monolingual, non-historical — i.e. synchronic — word/dictionary database; but, as is evident from the very existence of both the BONNLEX system and the MDW draft, there are two different classifications of information categories and thus two different metalexicographical apparatuses for establishing such a word database. This is of course because the systems in question are apparatuses designed to encourage discussion in connection with a developing project.

2.3.2 Descriptive apparatuses for monolingual dictionaries

2.3.2.1 Schaeder's proposal for a "Gestaltung der lexikalischen Mikrostruktur"

After discussing the BONNLEX system/MDW draft, it seems appropriate to cite Schaeder's systematic list (1981: 101 ff) of the specifications or information expected for each lexeme in a dictionary entry, as Heß/Brustkern/Lenders (1983: 31 f) take Schaeder's list as their point of departure in arguing against the inclusion of features like the above-mentioned etymological information in a word/dictionary database intended for working with the modern language.

Schaeder's proposal for a "Gestaltung der lexikalischen Mikrostruktur" is aimed at the computer-aided production of a traditional, i.e. printed, dictionary of the semasiological, monolingual, synchronic type, but including information on the history of the language. His ideal requirements for such a dictionary consist of the following information categories — which do not, however, have to be in the order specified and do not all have to be present simultaneously in a given dictionary entry:

1. Repräsentation

   1.1 Lemma
   1.2 Aussprache, Betonung, Silbentrennung
   1.3 Wortformenvorkommen
   1.4 Orthographische Variante(n)
   1.5 Kennzeichnung als Kurzwort, Abkürzung etc.
   1.6 Verweise auf Zentralartikel

2. Explikation

   2.1 Erzählerische und/oder ikonische Darstellung
   2.2 Grammatische Angaben
   2.3 Paradigmatische Relationen
   2.4 Syntagmatische Relationen
   2.5 Phraseologischer Gebrauch
   2.6 Angaben über stilistische, areale, fachsprachliche, sondersprachliche Zuordnungen
   2.7 Angaben zur Wortbildung
   2.8 Angaben zur Wortgeschichte (Bezeichnungs-, Bedeutungswandel, fremdsprachlicher Einfluß, Etymologie)

3. Demonstration

   3.1 Ausgewählte Belege des Gebrauchs
   3.2 Statistische Angaben
   3.3 Bibliographische Nach- bzw. Hinweise

Elsewhere in his thesis (1981: 193 ff) Schaeder uses a slightly altered scheme in the form of a grid or matrix for the presentation of the lemma *Betrieb*, and at one point fills out an information category somewhat differently from what one would expect, given its name.

This applies to the following items in the above list. Item 1.2 is filled out with

Be|trieb, der; -(e)s, -e

so that grammatical information — on gender and inflection — is also given here. This placing of grammatical information seems to be connected with the fact that Item 2.2, called "Grammatische Angaben" above, has been replaced by "2.2 Bedeutungserklärung", while "Grammatische Angaben" no longer exists as an independent information category. The text for Item 1.5 has now become "Kennzeichnung als bzw. Hinweise auf Kurzformen"; while Item 1.6 is now "Verweise auf andere Wörterbuchartikel"; in both cases the new category names seem to be clarifying improvements. In the text for Item 2.6 "sowie historische" has been inserted between "sondersprachliche" and "Zuordnungen", so that allowance now also seems to have been made for the temporal dimension.

Schaeder undoubtedly uses two slightly different metalexicographical descriptive schemes because, as with the BONNLEX system and the MDW draft, this is a tentative scheme connected with work in progress.

Schaeder's two descriptive apparatuses include quite a number of elements not found in the BONNLEX/MDW complex. This is true, for example, of "Verweise"; "Erzählerische und/oder ikonische Darstellung"; "Phraseologischer Gebrauch" as an independent category; and "Angaben zur Wortgeschichte" with its subcategories. In addition Schaeder's metalexicographical universe is differently structured; for example, "Statistische Angaben" — which does not exist in the BONNLEX system and which in the MDW draft appears as pragmatic information under "Frequenz" along with "(Angaben zur) Stilschicht" — appears in Schaeder's list as an autonomous category.

Schaeder's universe is structured in the three main sections "Repräsentation", "Explikation" and "Demonstration", grouped together as "Das Wörterbuchartikeltrias"; this structure seems to be predicated on the text comprehension functions of the lexicographical information, since "Wörterbuch-artikel" is regarded as a "Textsorte" (1981: 101 ff), where "Repräsentation des Lexems" as a superordinate category includes "Angaben zu ... Erscheinungs- bzw. Ausdrucksform", "Explikation" includes the various forms of "Erklärung", and "Demonstration" covers any type of "Nachweis des Vorkommens des Lexems als Wort in Texten".

The BONNLEX system, however, operates exclusively with linguistically derived categories like "graphemics", "phonology", "lemma", "word class", "morphology of inflections", "derivation", "syntactic environment", "deep case" and "semantic information", which the MDW draft restructures into "Wortlaut", "Phonetik, Phonologie", "Wortklasse", "Morphologie", "Syntaktische Angaben", "Semantische Angaben" and "Pragmatik".

Schaeder's and the BONNLEX/MDW metalexicographical descriptive apparatuses thus have a lot of elements in common, but with different names and ordered differently. This can be assumed to be due to their different functions, i.e description for the purposes of a traditional printed dictionary and automatic language processing respectively — although in both cases the intentions are monolingual-synchronic.

2.3.2.2 The Longman Dictionary of Contemporary English (LDOCE)

The LDOCE (1978) is a semasiologically-orientated, monolingual, synchronic "learner's dictionary", published in traditional printed form, but produced with extensive use of computers (1978: ix). Thus the LDOCE has its semasiological orientation and monolinguality as well as its synchronicity and computerization in common with the above-mentioned dictionary systems and ideals. But the metalexicographical descriptive apparatuses used in connection with the LDOCE differ substantially in certain respects from those mentioned above.

Besides this, the relationship between the names and the number of information categories that appear in the LDOCE's front matter for the user (1978: viii ff) and those used for the database storage of the dictionary provides us with an interesting insight into the use of different metalexicographical descriptive schemes according to the purpose of the description.

Michiels/Noël (1984: 386) have a figure showing the following database information categories for the LDOCE:

1. HEADWORD
2. PRONUNCN
3. POSINFLE (Part of Speech + inflections)
4. ENTRYCOD (grammatical and other codes for whole entry)
5. DEFINCOD (codes applying to a single definition)
6. DEFINTXT (text of the definition; also includes examples)
7. USAGNOT (usage note)
8. ENTRYTYP (includes homograph number and information on number of words and respective POS in multiple word entries)

But in the contents of the LDOCE'S "Guide to the Dictionary" we find the following set of more or less familiar names for lexicographical information categories:

3 Types of word
4 Syllable division
5 Variant
6 Pronunciation
7 Inflections
8 Labels
9 Punctuation in the dictionary
10 Examples
11 Cross-references
12 Idioms
13 Collocations
14 Related words listed without explanation
15 Affixes and combining forms
16 Usage notes
17 Grammar in the dictionary

Another set of rather less familiar names for lexicographical information types appears in the "Explanatory Chart" in the first section of the "Guide to the Dictionary", where framed sections of dictionary entries are identified for the user. A number of examples of the terms used for information types are "main entry"; "a different word that may be used, in American English, instead of this one"; "grammatical information about a noun; not the same for all meanings"; "the phrase in which this word nearly always appears when it has this meaning, with more explanation if necessary"; "note giving more information about grammar or meaning"; "many clear examples of the use of the word, with a line between each example"; "example showing how the same meaning can be understood when used of things not seen or touched"; "special expression (idiom)"; "word with the opposite meaning"; "part of speech"; "word for person or animal when female"; "shortened form (ABBREVIATION) shown at its own place in the dictionary"; "verb that is always used with another word such as *with*, *on* or *into* (a PREPOSITION), or with an adverb. These are always shown as a separate entry"; "example taken from a collection of real speech and writing"; "information about the use of a grammatical word, given either before the meaning, as here, or instead of a meaning"; "information about how words are built up by adding an ending (SUFFIX); in this case, that when it is added to an adjective it forms a noun of the stated kind"; "pronunciation, with

American form after the double line (||)"; "irregular plural and its pronunciation"; "double consonants in the past and present participles of a verb (*lagged, lagging*)"; "grammatical information about a verb; used sometimes, but not always, with other words such as *with*, *on*, or *into* (PREPOSITIONS), or with certain adverbs"; "type of object with which this verb is used"; "use in English limited to the country stated", "information about possible other forms of the word (in this case, that *leaner* and *leanest* are possible forms); the same for all meanings"; etc.

All these explanations are provided with page references to more thorough treatments in the front matter, which makes up a total of about forty pages.

The striking thing about these three descriptive systems is the extreme differences in the number of elements and degree of formalization. In the Explanatory Chart a descriptive scheme with very little formalization is used: everyday phrases with a slight admixture of lexicographical terminology are used to explain to the user in detail how the various framed lexicographical data are to be understood. The LDOCE is a "learner's dictionary"; so the descriptive apparatus employed in the LDOCE's "Guide to the Dictionary" is not assumed to be familiar to the reader already, but can be learned by using the dictionary. For this descriptive apparatus consists of the most widespread English lexicographical terms — those that can be found, for example, in the "Glossary of English Lexicographical Terms A - Z" in Kipfer (1984) and the "Terminological Index" in Hartmann (1983). In this connection it can be mentioned, for example, that "main entry" is just one of the many names for what in English alone is called "entry word", "lemma", "headword", "guide word", "entry-head", "keyword", "word-entry" or "entry", as can be seen from Kipfer (1984).

There has thus been consideration for the communicative needs of both the lexicographically naive and the lexicographically aware user: for the one, a very informal and minutely detailed descriptive scheme with a very large inventory of information categories and thus a strong explanatory effect; and for the other a fairly formalized traditional descriptive apparatus with a much smaller inventory of information categories and only the minimum necessary explanatory power provided by keywords. The descriptive apparatus for the advanced user is incidentally quite reminiscent of Schaeder's systems in terms of both the degree of formalization and the extent of the inventory.

What is notable about the LDOCE's database-orientated metalexicographical descriptive apparatus is its small inventory, both compared with the two user-orientated systems and with the descriptive schemes of the BONNLEX system and the MDW draft. The latter two also allow for several subcategories of their respecttive nine and seven main categories. The other machine-readable dictionary that Michiels/Noël use in the study described in their article is *The (New) Collins Concise English Dictionary* (1982), which manages with only three database-orientated information categories, in the order "HEADWORD (headword number and identification)"; "POSINFLE", with information on part of speech and inflections; and "DEFINTXT", containing definitions and text. Great differences can thus be observed in the degree of detailed information categorization required by these various dictionary projects in order to enable electronic processing.

Communication with the users and electronic processing factors thus both play a role for the design of the three different metalexicographical schemes used for describing the LDOCE's lexicographical data.

2.3.3 Descriptive apparatuses for translation dictionaries. The Canadian Dictionary: An Experiment in Automated Lexicography

If we now turn to the bilingual translation dictionary, we can find in Wilton (1978) both an example of a metalexicographical descriptive apparatus that is explicitly designed for computer processing of bilingual lexicographical data (English-French/French-English); and a rather different metalexicographical descriptive apparatus used for broader discussions of the bilingual data.

Wilton (1978: 408) uses the following computer-orientated system of information categories:

A	(ENTRY)	Phonetics	Graphics
B	(GRAMMAR)		

C (FIELD)
D (LANG.LEVEL)
E (DIALECT)
F (EXTENSION)
G (TRANSLATION)
H (USAGE)
J (X-REFERENCE)
K (INVERSION)

— where F includes combinations and compounds containing the headword, and K is a project-internal field with information on whether the "ENTRY"—"TRANSLATION" relationship has been inverted for the purposes of a bilingual dictionary going in the opposite direction. The one category that is itself subdivided is "ENTRY", which has pronunciation and spelling fields associated with it.

As was the case above with the names and degree of detail of the types of lexicographical information in the list of contents for the LDOCE's "Guide to the Dictionary", compared with those of its database-orientated categories, Wilton uses another set of names and a different degree of detail in the metalexicographical descriptive scheme used for the discussion in the article itself. Here we find names or terms like "entry word", "level of formality", "field of reference", "dialect type", "translation equivalent", "explanatory rubrics", "warning devices", "morphological paradigms", "subject field", "syntagmatic expressions", "semantic level", "homographs", "exponent numbers" [i.e. homograph numbers], "derivative forms", "canonical form", "compounds", "simple phrases", "locutions figées", "proverbs", "metaphorical expressions", "usage note" — that is, considerably more, different and more detailed terms than in the descriptive scheme intended exclusively for computerization.

It is incidentally striking that the information category "TRANSLATION" can contain not only one translation, but several at once, and that these are furnished with grammatical comments, as can be seen from a diagram of the data file for the headword *horn'* (1978: 411). There has thus been no intention of splitting grammatical information on equivalents off into their own categories. Similarly, the numbering of polysemic variants has been integrated into the information category "FIELD" along with the field labelling of specialized uses.

It is thus clear that the function (data processing/discussion) of a metalexicographical descriptive apparatus plays a role in its design.

2.3.4 Descriptive apparatuses for onomasiological dictionaries

2.3.4.1 The DANTERM record

The DANTERM record (1986)(see Fig. 2.3.4.1-1) is a format for the construction of an individual record in a computerized filing and retrieval system which is to form the basis of a term bank. The individual records are intended for the registration of specialized, i.e. terminological, information. The structure and inventory of information categories in the DANTERM record therefore primarily reflects a terminological working method, i.e. one that takes its point of departure in the *concept* and attempts to catalogue and describe its potentially different *expressions* — the *terms*. It is thus an onomasiological method, rather than the semasiological method characteristic of traditional monolingual and bilingual dictionaries. In addition, it registers and describes terms from several different languages.

Fig. 2.3.4.1-1 The DANTERM record

DANTERM record

PROJ	project name
CLASS	DANTERM classification
LANG	the languages covered in the record
NUM	identification number
TERMS	all registered terms
APPL	area of application
DEF	definition
ADD	additional definition
EXPL	explanation
ILL	illustration

ITERATIVE INFORMATION

TERM	(including information on suggested translations)
GRAM	grammatical information on the term
PHON	pronunciation
REG	linguistic region
ALT	alternative form of term, including:
ABBR	abbreviated form
NONABBR	non-abbreviated form
ORTGR	orthographic variant
SYMB	symbol
SPEC	special usage
STYL	style register
REF	source reference for term
EX	example(s)
TEXT	context(s)
TEXT {language}	language-pair related parallel texts
SYNTAG	syntagm(s)
SYNTAG {language}	language-pair related syntagms
NOTE	notes on the term
THES	thesaurus, including:
USE	descriptor
UF	(used for) non-descriptor
BT	broader term
NT	narrower term
RT	related term
AT	associated term

COM — comments on several terms or the whole record
QUASYN — quasi-synonym(s)
QUASYNOTE — notes on quasi-synonyms
DEPR — deprecated term

ITERATIVE INFORMATION

SYST	name of conceptual system
POS	position number of concept in conceptual system
REL	conceptual relations, including:
BC-GEN	broader concept (generic relation)
BC-PART	broader concept (part-whole relation)
BC	broader concept (no relation type specified)
NC-GEN	narrower concept (generic relation)
NC-PART	narrower concept (part-whole relation)
NC	narrower concept (no relation type specified)
PREC	preceding concept (successive relations)
SUCC	succeeding concept (successive relations)
CAUS	causal relation
ANTO	antonym
RC	related concept

EQ<language>		comments on equivalence in language pairs
EQADD<language>		additional comments on equivalence in language pairs
REV		information on reversibility
SUPPL		reference to supplementary information (drawings, tables, etc.) (drawings, tables etc.)
FACTS		supplementary factual information
FACTS<language>		supplementary factual information, language-pair related
INST		institution of origin, including:
	CLASSF	non-DANTERM classification
	DATE	date of concluding terminological processing
	COPY	copyright
	RESP	terminologist responsible
	METHOD	working method
ADM		administrative information (for use in sorting etc.)
	#CLASSA	key for sorting by subject (verbal description)
	#CLASSB	key for sorting by subject (alphanumeric code)
	#NUM	key for sorting by identification number
		ITERATIVE INFORMATION
	#TERM	key for sorting by term (alphabetical)
	#POS	key for sorting by position (systematic)
	#CLASSF	key for sorting by non-DANTERM classification
	#DATE	key for sorting by processing date
	#INPUT	date of first input
	#UPDAT	information on last and previous updates

In particular, names and terms like "term", "concept" and "conceptual system" and their degree of detail are striking, as is the term "thesaurus" and its degree of detail, in comparison with the lexicographical terms that were used in the metalexicographical descriptive models exemplified above.

The conceptual information categories are central to the theory of terminology, as its object is to define precisely, on the basis of an accurate description of the conceptual system or systems in a given special field, the concepts used and their interrelations within one or more closed systems, and to assign linguistic expression — *terms* — to them. This ensures the existence/development — if necessary by means of actual standardization — of an unambiguous specialized communicative apparatus. For this reason the theory of terminology and its lexicography — now frequently called terminography, as in Felber (1984) — is often normative or prescriptive by nature, unlike general lexicography with its monolingual and bilingual dictionaries/databases, which are primarily descriptive. The presence of the terminographical or lexicographical term DEPR (short for "deprecated term") can be attributed to this prescriptive aspect. The DANTERM record is primarily used, however, for the purely descriptive registration of terms. In Section 4.3 the categories of the DANTERM record are explained and exemplifed in more detail.

"Classification", "thesaurus" and thesaurus-related lexicographical terms appear in connection with both terminological theory and the information and documentation (I&D) area; but not to any great extent in general lexicography. For terms that are to be included in classification terminologies and thesauri, precise definition is still more essential than it is for the above-mentioned concept-related terms; in thesauri their meanings or definitions may even be arbitrarily demarcated, since their only context is the closed system in which they are elements, as Picht remarks (1983: 63).

The object, and consequently the function, of a metalexicographical descriptive apparatus is thus here too a determinant of its design.

2.3.4.2 *Roget's Thesaurus*, and thesauri or conceptual dictionaries of the vocabularies of individual authors

Two other products of the methodology of onomasiological lexicography are the two main types of conceptual dictionary, described by Dixon (1983: 49 ff) as follows:

> Basically, and in simplified distinction, there are two kinds of conceptual glossary: one sets out to present and classify a whole language, the other the vocabulary of a single author. (Variations and modifications of these two basic kinds may be envisaged.)

Roget's *Thesaurus of English Words and Phrases* (1974) is a conceptual dictionary of English based on a classification of concepts which attributes a series of more or less synonymous words or phrases to each concept created by the system. Sometimes antonyms are also listed. Dixon's account (1983: 49) of the purpose of this thesaurus or conceptual dictionary of the natural language English is as follows:

> To what end did Roget compile his *Thesaurus*? To the exclusively practical end of consultation by a writer or speaker, who would find in it, under the appropriate heading, the word he needed in a given context and for a given occasion.

In the user's instructions "How to use this book" in the 1974 Penguin edition of Roget, a metalexicographical descriptive apparatus with the following inventory is used: "idea", "meaning", "word", "expression", "keyword", "index", "reference in the index", "number", "part of speech", "head in text that bears the number given by the reference", "division corresponding to the part of speech", "paragraph headed by the same keyword as in your reference", "subhead", "All the words in the subhead have meanings which are related, usually in a very obvious way, to the meaning of the keyword", "cross-reference", "general topic", "allied topics", "scheme of classification". In the thesaurus itself terms like "class" and "section" can be found.

This apparatus is user-orientated, and thus typically has a fairly colloquial explanatory vocabulary. As rather a contrast to this we have the apparatus that Dixon (1983: 49 ff) uses in his scholarly discussion of *Roget's Thesaurus*; this includes lexicographical terms similar to those used in the DANTERM record, like "concepts", "fundamental classes of concepts", "conceptual class", "conceptual system", "primary, secondary & tertiary groups", "classification system", "synonymity", "antonymity".

In his article Dixon also gives an account of his work on the production of a conceptual glossary or thesaurus of Rabelais' vocabulary, which is not to be done on the basis of a pre-defined and pre-established conceptual classification of the type used by Roget; only the classificatory terms which themselves are part of Rabelais' vocabulary are to be used.

This work is to be done in several stages with the help of a computer, and so far has resulted in alphabetically sorted lexicographical word lists with the following information categories:

Column 1: the number of words on file, for identification
Column 2: vocabulary item
Column 3: the absolute coefficient of occurrence
Column 4: the grammatical category (required for subsequent sorting)
Column 5: a tentative classification

On the basis of the tentative classification it will be possible to produce lexicographical lists sorted by classification or subject with the information categories:

Column 1: identification number
Column 2: the term
Column 3: grammatical category
Column 4: number of occurrences
Column 5: classification
Column 6: reference of first textual occurrence

We thus have here yet another two slightly different working descriptive apparatuses, distinct from those for conceptual dictionaries discussed above.

Here too it is the function of the metalexicographical descriptive apparatus that determines its form.

2.4 The need for a *tertium comparationis*

The examples reviewed show that metalexicographical descriptive apparatuses are many and vary greatly, even when they are connected, like the three LDOCE schemes, with the same product.

Further articles and papers on various dictionaries, and the dictionaries themselves could easily be used to multiply examples of more or less differently structured metalexicographical descriptive apparatuses; but those that have been dealt with here may at least suggest the broad range of variation in lexicographical terminology.

All the purely computer-orientated descriptive models cited have one feature in common: they provide at once a structure and its possible content. This is true of the descriptive apparatuses for the BONNLEX system and the MDW draft for lexical microstructure; of Schaeder's *Raster* for a lexicographical presentation of the lemma *Betrieb* (cf Section 2.3.2.1 above); of the database information categories of the LDOCE and *The (New) Collins English Dictionary*; of Wilton's computer-orientated information categories, the DANTERM record and Dixon's two overviews of the information categories for his thesaurus of Rabelais' vocabulary. These models thus impose on their users both the content the dictionaries are to have and the way that content is to be structured. If the concept of a format is defined as a specification of content and structure for the individual dictionary, all the descriptive models cited immediately above have been formats. On the other hand, Schaeder's proposal for a "Gestaltung der Mikrostruktur", despite both its name and its computer-related nature, stands out from these because Schaeder states explicitly that his ideal arrangement includes a number of information categories that need *not* be kept in the order in question. This ideal structure is thus primarily content-orientated, and only secondarily structure-orientated, so it cannot be regarded as a format. The descriptive apparatuses that appear in the LDOCE's "Explanatory Chart" and the list of contents of the "Guide to the Dictionary" are exclusively content-orientated, like Wilton's and Dixon's terms for discussion and the user's instructions for *Roget's Thesaurus*. There is thus no question of these being formats either.

If different lexicographical projects are to be capable of exchanging their data in machine-readable form, it is necessary to establish comparability. Detailed formats have been drawn up for exchanging information — for example the lexicographical/terminological exchange format MATER (1980) and Sherman's standardized format for dictionary entries, WEBMARC (1974), based on the Library of Congress MARC (machine-readable cataloging) format. Yet the use of such detailed exchange formats with predefined information categories has not proved suitable, as they have difficulty in accommodating the great variety of dictionary types already in existence, and even more so those that may be created in future. Amsler (1984) also says that WEBMARC has not won acceptance to any great extent in American lexicography; and Heß/Brustkern/Lenders (1983: 175 ff) demonstrate in connection with MATER (1980) that it is difficult to place strongly differentiated lexicographical data in this format, which means that important information types can only be partially accommodated. Later versions of MATER (1982, 1984 and 1985) operate with exclusively user-definable information categories within each of nine pre-defined classes of data categories, and no longer with both pre-defined and user-definable categories within each of the nine classes, as in the 1980 version. MATER (1982) and MATER

(1984, 1985) have as appendices examples of the naming and definition of a number of data categories within six and eight of the nine pre-defined classes of data categories respectively. The examples can be used as guidelines for category definition, and their proposed data categories can be used wholly, partially or can be completely ignored according to the needs of the user.

Thus the problems of defining detailed exchange formats have almost led to the abandonment of the attempt to provide guidelines for the types of information one finds in dictionaries. If one resigns oneself to letting each user specify his own categories freely, the result is a great deal of sorting work whenever one dictionary is to use information from another dictionary. Both the supplying and receiving dictionaries must work out precise descriptions of the types of information they work with and of how these information types are placed and marked in their data material before it can be decided whether there is a basis for the exchange of data. If, on the other hand, the individual dictionaries are described in terms of a set of generally defined types of information, cooperation is made considerably easier.

It is an open question whether it serves any theoretical or practical purpose to try to specify such a set of general information types for the universal use of lexicographers, no matter which language or languages they are dealing with. But it seems obvious that a set of information types that can be used within a single language or a group of related languages irrespective of the nature of the particular dictionary will be of great practical importance by facilitating the exchange of information among different dictionaries.

In this book, a distinction is made between the description of content and the description of structure. First, in Chapter 3, we establish a taxonomy of general content categories that can be used to describe all types of dictionary involving the Danish language. Examples in Chapter 4 show how these content categories can be used in various types of dictionary. Then in Chapter 5 we review various formal systems for the description of the structure of dictionary entries, giving examples.

This division into content description and structural description makes it clear that the constitutive factor for any type of dictionary is the particular subset of the general content categories that is used in that type of dictionary. The structure of the individual dictionary depends less on the type of information it provides than on the way it is presented. Thus the same taxonomic content category may appear in many different structures in widely differing positions; and a format only emerges through the interplay between the particular subset of the general content categories used in that type of dictionary, and the structure selected for the dictionary in question and described by means of a formal system indicating the way the dictionary is to be presented.

3. A TAXONOMY FOR LEXICOGRAPHICAL DATA

The taxonomies of the sciences consist of small sets of very general classes delimited from one another by means of a few precise criteria. Consider, for example, the biological taxonomy with its distinctions among plants and animals. Each of these general classes again consists of a hierarchy of classes with many levels. In principle it is possible to define every living organism in terms of these hierarchies. The aim of the lexicographical taxonomy is to provide a description of the lexicographical universe, enabling us to assign a type to every item of information in lexicographical works and data collections.

As a point of departure for the establishment of a taxonomy it would be desirable to have a precise idea of the conceptual area the taxonomy is to deal with. How does one define lexicographical data? In this context we cannot avoid some discussion of the concept of the *word*.

It is a well known fact that all linguists use the term *word* although they are fully aware that its exact definition varies from discipline to discipline within linguistics. In lexicographical contexts one often sees the terms *lexical unit* or *lexeme* used of the units described in the individual lexicographical work (Kipfer 1984: 181). But there is no agreement among users on the exact meaning of these terms either. It is difficult, then, to find a good general account of the units described in lexicographical works. Yet there is a fairly wide area of consensus on the features these units exhibit and how they are to be described, and it is this area that we are attempting to isolate in proposing a general taxonomy for lexicographical information.

The units for whose features we wish to establish a general description can tentatively be defined as *meaning-bearing units up to sentence level, and the meanings represented by these units.*

One can see clearly from the descriptive apparatuses discussed in the preceding chapter what lexicographical research has considered to be the lexicographical work *par excellence* — the large, ideally exhaustive, national monolingual dictionary in printed form. But if one wishes to establish an apparatus for the description of all types of lexicographical data, one must include other kinds of work: translation dictionaries, specialist dictionaries, historical dictionaries, and collections of lexicographical data primarily meant for use in information technology systems. In the proposed taxonomy we attempt to identify and describe all the categories of information in lexicographical works and data collections involving lexical units in Danish, whether they exist, are in the planning stage, or are conceivable in the near future. The taxonomy has primarily been built up and checked on lexicographical works in which the Danish language is included. It is our view, however, that it will be possible to use it without substantial expansions and modifications for related languages like the Scandinavian languages, and western European languages like the Germanic and Romance languages.

Lexicographical data are a product of culture, not of nature. Language itself may perhaps be seen as a product of nature. For the possession of language may be said to be a characteristic of the species *Homo sapiens* — sometimes also known as *Homo loquens*. Yet there are many human communities without lexicographical works, even though our western European culture has a centuries old lexicographical tradition.

Having described lexicographical data as a product of culture, we can look around us for lexicographical cultures. It emerges that the lexicographical world considers itself to consist of many different cultures. There is a culture of specialized languages, associated with a terminological culture. There is an ordinary-language culture, which considers itself distinct from specialized lexicography, but which is itself usually divided up into the lexicography of monolingual dictionaries (i.e. national dictionaries), that of foreign-language dictionaries (i.e. translation dictionaries), that of elementary dictionaries, that of conceptual dictionaries, etc. We have seen it as our task to find the types of information that are common to all the different lexicographical cultures, and to identify those cultural features which are so specific to the view of lexicographical data in the individual work that they must be dealt with outside the taxonomy.

Quite apart from the variety of the many lexicographical cultures, it is necessary when characterizing lexicographical data as a phenomenon to be aware that one cannot find lexicographical data in free form. Lexicographical data are found in structures, either in dictionary entries or in lexicographical data collections structured for use in a computerized system.

The study of descriptive apparatuses from the various lexicographical cultures, and of many examples of lexicographical data in the structures where they can be found, i.e. dictionaries and term banks, has led us to extract three features that are characteristic of whole collections of lexicographical data and which are closely connected with the lexicographical culture of which the individual work is a part: these are *approach*, *language* and *medium of expression*.

What we are proposing is a descriptive apparatus that is independent of the issue of what a *word*, a *lexeme* or a *term* is. For the meaning of these expressions is closely connected with one's intentions with the lexicographical material and the philosophical view one has of language. One chooses one's point of departure for each different work or project; that is, one selects the units one wishes to give information about. In the type of specialized lexicography that has close connections with terminological theory, one normally begins with *concepts* and describes these in terms of the words and expressions used to refer to them. One takes the onomasiological approach. In most general lexicographical works the point of departure is *words and expressions* whose usage and meaning one wishes to describe. One chooses the semasiological approach. More specific definitions of the types of words and expressions to be described in general lexicography are in no small degree dependent on whether the dictionary in question deals with a contemporary language, with different stages of the same national language, with regional variants of the same national language or with translation to a foreign language. The choice of approach, onomasiological or semasiological, and the precise nature of the units to be dealt with must, then, be decided for every work or project. These factors vary in ways that are not amenable to treatment in a general taxonomy.

There are two other elements in the description of lexicographical works and projects that belong to the characterization of works as a whole rather than that of the categories of information they contain: information about the types of language dealt with in the work, and information about the way the work is presented.

Below is an overview of the proposed taxonomy. It is divided into three project-specific types of information and the general types.

3.1 Taxonomy for lexicographical data

Project-specific information types:

Language	- national language - sociolect - dialect - language stage
Approach	- semasiological - onomasiological
Medium of expression	- speech - writing - picture

General information types:

Main group	Categories
Etymological information	- parallel(s) - origin
Graphic information	- orthography - graphic symbol

Grammatical information	- part of speech - inflection - word formation - syntax
Phonetic information	- prosodic features - segmental features
Pragmatic information	- contextual information - usage - external reference - evaluative information - administrative information
Semantic information	- subject classification - semantic relations - content specification - equivalence

The taxonomy builds on comparative studies of a number of different types of lexical work where the Danish language is involved (Hjorth 1984 and 1985); on a review of various proposed formats for lexical data (Jacobsen 1984; Allén 1981; Grundt 1983; Midtvedt 1983); and on lexicographical scholarship in general. The differences in the fineness of distinctions in the main groups and the categories is related to needs as we perceive them and the consensus on subclassification registered in our surveys.

3.1.1 Project-specific information types

The three project-specific types of information, *language*, *approach* and *medium of expression*, determine the nature of the lexical units one deals with in the specific work, and assign the work to a particular lexicographical culture with its traditions.

Language

Every lexicographical work deals with one or more *languages*. The definition of "language" depends on the nature of the lexicographical work; one can define different chronological stages of a language as "languages", as one does in historical dictionaries; or the languages of different regions, as in dialect dictionaries; or different national languages, as in all translation dictionaries. A work may also deal with one or more languages. In monolingual dictionaries, as a rule, one only knows from the title which language is covered. This is true of *Nudansk Ordbog* (1984); and in the case of *Retskrivningsordbogen* ("The Spelling Dictionary") (1986) one can deduce the language dealt with from the publisher, *Dansk Sprognævn* ("The Danish Language Council").

Approach

The basic dividing-line here goes between, on the one hand, a lexicography that takes *words* for granted and thus takes the semasiological approach; and on the other, lexicography that takes concepts for granted — the onomasiological approach. Works that take the semasiological approach are committed to the definition of *word, expression, lexeme, lemma, headword* or whatever they call the units to which they attach information. In contrast, works that take the onomasiological approach must define *concept* and *term*. As examples of lexicographical works with the onomasiological approach we can mention terminographical works like term banks, or thesauruses and synonym dictionaries. Typical examples of lexicographical works with the semasiological approach are the big national monolingual dictionaries like *Ordbog over det Danske Sprog*, *The Oxford English Dictionary* and *Grimms Deutsches Wörterbuch*.

Medium of expression

Hitherto lexicographical works have been presented in the form of printed books. The written word has been the predominant medium, with occasional examples of the use of pictures, as in illustrated or pictorial dictionaries. In future a combination of writing, pictures and sound is conceivable. For example, one could have a translation dictionary available in an information retrieval system where one could listen to the pronunciation of the word one looked up. So the authors of a lexicographical work must now consider which medium of expression is best suited to their data and users.

This vision of the future has already been realized in at least one encyclopædia (the American *Grolier's Encyclopedia*). The medium is the CD-ROM, physically identical to the compact disc for audio reproduction; it can store data, pictures and sound. At the Frankfurt Book Fair in 1986 Sansyusya Publishing presented a database in CD-ROM form including dictionaries in nine languages, for example Harraps' English, French and German dictionaries, and Brandstetter's German technical dictionaries.

3.1.2 General information types

The central feature of the general component of the proposed taxonomy is a number of independently defined, mutually exclusive categories of information. Any given item of lexical information can be assigned to one and only one category.

On the basis of their dominant features the categories are arranged in main groups corresponding to the various linguistic disciplines: etymology, grammar, orthography, phonetics, pragmatics and semantics. This grouping is based on one overall view of the interrelations among the different linguistic disciplines. There is less general agreement, however, on the exact placing of some of the linguistic categories in the main groups. For example, information about word formation is sometimes considered to be etymological, like information about cognate words etc., and sometimes, as here, to be grammatical, like information on inflection. The fact that it is possible to classify some categories in one or the other main group does not detract, however, from the mutually exclusive nature of the categories. It is rather a symptom of a certain amount of competition between the linguistic disciplines.

In the above overview of the proposed taxonomy the main groups are ordered alphabetically to bring out the mutually exclusive nature of the categories. We will now describe the general information categories in more detail. The individual categories are quite comprehensive and can be subdivided in different lexicographical works according to the work-specific degree of specialization in particular types of information. However, it should be ensured that the subdivisions also result in mutually exclusive categories. In the following we have made a division into subcategories which should be sufficient for the great majority of dictionaries, but they should not be considered exhaustive. Their realization in actual formats will of course require further subdivisions, examples of which will be given in Chapter 4. In the choice of examples we have tried to represent various types of dictionary. Many of the specialized-language examples will be commented on in Section 4.3.

Etymological information

Etymological information can be in one of two categories: *origin* and *parallels*. *Origin* gives information about the historical origin of a word either at an older stage of the language or in the language from which it was borrowed. The *parallels* category gives information on cognate words or expressions in other languages.

For example, the entry on *mand* in *Dansk Etymologisk Ordbog* ("The Etymological Dictionary of Danish") has *origin*: ODan. *man*, from Germ. *mannaz*, Pr. Germ. *mannuas*; *parallels*: Norw. *mann*, Sw. *man*, ON *maðr*, OS, OHG *mann*, Germ. *Mann*, OE *mann*, Eng. *man*.

Graphic information

Graphic information tells us how words and concepts appear in writing. The main group includes two categories: *orthographical information* and *graphic symbol*. *Orthographical information* gives us the alphabetical form of a word or expression. The orthographical information given can be variant spellings like Danish *fosfor/phosphor*, *klor/chlor* (chlorine) or abbreviated forms like *ODS* for *Ordbog over det danske Sprog* or, in the Danish-English Dictionary, the abbreviation CPI for "consumer price index" under the equivalent Danish headword.

Graphic symbol specifies the symbol used for a given word or concept, for example *§* for *paragraph*, *+* for *plus*, *Ω* for *Ohm*.

Grammatical information

Grammatical information includes morphological and syntactic categories: one can distinguish between information on parts of speech, inflection, word formation and syntax.

The *part of speech* category gives information on the parsing of the unit described. This is one of the few categories where there is relatively wide agreement among lexicographers on its members: *noun, verb, adjective, adverb, pronoun, numeral, preposition, conjunction, interjection.*

The category *information on inflection* includes the subcategories *paradigm information* and *inflectional form. Paradigm information* gives an overall description of the inflectional forms of a given lemma. In the case of the Danish noun *æble* 'apple' it is the fact that it has an inflected plural *æbler*. Given this information and information on gender (a sub-classification of *part of speech*) — in this case neuter — one can construct the other inflectional forms. The subcategory *inflectional form* is used for single-word forms. Here one finds members of the categories the word is inflected in: for example, a former Danish masculine singular form *unger* of the adjective *ung* 'young'.

Word formation specifies how the word in question is formed or can be used to form other words. Here we can place information on the components of compound words, or on the kinds of words the headword can enter into compounds with. Similarly, with derived words there is information on the words they are derived from and the derivational affix or morpheme. In the case of non-derived words, information can be given on the affixes or morphemes they can be combined with to form derived words.

The *syntax* category includes the subcategories *valency* and *syntactic function. Valency* tells us about the range and type of segments that a given word can be combined with. For example, quantitative words are combined with phrases specifying the quantity: *a sum of 12,000 Ecus, a distance of 200 metres*. Another example of valency is the information that a verb is intransitive, e.g. the *i* in *vi* (verbum intransitivum) after *gnistre* 'sparkle' in *Dansk-Engelsk Ordbog (1976)*. Information on *syntactic function* tells us that the word can perform a particular grammatical function in a sentence: e.g. *fode*, an old inflected form of *fod* 'foot' governed by a preposition in fossilized expressions like *komme på fode* 'get on one's feet' or *træde under fode* 'tramp underfoot'. An example from *Dansk-Engelsk Ordbog* is the information *alm kun prædikativt* 'normally only predicative' given for the adjective *glad*.

Phonetic information

Phonetic information consists of two categories; *prosodic features* and *segmental features*. *Prosodic features* informs us about stress, intonation and accent. This is the type of phonetic information one most often finds in lexicographical works. Very few dictionaries can manage without indicating the stress in some words. For example, there is the distinction in Vinterberg and Bodelsen's Danish-English Dictionary between *'fortegning* 'model' and *for'tegning* 'incorrect drawing, distortion'.

The other phonetic category indicates the pronunciation of segments, using a phonetic notation like the IPA or an orthographical notation that approximates the pronunciation. This category is called *segmental features*. An example from *Ømålsordbogen* (a dictionary of Danish island dialects being edited by the Department for Danish Dialect Research at the University of Copenhagen) is the standard Danish *abe* pronounced [a.b] or [a.w] .

Pragmatic information

Pragmatic information collects together the information categories that indicate use in the broadest sense - both the usage of the words and concepts described and the use of the lexical information. The main group includes *contextual information*, *usage*, *external reference*, *evaluative information*, and *administrative information*.

Contextual information comprises the subcategories *citation* and *possible context*.

Citations are authentic examples of the use of words and expressions, with the actual wording of the source. An example of a citation for the word *standhaftig* 'constant', from the ODS is *Deres Dyd, som giør Dem standhaftig imod Lykkens umilde Anfald (kilde: Skuesp. VI 110)* 'your virtue, which renders you constant in the face of the unkind cuts of Fortune' (+ source reference); or a citation for *veksel* 'bill of exchange' from the bill-of-exchange terminology in the Danish term bank DANTERM (cf Section 2.3.4.1 and Section 4.3) — *En veksel kan trækkes på et firma, et aktieselskab, en forening o. lign. (kilde: Helper, A.: Vekselloven og checkloven af 1932, kommenteret udgave, Kbh. 1932* 'A bill of exchange may be drawn on a firm, a joint-stock company, an association, etc.' (+ source reference). The source reference itself is an *external reference* (see below). An example from the entry on *if* in the LDOCE is *We can send you a map if you wish (SEU S.)*

Possible context gives examples of the use of a given word or expression. An example for *abe* 'monkey, ape' from *Ømålsordbogen* is *den ene abe får den anden til at gabe* 'one ape makes another gape'; or, from bill-of-exchange terminology, *trække veksel på* 'draw a bill on'; or, from *Dansk-Engelsk Ordbog* (1976), under the headword *advokat* 'lawyer' the example (*fx* the devil's advocate) to show when *advokat* can be translated by *advocate*.

Usage places the use of a given word or expression in a *temporal, spatial* or *social* dimension, or tells us about how often a word or expression is used - its *frequency*. *Usage* includes the subcategories *temporal*, *spatial* and *social*, along with *frequency*.

In the *temporal dimension* we can be informed, for example, that a word or expression was used in former times. An example from the ODSS is *Baad//til baads: aftagende brug i 20. årh.* 'the phrase *til Baads*, "on a boat" has been used decreasingly in the 20th century'.

An example from DANTERM is the note on *helautomatisk regulering* 'fully automatic control', which says that the term was formerly in wider use to emphasize the difference between semi-automatic and fully automatic control, but is now rare, as anything that is not automatic control is now called 'manual control'.

As far as the *spatial dimension* is concerned, we can be told that a word or expression is used in a particular geographical area, e.g. that *plow* is an American English form of *plough*. An example from *Dansk-Engelsk Ordbog* (1976) is the information in the entry on *fandens* (an expletive) that the British English equivalent *bloody* does not have the same meaning in the USA.

In the *social dimension* we register usage in specific social strata or specific contexts, for example slang.

To take an example, DANTERM has a note on *den trukne veksel* 'drawn bill of exchange' and *tratte* 'draft', saying that legal documents do not use *tratte*, while legal commentaries and more general works use *den trukne veksel* and *tratte* interchangeably. The word *svensknøgle* 'shifting spanner' is marked *populær* 'popular'.

Examples from *Dansk-Engelsk Ordbog* (1976) are *adjøs: T* (for *talesprog* 'colloquial') — i.e. a colloquial word for 'goodbye', and *dask* S ɔ: *kroner*, corresponding to the English 'bob' (slang).

As an example of *frequency*, DANTERM has a note on the words *bigami* 'bigamy' and *dobbeltægteskab* 'double marriage' stating that the word *dobbeltægteskab* is only found in one source (and giving a reference to the source). On *stedlig rømning* and *svigagtig rømning* — two phrases meaning 'matrimonial desertion' it is remarked that the two expressions are about equally common in phrases meaning 'divorce on the grounds of desertion'. An example from the ODSS is *Baad//til Baads: aftagende brug i 20. årh.* 'used decreasingly in the 20th century'

External reference includes the subcategories *literature reference* and *source reference*. A *literature reference* indicates where more information can be found in another work. In *Etymologisk Ordbog* there is a literature reference on the word *angst*: *Litt.: W. Porzig: Die Gliederung des indogermanischen Sprachgebiets (Heidelberg 1954) 143-144.* In DANTERM, for example, there is a reference to an illustration for *trailed plough: Illustration BSI 2468 p 27.*

A *source reference* also refers to a source outside the given lexicographical context. As a source for the old medical term *dræg*, the GLDO gives *Lægeb. [AM] .97,11* (i.e. the Arnamagnæan Octave MS No. 187 containing an old Danish leech-book, published by Viggo Såby, Copenhagen 1886). For *bugseret plov* 'trailed plough', DANTERM has the source reference *JenM 64-65 p. 1* (i.e.

Ole Jensen, *Maskinlære* — a mechanical engineering textbook). The quotation in the LDOCE *We can send you a map if you like* is provided with the source reference *SEU S* (cf *citations* above).

Evaluative information is especially found in normative lexicographical works, in the form of recommendations of particular words or phrases. DANTERM is not normative, but does allow for evaluative comments from the terminologist, for example *Løs føler bør ikke anvendes, da føleren ikke sidder løst og ikke kan fjernes* '*løs føler* should not be used, as the sensor is not loose and cannot be removed'. The recommended term is *fjernføler* 'remote sensor'. Of the term *luftkonditionering* 'air conditioning' it is stated that one should not use *ventilation* as a synonym (= deprecated term). There is an example in *Dansk-Engelsk Ordbog* (1976) in the entry on *advokatfirma* 'firm of lawyers' stating that "firm of barristers" is not used.

Administrative information includes the subcategories *information on collection and processing of data*, *internal reference*, *homograph number* and *technical information*. *Information on collection and processing of data* indicates the collector, editor or other processor of the data described, and the compilation and data entry dates. *Internal reference* is used for references to other information in the same collection of data and *homograph number* is also considered to be administrative information. *Technical information* is information about the use of type-faces like semi-bold for the lemma or punctuation marks like brackets around usage information.

Semantic information

Semantic information serves to identify and describe the content of a linguistic sign — its meaning — and corresponds to what in lexicography is normally called the description of meaning in the broadest sense. *Semantic information* can be subdivided into the categories *subject classification*, *semantic relations*, *content specification* and *equivalence*.

Subject classification

Subject classification provides information about specialized fields or subjects. Use in a specialized field can be regarded as a characteristic feature similar to other features describing properties (for example, function, position, construction, purpose, components) and can thus be included in *content specification* (see below). But this information can also be given separately, for example as a notation or code belonging to a more or less detailed classification system, whether general or worked out for a given collection of data. Examples of classification systems that can be mentioned are Lenoch's classification, used by the EEC Terminology Bank EURODICAUTOM; the DANTERM classification (see bibliography) now being drawn up for the Danish term bank; and the UDC - the Universal Decimal Classification, actually intended for classifying documents, but also used in some collections of terminological data.

Using the DANTERM classification one can classify a concept like *radiatortermostat* 'radiator thermostat' under the subject *K8840, Thermostats*. The same concept is found in Lenoch's classification under *PHA Wärmelehre* and is classified in the UDC under *536.581:697.35* (heating and plumbing).

In many dictionaries there is no more than a rough subject classification in the form of an alphabetical list of subject abbreviations, for example *med.* for medicine, *techn.* for technical. Finally, subject information may also be given by the title of a specialist dictionary or data collection, for example *Dansk/tysk vekselterminologi* ("Danish-German Bill-of-Exchange Terminology").

Semantic relations

By information about *semantic relations* we understand specifications of the relationships between the contents of lexical units. General lexicography operates with *hyponymy* and distinguishes between the relationships *hyperonymy* and *co-hyponymy* for subordinate, superordinate and co-ordinated units respectively.

In terminological and specialized lexicography one works with relations between concepts, and they can be systematically ordered in a conceptual system (DIN 2331, 1976).

The category includes the following subcategories: *generic superordinate/subordinate relation*, *partitive relation*, *successive relation*, *causal relation*, *antonymy*.

The *generic superordinate/subordinate relation* is often formulated in terms of set theory (cf Lyons 1977: 291 ff.). According to Dahlberg (1976) this relation pertains between two concepts when they have identical characteristic features and one concept has one or more specific features that the other does not have.

For example, *Dansk-Engelsk Ordbog* (1976) uses information on superordination or subordination for meaning differentiation. The gloss for the first meaning of *flod* 'river' is *vandløb* 'waterway'; and under *skade* 'damage, harm' etc. the subordinate concepts *legemsskade* 'bodily harm' and *maskinskade* 'engine damage' are differentiated by the glosses *legems-* and *maskin-*.

An example of a conceptual system involving generic relations is a system for bicycle terminology worked out for a terminological project (Bock 1979).

Fig. 3.1.2-1 Extract from conceptual system for bicycle terminology: Superordinate/subordinate relations

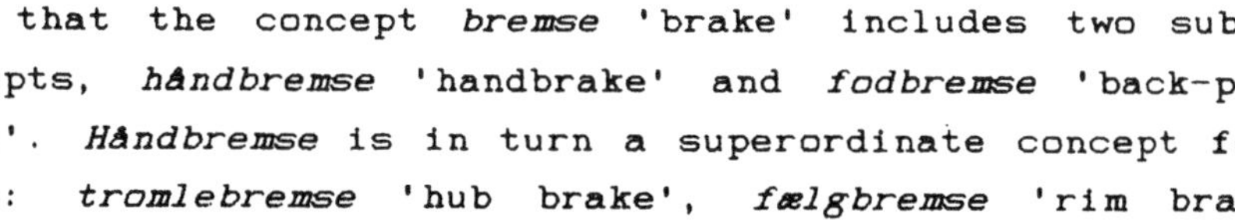

Fig. 3.1.2-1 illustrates part of this system. It can be seen here that the concept *bremse* 'brake' includes two subordinate concepts, *håndbremse* 'handbrake' and *fodbremse* 'back-pedalling brake'. *Håndbremse* is in turn a superordinate concept for three types: *tromlebremse* 'hub brake', *fælgbremse* 'rim brake' and *skivebremse* 'disc brake'.

Partitive relation specifies relations between components and the whole of which they are a part. There are also partitive relations in the conceptual system for bicycle terminology, cf Fig. 3.1.2-2.

Fig. 3-1.2-2 Extract from conceptual system for bicycle terminology: Partitive relations

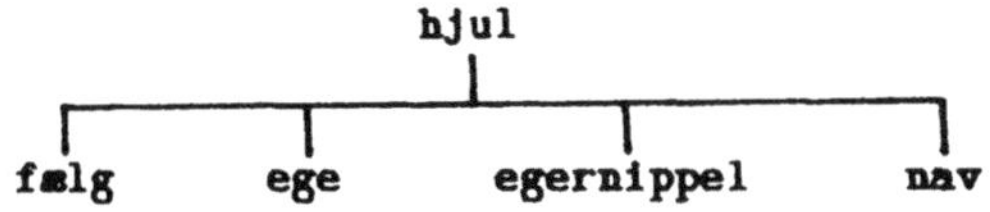

The components of *hjul* 'wheel' are given as *fælg* 'rim', *ege* 'spoke', *egernippel* 'spoke nipple' and *nav* 'hub'.

Successive relation (temporal) specifies the preceding and succeeding concepts in a sequence or process. An example (greatly simplified) of successive relations is the progress of a bill of exchange:

***udstedelse* 'drawing' → *accept* 'acceptance' →**

***endossement* 'endorsement' → *indfrielse* 'payment in due course'**

Causal relation is used to specify a cause-and-effect relation between the concepts.

Antonymy (the relation between opposites) is used for two concepts whose characteristic features are in a relation of opposition (cf for example Dahlberg 1976). An example of antonymy can be seen in *Dansk-Engelsk Ordbog* (1976), where the polysemic headword *ret* 'right' has the distinguishing gloss *(modsat uret)* 'the opposite of wrong' for meaning number 1.

As can be seen from the above examples, the system used is often one specially ordered for the internal use of dictionaries and data collections.

A special type of lexicographical data collection is the *thesaurus* for information and document retrieval. Such a thesaurus lists the permissible expressions, the *descriptors* for indexing and accessing information in databases. The descriptors are ordered systematically to show the relations between them. In addition, non-admissible expressions, synonyms and non-descriptors are are listed.

The numbering of meanings in dictionary entries can also be regarded as a form of semantic structuring. Often a special significance is attached to the order of the meanings.

Content specification

By *content specification* we understand the description of meaning in the narrow sense (definitions). The category includes the subcategories *lexical paraphrase*, and *analytic*, *synthetic*, *denotative* and *ostensive definition types*. With this type of information too one finds differences in practice in the two lexicographical cultures, general and terminological.

Traditionally, both cultures operate with the term *definition* for the description of meaning — the lexicographical and the terminological definition. But there are differences in both the objects and methods of definition. The object of definition in general dictionaries is the word (see for example Zgusta 1971; Kipfer 1984) while in specialized dictionaries and data collections it is the concept (cf Dahlberg 1976; DIN 2330, 1979; Wüster 1979; Felber 1984) — i.e. the semasiological versus the onomasiological approach.

To a certain extent, works on general and specialized lexicography describe the same methods of definition: the analytical method (intensional and extensional definition); the synthetic method (relational definition); the denotative method (exemplification); the ostensive method (for example, an illustration); the implicative method (definition by context) and the synonym method. Thus Kipfer (1984), referring to Robinson (1962) mentions the analytic, synthetic and synonym methods as correct methods of definition in general lexicography.

Wiegand (1985), however, says that in the great majority of cases it is not possible to give an analytic definition of ordinary-language expressions, and argues that one should not use the term definition of the description of meaning in general dictionaries. Instead he proposes the use of the terms *lexikalische Paraphrase* 'lexical paraphrase' and *lexikalische Bedeutungserläuterung* 'explanation of lexical meaning'. Each of the meanings of the lemma is provided with a lexical paraphrase, and the lexical paraphrases of the various meanings of the lemma together make up the *Bedeutungserläuterung* of the lemma.

Wiegand also says that synonyms are not part of the *Bedeutungserläuterung*, but are rather part of what he calls

Bedeutungsangabe 'meaning specification' (Wiegand 1985: 60 ff). As an example of a lexical paraphrase we can give the gloss *forkert tegning* from the entry *for'tegning* 'incorrect drawing' in *Dansk-Engelsk Ordbog* (1976).

In the terminological lexicographical culture, however, it is necessary to use both the analytic and synthetic method as well as the ostensive method. In this culture a *definition* is itself defined as *an unambiguous determination of a concept for factually descriptive or normative purposes* (see for example Dahlberg 1976, who defines *Definition* as *Feststellung oder Festsetzung eines Begriffsinhaltes*).

In accordance with the present taxonomy's rigorous classification into mutually exclusive categories, the implicative method and the synonym method are not regarded as content specification, but as other types of information (pragmatic information and information on equivalence respectively). This accords well with the terminological view.

If one followed the definitions of *definition* quoted above the denotative method would have to be rejected. However, it is included here, as it is in fact a type of information describing meaning.

Information on conceptual content also includes information on subject field and semantic relations. These types of information are therefore often included in definitions, but can also appear separately. A subject field can be labelled by using some form of notation or code, and semantic relations — for example the superordinate and subordinate concepts of a concept — can appear from a conceptual system (see above).

Examples of terminological definitions are:

Analytic definition

a) The *intensional definition* specifies *genus proximum* and *differentia specifica*:

For example, for the term *tratte* 'draft' a definition is given stating the *genus proximum*: *en i vekselform udstedt anvisning* 'an order in the form of a bill of exchange'; and the *differentia specifica*: *hvorved udstederen (trassenten) anmoder en anden (trassaten) om at betale et vist beløb til tredjemanden (remittenten)* '...whereby one person (the drawer) requests another (the drawee) to pay a given sum to a third (the payee)'. (Source: *Juridisk Ordbog*, Borum, O. A. and v. Eyben, W. E., 1976).

b) The *extensional definition* specifies the components of the definiendum:

In connection with the DANTERM project on ploughs, for example, *plovlegeme* 'plough body' is defined as follows: *et plovlegeme består af plovskær, landside, muldplade* 'a plough body consists of share, landside and mouldboard'.

Synthetic definition

The relations of the definiendum to other concepts are specified (relational definition). An example is *100°C ist die Temperatur, bei der Wasser unter einem Luftdruck von 760 Torr siedet* from Weinberger (1970) in Frandsen (1982).

Denotative definition

Exemplification

Datamedium 'data storage medium' can be exemplified as follows: *Datamedium kan være hulkort, hulbånd, magnetbånd* 'a data storage medium may be a punched card, punched tape or magnetic tape' (Source: *DS EDB-ordbog*, 1975).

Ostensive definition

An ostensive definition refers to an illustration. An illustration often says much more than a long explanation. The term *skruetrækkerindsats med udvendig sekskanttilslutning til kryds-kærvskruer* 'screwdriver bit for recessed head screws, hexagon shank' is illustrated as follows:

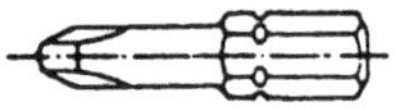

(Source: DS/ISO 1703 1980)

As far as rules of definition are concerned — i.e. rules for the formulation of definitions after the method has been chosen — there is wide agreement between the two lexicographical cultures. Examples are the rules on adequacy, simplicity, clarity, and the avoidance of circular definitions (see for example Landau 1984; Weinberger 1970; Dahlberg 1976; DIN 2330, 1979; Wüster 1979).

Equivalence

Equivalence informs us about similarities and differences between concepts, i.e. common and distinctive semantic features, relations of equivalence. The category has two subcategories: equivalence relations *within one language* and equivalence relations *between two or more languages*. In both categories one can speak of full, partial or zero equivalence.

Using information on relations of equivalence within one language one can describe synonymy. It is often said that full equivalence, i.e. full synonyms, do not exist. In the terminological context, however, it is possible to speak of full synonymy, as style level, for example, is not regarded as a meaning-differentiating feature. Partial equivalence is called *quasi-synonymy*.

In *Dansk-Engelsk Ordbog* (1976) the expression *tage fast form* is given as a synonym for the sublemma *fæstne sig* 'assume definite form'. The synonymy is marked by an equals sign. Synonyms and near-synonyms in the target language of a bilingual dictionary are often listed separated by a comma. For example, *Dansk-Engelsk*

Ordbog lists the equivalents 'fierce, grim, gruff' under the lemma *bister*.

An example from DANTERM of a comment on quasi-synonymy is *'Radiobølger' kan ikke betragtes som fuldgyldigt synonym med 'elektromagnetiske bølger', da de elektromagnetiske bølger også omfatter f.eks. lysbølger* 'radio waves cannot be regarded as a full synonym of *electromagnetic waves* as electromagnetic waves also include, for example, light waves'.

In many cases a synonym is given as for the sake of meaning specification or differentiation.

Translation equivalents indicate relations of equivalence between two languages. *Full equivalence* is often signified by zero marking. Partial equivalence is specially marked, for example with a comment on differences. Non-equivalence or zero equivalence may be expressed by the fact that there is a suggested approximate translation or explanation.

In *Dansk-Engelsk Ordbog* (1976) partial equivalence is marked by *omtr* (for *omtrent* = 'approximately the same as'), for example to state the relation between *frugtgrød* and *stewed fruit*. As an example of zero equivalence we can mention that *folketingstidende* is explained in *Dansk-Engelsk Ordbog* by [*official report of parliamentary records*] .

In DANTERM partial equivalence can be indicated by a comment like *begrebet separation eksisterer ikke i Tyskland, men p.g.a. ligheden mellem definitionerne på og forholdene omkring begreberne 'separation' og 'Trennung' kan det lade sig gøre at oversætte 'separation' med 'Trennung', hvis man samtidig i en fodnote forklarer, at separation i Danmark sker ved en offentlig myndigheds dekret* 'the concept of legal separation does not exist in Germany, but because of the similarity between the definitions of, and circumstances surrounding the concepts 'legal separation' and 'Trennung', 'legal separation' may be translated by 'Trennung', as long as one explains in a footnote that separation in Denmark is effected by a court order'.

An example of zero equivalence from DANTERM is found under *Behördenmodell* where the suggestion is *institutionsmodel (oversættelsesforslag)* 'institutional model (suggested translation)'.

3.2 The linking of information

The choice of approach will entail that the central units in each lexicographical work will be delimited and defined. To a certain extent these central units will determine how the various types of information will be linked together.

But the linkage possibilities also depend on the storage medium and the form of presentation. Storage in computer systems enables us to link various types of information in a multi-dimensional structure. Both network databases and relational databases offer this kind of multi-dimensional linkage.

In the presentation of related information types, however, one must be content with a one-dimensional structure. The classic dictionary entry has a tree structure where the headword is the root of the tree. The branches of the tree are usually marked typographically. One achieves something more like the more flexible network structure by using cross-references which act as pointers from one place in a tree structure to another point in the same or another tree structure.

Items of information that can be described as variants and subclassifications will often be linked information. When one describes an orthographic form as a variant, one does so because of its association with another orthographic form, i.e. the lexical unit. In the group for grammatical information, for example, *part of speech* can include a subclassification that gives information in compressed form on valency, e.g. *vt* for *verbum transitivum*.

We conclude this review of the taxonomy with an overview of the general information types, with the proposed subcategories specified for each category.

3.3 Overview of the main groups for general information types, categories and subcategories

MAIN GROUPS	CATEGORIES	SUBCATEGORIES
Etymological information	- parallel(s)	
	- origin	
Graphic information	- orthographical information	
	- graphic symbol	
Grammatical information	- part of speech	
	- information on inflection	, paradigm information
		, inflectional form
	- word formation	
	- syntax	, valency
		, syntactic function
Phonetic information	- prosodic features	
	- segmental features	
Pragmatic information	- contextual information	, citation
		, possible context
	- usage	, temporal
		, spatial
		, social
		, frequency
	- external reference	, literature reference
		, source reference
	- evaluative information	
	- administrative information	, collection and processing of data
		, internal reference
		, homograph number
		, technical information
Semantic information	- subject classification	
	- semantic relations	, generic super-/subordinate relation
		, partitive relation
		, successive relation
		, causal relation
		, antonymy
	- content specification	, lexical paraphrase
		, analytic definition
		, synthetic definition
		, denotative definition
		, ostensive definition
	- equivalence	, equivalence within one language
		, equivalence between two or more languages

4. USING THE TAXONOMY

This chapter describes various lexical works and the types of information they contain. It thus serves both to exemplify and test the taxonomy. In the discussion of the dictionaries selected there are many examples of the different categories of the taxonomy, and we show how it is possible to relate the information types in each work to the classification of the taxonomy. Three very different types of lexicographical work have been chosen: an academic historical dictionary in the process of compilation; a substantial translation dictionary that has existed in book form since 1956; and a specialized, electronically stored term bank.

In the previous chapter we set up a taxonomy for lexicographical information. Its form can be described with the help of concepts from mathematics.

The taxonomy has three levels of abstraction. At each level there is a set of elements. At the highest level of abstraction we have called these elements *main groups*. At the next level the elements are called *categories*, and at the third level we have called the elements *subcategories*. At the two highest levels of abstraction the sets include only the pre-defined elements. At the subcategory level the individual dictionary editor can add new elements, as long as it is made sure that they are properly delimited from the pre-defined elements. The following relation pertains between the elements at the different levels of abstraction: an element at a higher level maps on to a set of elements at the next level down. In addition, the value sets for elements at any level are disjunctive.

In the preceding chapter we described elements at the two highest levels by specifying their value sets; at the two lower levels we also characterized the individual elements in each set, mainly by means of examples from lexicographical works.

In what follows we will explain the taxonomy in more detail by applying it to various lexicographical works. It should thus be possible to identify and place all the information types of a work, so that each of them has one position and one only in the taxonomy.

In the course of this work one encounters difficulties closely connected with lexicographical practice and tradition, i.e. the aspect of lexicographical practice concerned with concentrating as much information as possible in as few printed lines as possible. The authors of dictionaries are masters of the art of compressing information.

When one wishes to give an unambiguous description of the information in a dictionary — as one must if the information is to be used in a computerized system — one has to "unpack" the dictionary entries. It often emerges that an abbreviation or a citation provides several different items of information that belong to quite different categories in the taxonomy. A very common abbreviation like *vt* — for "transitive verb" — provides two items of information: one about the part of speech, and one syntactic. One can also get into difficulties describing the information provided by a citation: in many cases a citation, which comes under the category "contextual information", will be chosen so as to illustrate some feature or features of the word that belong in other categories of the taxonomy. In these cases the object language — the language dealt with in the dictionary — is used to give information that could be provided otherwise in a metalanguage. For example, the information conveyed by the abbreviation *vt* is in some cases given implicitly in the form of a citation where the verb in question appears with a subject and object. Besides explicit contextual information, then, citations can contain implicit information from many of the other taxonomy categories: for example, in general dictionaries it is not unusual to find a citation instead of an actual meaning specification as an illustration of a sub-meaning

The various forms of compression help the dictionary user, in that she is given many items of information without having to read very much. On the other hand, compression and implicit information often demand a great deal of previous knowledge from the user. By unpacking the information in the existing dictionaries we get a very clear picture of the demands each work makes on the user. The resulting description of entry structure and notational conventions can also form a basis for reflections on how one can process the dictionary automatically, and reveal the information types that are specified so often and so consistently that they can be of value to other dictionaries.

4.1 Academic dictionaries

4.1.1 Use of the taxonomy to classify lexicographical information for establishing a format for an academic dictionary

In the following we will describe how the taxonomy for lexicographical information has been used to establish a format for the academic dictionary *Gammeldansk Ordbog* (the GLDO), which is a work in progress.

4.1.2 General points about *Gammeldansk Ordbog*

The *purpose* of *Gammeldansk Ordbog* ("The Dictionary of Old Danish"), which is being compiled under the auspices of *Det danske Sprog- og Litteraturselskab* ("the Danish Society for Language and Literature") is:

- to provide a linguistic description in lexical form of the Danish language in the Old Danish period, i.e. from c. 1100 to 1515 AD;
- to create a philological handbook to serve as an aid to reading texts from the Old Danish period.

The *project-specific* information types (cf above, Chapter 3) — language, approach and medium of expression — are thus defined, as can be seen from the statement of the purpose of the work, as follows.

Language

As mentioned above, the GLDO has a dual purpose. On the one hand it is to be a linguistic description of the Danish language in the middle ages, i.e. a description of the *language stage Old Danish*; on the other the GLDO is to serve as an aid to reading texts from the Old Danish period, i.e. the semantic content of the Old Danish words is to be described by means of the *language stage Modern Danish*. Or, to put it in other terms, words from the *language stage Old Danish* are translated into the *language stage Modern Danish*. The GLDO is thus at once a native-language and a translation dictionary.

Approach

The lexical unit in the GLDO is the word — any word which can have an independent or superordinate function in the context. In contrast to this, prefixes and suffixes cannot be headwords; nor can multiword units. The approach in the entries is *semasiological*, and the entries will be in strict alphabetical order: *dughe* and *dyghth* (a verb and noun formed from the same root) are thus kept separate, as are *dvale* and *dvælje* (noun and verb from the same root). Compound and derived words are dealt with in separate entries, for example *drøveful*, *drøvelik*, *drøvelikhet* and *drøvelsedagh*.

Medium of expression

The medium of expression for the GLDO is *writing*. At the moment there are no plans for eventually replacing semantic descriptions with illustrations.

The *main material* on which the GLDO is based is the linguistic material handed down to us directly from medieval times, either as manuscripts or in the form of printed texts.

The *work of compiling the collection of slips* which will form the basis for the editorial work began in 1953. The collection of slips was planned and built up according to well-tried principles:

- the selection of lexicographically relevant words in extant texts;
- the transcription of the extant sources, either from manuscripts in the case of unpublished texts, or from modern

critical editions after collation with the manuscripts;

- the reproduction of the transcriptions;
- the final identification of the relevant words;
- philological processing of the dictionary slips (i.e. the work of adding information to the individual slips concerning
  - the wording of an original text, if any;
  - the wording of any parallel translations;
  - palaeographic aspects;
  - textual corrections etc.);
- alphabetization etc.

Each process involved in producing the slips is subject to meticulous checks to prevent errors. The method used to establish the GLDO slip archive has meant that the *one-million slip* collection has the following features:

- each word appears on the slip with so much of its context that in the great majority of cases it will be unnecessary to go back to the source from which it is excerpted to assess it;
- each slip is furnished with an orthographically standardized headword and a specification of the part of speech;
- on each slip, where it is useful for evaluating the word in question, variants from other transcriptions of the same text are given;
- wherever the information helps with the evaluation of the word in question, the wording of the original from which the Old Danish text is translated, or on which it is otherwise dependent, is given;
- on any slip where it is relevant, editorial information of a palaeographic, critical, semantic or encyclopaedic nature is given.

If all goes according to plan, this slip collection will result in an academic, historical dictionary in nine volumes.

4.1.3 Establishing editorial principles for the GLDO

Establishing a format for the GLDO on the basis of the general taxonomy involves *two different types of working procedure*.

One procedure ensures that each information type in the dictionary entries can be assigned to one and only one category in the taxonomy; the other is the definition of the subcategories necessary for the GLDO. The *working method* to be used in working out a format, which will be demonstrated below, can be described briefly as follows:

1. provisional editorial principles are drawn up on the basis of the lexicographer's general lexicographical experience;

2. the information types of the provisional format are confronted with the general taxonomy to establish whether the information types of the format can be assigned to one category of the taxonomy and one only; this confrontation helps the lexicographer to sort things out in his or her mind, to reach a higher level of "lexicographical awareness";

3. the lexicographer is then able to revise the structure of the dictionary entries, and the revised editorial principles can then once more be confronted with the general taxonomy in order to

   - check that the information categories are unambiguous, and
   - define the subcategories.

   For all the information types of the entry, the processes described in Points 2 and 3 should be repeated as often as necessary to fulfil

   - the requirement of non-ambiguity, and
   - the subcategorization requirement.

4. Finally, the definitive format can be drawn up.

We have now briefly presented the work process involved in editing the GLDO, and will go on to describe it in practice.

During the last period of the collection phase (in 1975) a number of sample entries were compiled, and provisional editorial principles were laid down. In 1986, when the collection of material was on the whole completed, these sample entries and the provisional editorial principles could form the basis for attempts to establish a definitive format, i.e. the final editorial rules for the dictionary, formulated as the structured subset of the categories of the taxonomy required by the GLDO.

The sample entries and provisional editorial principles had then reached a stage where they were so well thought-out and complete that they could form a point of departure for reflections and decisions on the information types an entry in the GLDO should contain. At the same time, the number of sample entries was not too large to allow for any alterations growing out of the wish to adapt the entry structure to the general taxonomy.

The 1975 editorial principles state concerning the content of an entry: "Each entry comprises 1) the head, and 2) the body. The head of the entry consists of a) the headword, b) specification of part of speech, c) inflection, d) variants, e) etymology and history, f) usage specifications. The body of the entry contains an account of the meanings of the word, documented by citations."

The various types of information traditionally found in an entry in a historical dictionary fall into four main types:

- information serving to identify the headword — i.e. of the above, a) headword, b) specification of part of speech, and d) variants;
- information on the inflectional features of the word — i.e. of the above, c) inflection;
- semantic information about the word — i.e. the body of the entry above;
- information on the history and etymology of the word — i.e. of the above, e) etymology and history and f) usage specification.

These main types of information are documented in an academic dictionary by references and citations of various kinds:

- citations from or references to the sources on which the dictionary is based;
- references to or citations from the sources from which the dictionary's sources are translated or on which they are otherwise dependent;
- cross-references to other entries in the same dictionary.

The main information types entail that the entries fall naturally into four sections:

- an identification section which we may for convenience call the "I" section;
- an inflectional section which we can call the "B" section ("B" from Danish *Bøjning* 'inflection')
- a semantic section — the "S" section;
- an etymological/historical "E" section.

The "I" section

After renewed reflection on the provisional editorial principles, we want the "I" section, which forms a natural introduction to an entry, to contain the following information types:

- headword;
- coverage marker;
- part-of-speech marker;
- variants.

Headword

The headword, written in a standardized orthography, can be preceded in cases where there are homographs by a marker distinguishing between them.

Coverage marker

The coverage marker, consisting of the presence or absence of a plus sign, "+", indicates whether all the instances on the slips have been cited in the entry. This is hardly information on word identification, but it is practical information relevant to the whole entry, telling the user that it would serve no purpose to consult the slip collection for further instances of the headword: all the slip material has been covered in the entry. This information is most conveniently placed next to the headword.

Part-of-speech marker

As far as the indication of part of speech is concerned, the 1975 editorial principles, quoted here at length, but without references to examples in the sample entries, are as follows.

b) *Parts of speech* are to be identified by markers such as *sb.*, *adj.*, *part. adj.*, *adv.*, *vb.*, etc. For substantives (nouns) special rules apply (see under c) Inflection).

c) *Inflection*. For substantives, insofar as the material permits, the definite form should be given in the singular and the indefinite form in the plural:[3] in these cases, the marker *sb.* should not be used. If the plural is not documented, its form is not given. In cases where only the plural is documented, one can either construct a singular form for the lemma or — if there is uncertainty about whether the singular was in use — the plural form can be used as the lemma. If a substantive is not documented in the definite form, the marker *sb.* is used — also with compound words, even if the definite form of the second element of the compound is documented outside the compound. If attributive or predicative words show the gender of the substantive, this is marked with *fk.* [i.e. *fælleskøn* — common gender] or *n.* [neuter]; when these markers are used, there should be a reference to at least one source documenting the gender. After the general statement of inflectional forms, in the case of common-gender words, any examples should be given that show whether the word was perceived as masculine or feminine.

Variants

Variants are forms of words that require more detailed comment, first and foremost the most important orthographical variants, especially any that probably reveal phonetic differences. These variants are documented (cf above) in different ways:

- by reference to relevant specialist literature where the variant in question is discussed in more detail;
- by reference to the Old Danish source where the variant is found;
- by reference to other entries in the GLDO where variants of related words shed light on the variant in question.

[3. Danish nouns today have two genders - common and neuter. Old Danish also has traces of a division into masculine and feminine. As the Danish definite article is enclitic (*-en*, *-et*) it can serve as a part-of-speech and gender marker in labelling nouns. The form changes in the plural (*-erne*, *-ene*). There are thus both definite and indefinite plural forms of nouns. Morphemic variants of a substantive are usually cited in the order *canonical form - definite singular - indefinite plural - definite plural*, e.g. *by, byen, byer, byerne* (common gender), *hus, huset, huse, husene* (neuter). Scandinavian grammarians have traditionally classified these alternations as a form of inflection (Dan. *bøjning*)].

The "I" section's two information types, "headword" and "variant", can, as appears from the rather more thorough description of them, be classified into the following lexical information types:

headword	**homograph marker** **headword**
variant	**variant** **documentation**

So how do the lexical information types of the "I" section fit in with the proposed taxonomy's *general information* types? Is the requirement stated in Chapter 3, that a given item of lexical information should be identified as belonging to one category in the taxonomy, and one only, met?

Homograph marker

This information is uniquely classified as *pragmatic information* in accordance with the *main group* of that name, and in the category *administrative information*, i.e. it is an item of *pragmatic/administrative information*.

Headword

This is uniquely classified in accordance with the main group *graphic information* in the category *orthographical information*, i.e. it is an item of *graphic/orthographical information*.

Coverage marker

This information is uniquely classified as *pragmatic/administrative information* (in the following, classifications into main group and category will be abbreviated this way).

Part-of-speech marker

The quotation above from the 1975 editorial principles is an example of how the honing-down of lexicographical practice throughout many years has meant that in many cases lexical information is only implicitly present (a thorough demonstration of this space-saving practice is given below in Section 4.2).

If the 1975 editorial principles are followed in establishing the definitive set of editorial rules, the GLDO's information categories will only be in complete agreement with the information types of the general taxonomy if a substantive has *not* been preserved in the definite form. If the substantive is documented in the definite form the *sb.* marker should not be used as the part of speech marker according to these principles, as the information that the headword is a substantive is given implicitly by the citation of the definite singular form and (if documented) the indefinite plural form. In this case, then, the lexical information in the GLDO will not be assignable to one and only one information category in the general taxonomy, but could be classified as both *grammatical/part-of-speech information* and *grammatical/inflectional information*.

As the desirability of the implicit communication form is very much a moot point, and as more explicit presentation is necessary for the processing and exchange of data, part-of-speech information should be given by the labels *sb.*, *adj.*, *vb.*, *adv.*, etc., while inflectional information is assigned to the "B" section (see below for further details of this).

This would bring the GLDO information category into line with the information types of the general taxonomy, so that the indication of part of speech could be unambiguously classified as a *grammatical/part-of-speech* marker.

Variant

A variant can be uniquely classified as *graphic/orthographical* information.

Documentation

Documentation cannot be directly assigned to one and only one of the categories of the taxonomy. As stated above, a variant can be documented by one or more of the following three types of reference:

- to the relevant specialist literature;
- to the source from which the dictionary has it;
- to other entries in the dictionary.

Of these three, reference to specialist literature and source reference can be classified according to the taxonomy as *pragmatic/external reference*, while reference to the other entries in the dictionary can be classified as *pragmatic/administrative information*.

Is such a reordering of the documentation information into two categories — a *pragmatic/external* type containing references to specialist literature and a *pragmatic/administrative* type for references to other entries — desirable?

In terms of the utilization of data storage facilities for the editing and presentation of the GLDO (more on this in Chapter 6) a listing of all cross-references to other entries in the dictionary would provide useful checking possibilities. To achieve a similar facility for checking the correctness and consistency of source references and the possibility of an automatic complete bibliography of specialist literature quoted, it would be necessary to work with two parallel and mutually independent *pragmatic/external reference* types, i.e. to subclassify the category *pragmatic/external reference* into two subcategories, one for references to specialist literature, and one for source references.

Developments in the establishment of the format for the "I" section were — as will have emerged from the above — as follows. In the first phase of drawing up the format, which resulted in the 1975 editorial principles, the following types of information were described:

- headword
- part-of-speech marker
- variant

In the second phase, after renewed reflection, the work was done using the following information types:

- homograph marker
- headword
- coverage marker
- part-of-speech marker
- variant
- variant documentation

— and in the third phase of the establishment of the format, which took the general taxonomy as its point of departure, it proved both necessary and desirable to operate with the following information types:

- homograph marker (coded IHOM)
- headword (coded IOPO)
- coverage marker (coded IUDN)
- part-of-speech marker (coded IOKA)
- variant (coded IOPV)
- documentation, literature reference (coded IOVL)
- documentation, source reference (coded IOVX)
- cross-reference between entries (coded IHEX)

PHASES

I	II	III
- headword	- homograph marker	- homograph marker
	- headword	- headword
	- coverage marker	- coverage marker
- part-of-speech marker	- part-of-speech marker	- part-of-speech marker
- variant	- variant	- variant
	- variant documentation	- documentation, literature reference
		- documentation, source reference
		- cross-references between entries

Conclusion

This attempt, starting with the 1975 editorial principles, to draw up a definitive format for the "I" section of the GLDO with the help of the taxonomy for lexicographical information, left us with the following two main lessons.

In the first place, in order to meet the requirement that a given item of lexical information can be identified as belonging to one and only one of the categories of the taxonomy, it was necessary to split up the information type which in the 1975 editorial principles contained implicit part-of-speech information into proper, explicit part-of-speech markers, placed in the identification section, and inflectional information, assigned to the "B" section (see below).

Secondly, to maintain the degree of complexity in the GLDO, and to make use of all conceivable checking and sorting possibilities when using computer facilities in the editing and presentation of dictionaries (see Chapter 1), three of the categories of the taxonomy had to be supplied with subcategories:

- pragmatic/administrative information with the subcategories
    - homograph marker (IHOM)
    - coverage marker (IUDN)
    - cross-reference between entries (IHEX)
- graphic/orthographical information with the subcategories
    - headword (IOPO)
    - variant (IOPV), and
- pragmatic/external reference with the subcategories
    - specialist literature reference (IOVL)
    - source reference (IOVX)

Definitive format

The definitive format for the "I" section of the GLDO now looks like this — described in terms of the so-called ETTO notation (see 5.2.2 for more details of this):

```
(IHOM)
 IOPO
(IUDN)
 IOKA
┌ IOPV    ┐*
│ (IOVL)  │
└ [IOVX]* ┘
[IHEX]*
```

The establishment of the definitive format based on the general taxonomy for the other three main sections of the GLDO, the "B", "S" and "E" sections, will be described more briefly in the following.

The "B" section

After provisional reflection, it was decided that the "B" section should contain the following types of information.

As regards *inflectional information* on substantives we refer to the quotation from the 1975 editorial principles above. In the case of adjectives and verbs the editorial rules say (omitting references to examples in the sample entries):

> Normally, the inflection of adjectives is not given. With verbs, the preterite form is given. If the preterite is not documented the form is not mentioned.

Information is also given on the *usage* of the inflectional forms listed. This is primarily chronological information, but geographical distribution or information on register may also be given. Finally, there is *documentation* referring to the sources of the inflectional forms listed.

Comparison of the information types in the "B" section and the categories of the general taxonomy

A comparison of these three information types with the categories of the general taxonomy to see whether the requirement of non-ambiguity is met shows that the information type *documentation* includes elements of both *pragmatic/contextual* information, i.e. the form stipulated for the taxonomy subcategory *citation*, and the *pragmatic/external reference* type. The information type *documentation* should therefore be split into two parts: one for the *pragmatic/contextual* information, i.e. the actual source citation which contains or consists of the inflectional form to be documented; and one for the *pragmatic/external reference* information on the locus — the page and line of the source from which the inflectional form and/or citation has come.

The form is thus as follows:

Documentation { **citation** / **source reference** }

Establishment of subcategories

To achieve the advantages mentioned in Chapter 1 it was necessary to give thorough consideration to the content of the information types established for the "B" section, i.e.

- inflectional information;
- usage;
- citation;
- source reference.

This revealed a need to set up the following subcategories for the category *inflectional information*:

- part-of-speech subclassification
- inflectional marker
- inflectional form

The subcategory *citation* is realized as:

- *source citation*, i.e, the Old Danish citation containing or consisting of the inflectional form
- *original of source*, which, as the name suggests, is a citation of the original source from which the Old Danish source is translated, or on which it is otherwise dependent — the inflectional form of which may have influenced the Old Danish form

The types of information in the "B" section thus become

- subclassification (BSUB) (grammatical/inflectional information)
- inflectional marker (BFLE) (grammatical/inflectional information)
- information on usage (BØKO) (pragmatic/usage information)
- inflectional form (BØFO) (grammatical/inflectional information)
- source citation (BØCI) (pragmatic/contextual information)
- source reference (BØKX) (pragmatic/external reference)
- original of source (BFXX) (pragmatic/contextual information)

Conclusion

As with the "I" section above, the conclusion as far as establishing a format based on the taxonomy is concerned is that it will be necessary

- to subclassify the information type *documentation* for the sake of the non-ambiguity requirement (this corresponds to the first conclusion on the "I" section)

- to introduce subcategories under the categories *grammatical/ inflectional information* and *pragmatic/contextual information* to gain the advantages mentioned in Chapter 1 (this corresponds to the second conclusion on the "I" section)

Final format

The final format for the "B" section of the GLDO thus looks like this:

$$\begin{bmatrix} \text{(BSUB)} \\ \text{BFLE} \\ \text{(BØKO)} \\ \text{(BØFO)} \\ \begin{bmatrix} \text{BØCI} \\ [\,\text{BØKX}\,]^{+} \\ \text{(BFXX)} \end{bmatrix}^{*} \end{bmatrix}^{*}$$

The "S" section

Using the same procedure as for the "I" and "B" sections, the result of comparing the required information types, i.e.

- meaning number
- syntactic information
- information on phrases
- meaning specification
- cross-references between entries
- documentation

with the taxonomy categories is that the information type *documentation*, like the documentation category of the "B" section, will be subdivided into the types *citation* (pragmatic/contextual information) and *source reference* (pragmatic/external reference).

Like the "B" section's *citation*, the *citation* of the "S" section is also best divided into the following two categories:

- *source citation*, i.e. the citation from an Old Danish source that documents a given meaning, and
- *original of source*, i.e. a citation of the source text from which the Old Danish source is translated or on which it is otherwise dependent, and which can be helpful in assessing the semantic content of the Old Danish citation

The information types in the "S" section, once related to the categories of the taxonomy, thus become:

- meaning number (SBEN) (semantic information/semantic relations)
- syntax (SSGK) (grammatical information/syntax)
- information on phrases (SORF) (pragmatic/contextual information)
- meaning specification (SBEB) (semantic/content specification)
- cross-reference between entries (SIHX) (pragmatic/administrative information)
- source citation (SBCX) (pragmatic/contextual information)
- source reference (SCXX) (pragmatic/external reference)

This means that the category *pragmatic/contextual information* is supplied for the "S" section with three subcategories, i.e.

- information on phrases
- source citation, and
- original of source citation.

Conclusion

The conclusion on establishing the format on the basis of the general taxonomy is thus the same for the "S" section as for the "I" and "B" sections.

A further requirement for the "S" section is stated in the 1975 editorial principles:

> Large entries where it is possible to operate with clear semantic and/or syntactic differentiations should begin with an introductory *overview* of the classification.

This means that the "S" section is increased by three information types parallel with *meaning number*, *syntactic information* and *meaning specification*, i.e.

- overview meaning number (SOBN)
- overview syntactic information (SOGK), and
- overview meaning specification (SOBB)

This makes the final format for the "S" section

[SOBN (SOGK) SOBB]*
[(SBKN) (SSGK) (SORF) (SBKB) (SIHX) (SBCY) SBCX [SCKX]*]*

The "E" section

The GLDO is not really an etymological dictionary, so the bulk of the etymological information given in the dictionary will be references to occurrences in parallel languages. A comparison of the categories of the general taxonomy with those of the GLDO's "E" section —

- loan word/word formation information (ELDK), corresponding to the *etymological/origin* category of the taxonomy
- parallel(s) for native/loan words (see below)
- parallel(s) for younger compounds and derived words (see below)
- literature reference (EEHL), corresponding to the taxonomy category *pragmatic/external reference*, and
- usage information (EBRO), corresponding to the taxonomy category *pragmatic/usage information*

— shows, as already suggested, that the requirement that lexical information types should belong in one category only is met.

The wish to make use of the advantages mentioned in Chapter 1 entails that the information type *parallel(s) for native/loan words*, corresponding to the category *etymological information/ parallel(s)*, is realized as the subcategories

- donor language/language of parallel (ELPS)
- donor/parallel word (ELPO)
- information on donor/parallel word (ELPI)
- meaning of donor/parallel word (ELPB)
- core meaning of donor/parallel word (ELPG)

The information type *analogue(s)* of younger compounds and derived words, corresponding to the category *etymological/parallel(s)* is realized as the subcategories

- compare (EJSA)
- language of analogue (EJSS)
- analogous word (EJSO)
- meaning of analogous word (EJSB)

The format for the "E" section now looks like this:

```
┌  (ELDK)   ┐*
│ ┌ELPS  ┐* │
│ │ELPO  │  │
│ │(ELPI)│  │
│ │(ELPB)│  │
│ └(ELPG)┘  │
│ ┌EJSA  ┐* │
│ │(EJSS)│  │
│ │EJSO  │  │
│ └(EJSB)┘  │
│  (EEHL)   │
└  (EBRO)   ┘
```

Overall conclusion: the taxonomy as a useful tool

It will have emerged from the above account that it has proved useful to take the general taxonomy as a point of departure in formulating the editorial rules for the GLDO as a structured subset of the taxonomy needed by the GLDO.

The primary advantage of relating the information types of the GLDO to the categories of the taxonomy is that the editorial rules have now been formulated so that information types are uniquely defined and no implicit information is given in the dictionary entries. The unique information types and explicit formulation of the information in the entries are a necessary condition if data processing and exchange are to take place and the ensuing advantages gained, if optimal communication with the users is to be ensured, and if the editors are to have an apparatus based on the taxonomy that will guarantee quick, consistent editing of the dictionary.

The general taxonomy has been used, with the exchange of data with the GLDO in mind, to describe the entry structure in the alphabetically-ordered reference work *Danmarks Stednavne* ("Place Names of Denmark")(Hjorth 1986).

In establishing the format for the GLDO on the basis of the taxonomy, the following taxonomy categories were *not* used (categories are called by their category name alone here, not, as above in this chapter, by referring to both main group and category):

- prosodic features
- segmental features
- graphic symbol
- word formation
- evaluative information
- subject classification

That these particular categories were not used in the GLDO is primarily due to the fact that the dictionary describes a historically limited period, and that it is in the nature of things that the sources of the dictionary are exclusively written ones and represent a limited number of genres.

Only a few of the categories were *directly transferable* to the GLDO format without further division into subcategories. These were:

- origin → loan word/word formation (ELDK)
- part of speech → part of speech marker (IOKA)

With many of the taxonomy categories *subcategorization* has been necessary because of the complexity of the dictionary. The subcategorizations that it has been useful to make for the GLDO have in all cases proved to be different from those of the taxonomy (in the cases where subcategorizations have been made there). In some cases the GLDO subcategorizations are *much more detailed* than those of the taxonomy (for example, for contextual information, because of the scholarly character of the dictionary and its highly developed and minutely detailed documentation). In other cases subcategorization has been *less detailed* (for example, in the case of usage information, because of the limited extent and nature of the sources).

4.2 Translation dictionaries: describing Vinterberg and Bodelsen's *Dansk-Engelsk Ordbog* with the taxonomy

4.2.1 Describing an existing dictionary

Another potential use of the taxonomy is the description of existing dictionaries. "Why describe existing dictionaries at all?" one might ask. There are several possible reasons for doing so. For example, one might want to compare different dictionaries, in which case the taxonomy could function as the necessary *tertium comparationis*, since entries in different dictionaries — as shown in Chapter 2 — may be arranged in categories that are not congruent with one another, and since even congruent categories may have different names depending on the editorial practice of the dictionary in question.

Another incentive is the wish to use data processing facilities as a lexicographical, not just a typographical, aid in future revisions of the dictionary (Norling-Christensen 1982: 215f). The following account, where the taxonomy is applied to Vinterberg and Bodelsen's *Dansk-Engelsk Ordbog* (1976), concentrates on this aspect.

The dictionary already exists in machine-readable form for the purposes of computerized photocomposition. This typographical material is only coded for printing, i.e. with instructions on whether a segment of text is to be printed in a bold, italic or plain typeface. For lexicographical purposes, i.e. as an aid to editing, the usefulness of this material is limited. If one needs to access particular sections of one or more entries automatically, it can only be done by so-called free-text retrieval: that is, entries can only be accessed as identified text strings. Moreover, the editorial staff only has access to the results of such a search in the form of printouts.

An example of this is a list printed out as the result of a search on the text string ***mar*** (bold or italic typeface), for ***maritim***, the abbreviation used to label maritime words and expressions. This list has been used as material for the expert on maritime matters who has assisted the editors with the revision of words and expressions from this field. So it has not been necessary for him to read through all the 4000 columns of the dictionary to find the relevant material, which in itself is of course a very great advantage. But a search for the character string ***mar*** (bold or italic) and the printout of all the instances of this string with the text immediately surrounding it gives imprecise results in two ways: on the one hand text strings that are irrelevant to the purpose at hand, like *akvamarin* or ***marked***, with their surrounding context, are printed out; on the other, not all the relevant words and expressions are necessarily marked with ***mar***. On the face of it, one would think that a further specification of the contexts in which ***mar*** is to be printed out would solve the problem of the irrelevant text strings; but there was no way of providing the existing system with such a specification so that all the relevant occurrences of ***mar*** and only these will be printed out. The result of such an attempt at more detailed specification would only be new problems.

The use of a ready-made format for building up a dictionary entry with subdivisions of the entry text into independently labelled information categories would make the retrieval process easier and improve the results of the search, as it would also be possible to look for more than just a known, identified character string. In the case of *mar* above, one could first restrict the search to an information category coded as "specialized field" and *then* look for the content *mar*. This way irrelevant strings like *akvamarin* and *marked* would be excluded. Moreover, the editorial staff could operate with an internal coding — suppressed for external purposes — of all the relevant words and expressions with *mar* so they could be searched for and printed out on the basis of the information category coded "specialized field" and containing *mar*. The codes would not necessarily have to be in the final printed dictionary text — or visible in the dictionary available to users in database form.

Classification of the dictionary text into information categories for a format can be done in many ways — cf. Chapter 2 — and the classification should of course reflect any wishes the editorial staff may have as regards what it should be possible to find and print out as subsets of the dictionary text, or as regards cooperation with other dictionaries.

Thus if one wanted to work out a format for an existing dictionary like Vinterberg and Bodelsen's *Dansk-Engelsk Ordbog*, it would help the work greatly if one began by using the main groups and categories of the taxonomy to describe the existing dictionary text. This way one could be quite certain from the outset about the exact types of information that can be found in the dictionary, where in the dictionary entry they are to be found, and not least how they are presented.

At this point it is reasonable to ask whether such information on the types of lexicographical data and their arrangement in the dictionary cannot be found in the front matter and instructions for the user. It can indeed — but only in very rudimentary form; and there are no editorial rules in print. The dictionary was revised for the second edition in 1966, and a supplement was drawn up for publication in 1973. Both these revisions, and the one in progress now, have entailed changes of various kinds in editorial principles; but there is no full description of these changes. If only for this reason, an initial, clarificatory description making use of the taxonomy is desirable as an editorial aid.

4.2.2 Description using the project-specific information types of the taxonomy

Dansk-Engelsk Ordbog, as the title indicates, is a dictionary providing information on the two national languages Danish and English, with Danish as the source language and English as the target language. The medium of expression is writing, and the approach is semasiological: the lexicographical information is presented in the form of entries whose point of departure is one headword, whose potentially several English equivalents are recorded with necessary indications of differences in meaning or semantic classifications of the meaning content of the headword. In each entry where it is relevant one can also find a section on phrases containing the headword. Each of these phrases is supplied with one or more English equivalents. The dictionary thus features Danish words and phrases with their equivalents or translations — English words and phrases.

4.2.3 Lemma, sublemma and lexical units

In the review of the taxonomy, for the sake of generality, we omitted any discussion of lexicographical concepts like *headword*, *equivalent/translation*, *word*, *phrase*, *collocation* etc.; but concepts of this kind must be used — as seen above — as soon as the taxonomy is used for a specific lexicographical purpose.

In the specific description of a translation dictionary like *Dansk-Engelsk Ordbog*, it is useful to introduce and use the concepts *lemma*, *sublemma* and *lexical unit*.

What we understand by the *lemma* in this dictionary is the Danish character string (in semi-bold type) which introduces each entry — referred to above as the headword. In the vast majority of cases this character string consists of one word — understood as a unit consisting of at least one letter of the alphabet and surrounded by two blank spaces — for example *disparat* (see Fig. 4.2.4-1 a). Such a word may contain a hyphen, if the hyphen is not in initial or final position — for example *a-bombe*. Then there are character strings beginning or ending with hyphens (to show that they are potential elements in compounds) like *-apparat* (see Fig. 4.2.4-1 c) or *fabrik-*; and character strings containing or ending with a full stop like the abbreviations *eks.* and *M.F.* Both words and potential elements of compounds may contain vertical separators — like *destillations|anlæg* (see Fig. 4.2.4-1 c). Considerations of space entail that two synonymous lemmas, or two non-synonymous lemmas that can be translated by the same equivalent, wherever practical (i.e. alphabetically possible), may be "telescoped" by using brackets so they appear as one character string without intervening spaces, as is the case, for example, with *adams|figen(træ)* 'plantain' (but literally 'Adam's fig tree') which is a telescoping of the two words *adamsfigen* and *adamsfigentræ*. In a very few cases the lemma may consist of more than one word in the above sense, e.g. *a meta* 'on joint account', *hytte- og brofrontskod* 'poop and bridge front bulkheads', or *m. fl.* (for *med flere* 'and others, etc.') i.e. abbreviations with spaces between the abbreviated words.

The units that can be found as lemmas in *Dansk-Engelsk Ordbog* are uninflected words, the root forms (if possible) of regularly or irregularly inflected words, and irregular inflected forms of irregularly inflected words. The grammatical forms used as citation forms are the infinitive for verbs, indefinite singular (i.e. without the enclitic definite article) for nouns, and the indefinite singular, common gender, positive form for adjectives.

The concept *lexical unit* is used as an overall term for words, elements of compound words, abbreviations, idioms, collocations and set phrases. Combining *lexical unit* with the national language *Danish* gives us all the Danish words, elements of compounds or abbreviations making up the lemma or included in the lemma, when the space-saving compressions are "unpacked", along with the phrases in which the lemmatized unit is included: i.e., all the Danish units for which the dictionary supplies translation information in the form of equivalents. It should be noted that the Danish phrases in an entry are thus regarded as "sub-headwords" — *sublemmas* — (cf Manley/Jacobsen/Hjørnager Pedersen 1987) primarily distinguished from the lemma proper by being italicized and by not beginning the entry. Inflected forms of the lemma (without context) can also occur as sublemmas (not semi-bold and not beginning the entry) — for example *-t* for *afbleget*, with *afblege* as the lemma and 'faded, discoloured' as equivalents in an entry like

> **afblege** *vt* bleach (out); *-t* faded, discoloured; *en -t farve* a faded colour; *-t hår* peroxide hair; *en -t skønhed* a faded beauty.

But the great majority of sublemmas typically contain spaces between words, as for example *en -t farve* and *en -t skønhed* above.

Combining *lexical unit* with the national language English gives us all the English words, parts of words, abbreviations, phrases or combinations of words that occur as equivalents or translations of the Danish lexical units, whether the latter are lemmas or sublemmas.

4.2.4 Incorporating the general information types of the taxonomy

By relating the information in a few specific, very small dictionary entries from *Dansk-Engelsk Ordbog* to the main groups and/or categories of the taxonomy, we can indicate how compressed the information actually is in this traditional type of translation dictionary. In order to draw up a format, of course, a far larger number of entries — i.e. a representative sample — would have to be analysed (cf also Section 5.4).

Figs. 4.2.4-1 a-d show the dictionary material to be discussed below, and its description in schematic form. We can start with a very small, quite simple dictionary entry — the entry on *disparat* (Fig. 4.2.4-1 a).

The bold type-face and position in the entry of the lemma *disparat* give the information that there exists such a lexical unit in the national language Danish; through its form the lemma also gives orthographical information. The abbreviation *adj* specifies the part of speech as *adjective* and its position immediately after the lemma means that it applies to the lemma; *adj* thus gives information about the national language Danish. Between *adj* and *disparate* there is a zero-marked item of information, i.e. the inflectional information that *disparat* has no irregular synthetic comparative and superlative forms. But this is only evident from

Fig. 4.2.4-1 a Relation of entry on *disparat* and parts of entry on *god* from *Dansk-Engelsk Ordbog* (1976) to the main groups/categories of the taxonomy

Entries and parts of entries	Project-specific information types	General information types
disparat *adj* disparate		
disparat	lemma + lexical unit + national language: Danish	orthographical information
adj	national language: Danish national language: Danish	part of speech inflectional information
disparate	lexical unit + national language: English	orthographical information + equivalence
		administrative information
god *adj (bedre, bedst) (se ogs godeste, godt, I. gode, bedre, bedst)* 1 good (fx a good beginning...		
...		
( )		administrative information
bedre	national language: Danish	inflectional information
,		administrative information
bedst	national language: Danish	inflectional information
(se ... bedst)		administrative information (internal reference)
...		

a comparison with an entry like *god* (see Fig. 4.2.4-1 a) where the irregular comparative and superlative forms *bedre* and *bedst* are given explicitly. However, there is no way of knowing from the entry whether *disparat* has comparative and superlative forms at all, and if so what they might be.

The English word 'disparate' gives orthographical information on the lexical unit that is the equivalent of the lemma, and information on national language — that this lexical unit is English. Now the lemma equivalent has been mentioned — the English lexical unit given as equivalent to the Danish lexical unit of the lemma; but how do we actually know that the English lexical unit is in fact such a unit, and thus an equivalent? We know this because 'disparate' is in a plain typeface — neither semi-bold like the lemma nor italic like the editorial comments and Danish sublemmas. The instructions to the user in the dictionary incidentally do not mention that equivalents — the English lexical units that are direct translations of the Danish lexical units, are in plain type, and that information on their status as English lexical units and on equivalence between lexical units in the two national languages is given by typographical changes from the semi-bold of the lemma or the italic of the sublemmas to a plain typeface. The full stop immediately following this is administrative information to the user that the entry is now concluded.

As the next example to be described we can take another small entry — the one on *desperation* (see Fig. 4.2.4-1 b). This can be described in the same way as *disparat*. So we will continue with the information *en*. This is the Danish common-gender indefinite article and thus first and foremost gives information on national language. But its communicative function is to inform us that the Danish lexical unit constituting the lemma is a common-gender substantive. No explicit part-of-speech marker for *substantive* is thus present, as *adj* was for *adjective* in the entry on *disparat*.

There is in fact also inflectional information here about the Danish lexical unit *desperation*, i.e. the information that *desperation* has no plural form. This is given by the absence of explicit marking. That the information is present can be seen by comparing it with the entry on *despot*, for example (Fig. 4.2.4-1 b), where the lemma is marked with the plural ending *-er*. This zero-marked information on the absence of a plural form also applies to the English substantive 'desperation' given as an equivalent to the lemma *desperation*. In the entry on *despot*, *-er* also tells us implicitly that the English lexical unit 'despot', as the equivalent to the Danish lexical unit *despot*, has a plural form, even though this form is not cited explicitly. That the uncited

Fig. 4.2.4-1 b Relation of the entry on *desperation* and parts of the entries on *despot* and *anakoluti* from *Dansk-Engelsk Ordbog* (1976) to the main groups/categories of the taxonomy

Entries and parts of entries	Project-specific information types	General information types
desperation *en* desperation (fx do sth in d.).		
desperation	lemma + lexical unit + national language: Danish	orthographical information
en	national language: Danish national language: Danish	part of speech + subclassification of part of speech
	national language: Danish + English	inflectional information
desperation	lexical unit + national language: English	orthographical information + equivalence
(fx)		administrative information
do sth in d.	national language: English	contextual information + syntactic information
.		administrative information
despot *en -er* despot.		
...		
-er	national language: Danish + English	inflectional information
despot	lexical unit + national language: English	orthographical information + equivalence
	national language: English	inflectional information
.		administrative information
anakoluti *en -er* anacoluthon (*pl* anacolutha).		
...		
( )		administrative information
pl anacolutha	national language: English	inflectional information
...		

plural form of 'despot' is not irregular is in fact also conveyed by the absence of any explicit information between the English equivalent and the concluding full stop — it is assumed that the user will normally be familiar with the regular morphology of English substantives. The presence of the latter item of inflectional information can be deduced from a comparison with the entry on *anakoluti* (Fig. 4.2.4-1 b) where the equivalent 'anacoluthon' is followed by '*pl* anacolutha'.

The description of the equivalent 'desperation' is otherwise like that of 'disparate'. It is followed by '(fx)', which is an item of pragmatic-administrative information, in the sense that it tells the user how the information introduced by '(fx' and ending with ')' is to be treated or understood, i.e. as an example of the use of the English lexical unit. This English example, 'do sth in d.', where 'd.' for reasons of space is a compressed version of 'desperation', is a supplement to the English lexical unit 'desperation' and therefore appears in the same typeface — plain type for information on the national language English. The example is an item of pragmatic contextual information, since it shows a possible context for the lexical unit 'desperation'. At the same time it provides implicit syntactic information about the English lexical unit, since the example shows a construction into which it can enter. The full stop — administrative information — then tells us that the entry is finished.

The entry on *destillationsapparat* (Fig. 4.2.4-1 c) shows first and foremost how part of the lemma in an entry that comes as the second or later entry in a group of related entries is represented by a hyphen: *-apparat* here is to be read as *destillationsapparat*, and one only arrives at the Danish lexical unit underlying the representation in the lemma by making the substitution. This reading is only possible when the entry is seen as belonging with the preceding entry *destillationsanlæg*. The entry also demonstrates zero marking for both part of speech and inflectional information. The absence of explicit information can moreover be regarded as zero-marked administrative information (dictionary-internal reference) indicating to the user that information on gender and inflection is to be found in the entry on *apparat* — where the information that the listed equivalents have plural

Fig. 4.2.4-1 c Relation of the entry on *destillationsapparat* from *Dansk-Engelsk Ordbog* (1976) to the main groups/ categories of the taxonomy

Entries and parts of entries	Project-specific information types	General information types

destillations|anlæg distilling plant. **-apparat** distilling apparatus, still, distiller; *(i skib)* freshwater generator.

Entries and parts of entries	Project-specific information types	General information types
-apparat	lemma + lexical unit + national language; Danish	orthographical information
	national language; Danish	part of speech + word formation + administrative information (internal reference)
	national language; Danish + English	subject classification
distilling apparatus	lexical unit + national language; English	orthographic information + equivalence
	national language; English	inflectional information
,	national language; English	equivalence
still	lexical unit + national language; English	orthographical information + equivalence
	national language; English	inflectional information
,	national language; English	equivalence
distiller	lexical unit + national language; English	orthographical information + equivalence
	national language; English	inflectional information
;	national language; English national language; Danish	administrative information + equivalence + semantic relations
(i skib)	national language; Danish + English	subject classification (for meaning differentiation)
freshwater generator	lexical unit + national language; English	orthographical information + equivalence
	national language; English	inflectional information
.		administrative information

forms is also given implicitly (cf above on *desperation* and *despot*). But even without looking up the entry on *apparat*, zero marking has given two other items of information — on the part of speech of *destillationsapparat* (substantive) and information on word formation (that *destillationsapparat* is a compound). For it is specified in the user instructions that the markers *en* and *et* and plural forms are not given with compound nouns, since this information can be found in the entry on the last element of the compound, in this case *apparat*.

With respect to the subject-classifying, meaning-differentiating information *(i skib)* later in the entry, there is yet another zero-marked item of information between the lemma and the first English lexical unit listed — the equivalent 'distilling apparatus' — i.e. information to the user on subject classification along the lines of "*destillationsapparat* in the sense that, as far as the editors can judge, is most likely to occur to you first; that is, not an apparatus for distilling fresh water on board a ship". As this information also applies to the following three equivalents, it has dual reference in terms of national language.

After this, three English lexical units are listed as equivalents to the Danish lexical unit underlying the lemma representation. The description of each of these three lexical units in terms of the taxonomy would be no different from the preceding descriptions of English lexical units. But there is also information about the interrelations among these three lexical units. They are to be regarded as English synonyms, and this is marked by the punctuation, since commas have been placed between the three equivalents. Here the comma provides an item of language-internal equivalence information on the national language English, evident from the position of the commas.

The semicolon before the subject-classificatory, meaning-differentiating information *(i skib)* relates to the two national languages, as it applies to both lemma and equivalent. It is in the first place administrative information: it indicates to the user that something new is coming and attention should be paid. But at the same time the semicolon gives unspecified information about the semantic relations between the different senses of the

Fig. 4.2.4-1 d Relation of the entry on *detonere* and parts of the entry on *gå* and *afgå* from *Dansk-Engelsk Ordbog* (1976) to the main groups/ categories of the taxonomy

detonere *vi (eksplodere)* detonate; *(mus.)* sing (, play) false *(el.* out of tune); *-nde tændsnor* detonating fuse.

Entries and parts of entries	Project-specific information types	General information types
detonere	lemma + lexical unit + national language: Danish	orthographical information
vi	national language: Danish national language: Danish	part of speech + syntactic information inflectional information
(eksplodere)	national language: Danish + English national language: Danish	content specification (for meaning differentiation) + equivalence
detonate	lexical unit + national language: English	orthographical information + equivalence
;	 national language: English national language: Danish	administrative information + equivalence + semantic relations
(mus.)	national language: Danish + English	subject classification (specialized field)
sing false	lexical unit + national language: English	orthographical information + equivalence
(el.)	 national language: English	administrative information + equivalence
sing out of tune	lexical unit + national language: English	orthographical information + equivalence
(,)	 national language: English	administrative information + equivalence
play false	lexical unit + national language: English	orthographical information + equivalence
(el.)	 national language: English	administrative information + equivalence
play out of tune	lexical unit + national language: English	orthographical information + equivalence
;		administrative information

(Fig. 4.2.4-1 d continued)

Entries and parts of entries	Project-specific information types	General information types
-nde tandsnor	sublemma + lexical unit + national language: Danish	orthographical information
detonating fuse	lexical unit + national language: English	orthographical information + equivalence
		administrative information
gå *gik gået vi & vt* ...		
...		
gik	national language: Danish	inflectional information
gået	national language: Danish	inflectional information
vi	national language: Danish	part of speech + syntax
&		administrative information
vt	national language: Danish	part of speech + syntax
...		
afgå *vi* ...		
afgå	lemma + lexical unit + national language: Danish	orthographical information
		administrative information (internal reference)
vi	national language: Danish	part of speech + syntax
...		

Danish lexical unit represented by the lemma, i.e. the sense differentiated by *(i skib)* and the preceding zero-marked sense. The semicolon may also be said to provide the equivalence information that the three preceding English lexical units are not synonymous with the following lexical unit, the equivalent 'freshwater generator'. The semicolon thus also relates to the two national languages — it refers to both the Danish and English material.

After all four equivalents the absence of explicit marking gives the zero-marked inflectional information that none of the equivalents has an irregular plural form.

In the entry on *detonere* (Fig. 4.2.4-1 d) we can examine the marker *vi*, where *v* marks the lemma as a verb and *i* gives the syntactic information that the verb is intransitive.

Here too there is zero-marked inflectional information: that the non-compound verb of the lemma is regularly conjugated. If it had been an irregular non-compound verb, the full inflectional forms of the imperfect and perfect tenses would have been given as they are in the entry on ***gå*** (Fig. 4.2.4-1 d), where the forms ***gik*** and ***gået*** are listed explicitly. We must emphasize that we are talking about non-compound verbs here because a user of this dictionary is assumed to know whether a Danish verb is compound or simplex. The user who is unaware of this would for example be unable to find inflectional information on a compound irregular verb like ***afgå*** (Fig. 4.2.4-1 d), because this information is only to be found in the entry on the second element of the compound, ***gå***. Zero-marked information on regular conjugation only applies to the Danish lemma, not to the English lexical units or their parts. 'Sing' is irregular, but this is not stated either explicitly, implicitly or by zero-marking; the user is thus expected to be familiar with the morphology of English verbs.

The gloss *(eksplodere)* gives the content of the Danish lexical unit in the lemma: it differentiates meaning, contrasting this sense with the one marked by the specialized field label *(mus.)* 'musical', applying to both national languages; but *(eksplodere)* also specifies the content of the English lexical unit 'detonate'. This further constitutes an implicit language-internal item of information on equivalence — on synonymy between the Danish lexical unit of the lemma and the word used for meaning differentiation. It is not stated explicitly that they are synonyms.

There is nothing in particular to say about the English lexical unit, the equivalent 'detonate'. But it may be noted that the semicolon following it provides both administrative and semantic information — on equivalence and semantic relations. The semicolon indicates that something new is coming; it establishes an unspecified semantic relation between the two senses of the Danish lexical unit — 'explode' and the musical sense; and it indicates that the English lexical units corresponding to *(eksplodere)* and the musical sense respectively are not synonymous.

We have seen above how the comma can indicate synonymy between English lexical units. In this entry *(el.)* (for *eller*, 'or') has this function. At the same time *(el.)* can be seen as administrative information telling the user how the compressed or telescoped form of presentation is to be interpreted. The brackets and comma (,) also give administrative information to the user about the interpretation of the compressed presentation, and information on equivalence; but the equivalence information is that the lexical units containing 'sing' and 'play' are not synonymous — 'sing false' is not a synonym of 'play false', nor is 'sing out of tune' a synonym of 'play out of tune'. The telescoped presentation thus makes it possible to compress four different English lexical units, four equivalents, along with information about their semantic relations, all in very little space.

The semicolon following these is, unlike the semicolons mentioned above, an exclusively administrative marker; it only indicates that something new is now coming.

The new item is a sublemma consisting of a Danish lexical unit — a combination of words containing a form of the Danish lexical unit of the lemma: *detonerende tændsnor*. This, like the Danish lexical unit of the lemma, provides both orthographical and national-language information. Here *-nde* is a compressed version of *detonerende*, so the hyphen represents the Danish lexical unit of the lemma in precisely its lemmatized form. In principle, one could describe *detonerende tændsnor* as pragmatic/contextual information, since it is a possible context of the lemma; but the information is not included in the dictionary to show a possible context for the lemma; it is there because it does not have a predictable English equivalent, and it is placed as a sublemma in the *detonere* entry for indexation purposes. It might just as well have been placed in the entry on *tændsnor* — which simply refers to the entry on *detonere* without recording the sublemma. The typographical change from the italics of the sublemma to plain type indicates the equivalence between the Danish lexical unit of the sublemma and the English lexical unit 'detonating fuse'.

4.2.5 A brief account of the other information types in *Dansk-Engelsk Ordbog*

In *Dansk-Engelsk Ordbog* there is also prosodic information indicated by stress markers, but it is used exclusively to differentiate between certain lemmas and sublemmas when necessary — for example to distinguish between the lemmas *'forfald* 'failure to appear, absence' and *for'fald* 'decay, decline', or the sublemmas *'stå på* 'stand on' and *stå 'på* 'get on'. Segmental phonetic information is not given, either for Danish or English lexical units.

In a very few cases there is graphic information in the form of graphic symbols, for example + for the plus sign in the entry on *plustegn*:

> **plus|leder** *(elekt)* positive conductor. **-tegn** plus (sign) (+).

There are other types of grammatical information than those mentioned above, and other types of pragmatic information, for example several other types of contextual information, various types of usage information — see also Section 5.4 — i.e. on style register, frequency, geographical distribution and chronology; there are also various types of evaluative information, primarily in the form of warnings against, or advice on caution in the use of, certain English lexical units. For example, the information

> *(NB* "a dose" *kan betyde "en kønssygdom");*

(i.e. that 'a dose' can mean 'a venereal disease') has been added in the present revision after 'dose' in the entry

> **dos|is** *en -er* dose; *(= dosering)* dosage; ...

There is also administrative information for the user in the form of explicit internal references, both from entry to entry as in the entry on *god* (Fig. 4.2.4-1 a) and within entries, using various reference symbols like *cf.*, *jvf.* 'compare', *se* 'see' and =. In the case of the reference symbols the taxonomic description has revealed that several different symbols seem to be used with the same meaning, so closer editorial study is required here. External reference is not used in this dictionary.

One type of semantic information which should also be mentioned is the explicit information on equivalence given by editorial comments like *(kan gengives)* 'can be rendered', *(svarer til)* 'corresponds to' and *(omtr =)* 'approximately =', all marking approximate equivalence between Danish and English lexical units. In addition there is the use of square brackets, [ ] , around an explanation in English when neither full nor approximate equivalents can be found for Danish lexical units.

There is no etymological information of the type specified in Chapter 3 in *Dansk-Engelsk Ordbog*, nor would one expect to find it in a translation dictionary — although one could argue that information like *(fig.)* for *figurligt* 'figuratively', which would normally be classified as Danish national-language semantic information with a meaning-differentiating function, is in fact an item of etymological information (on the semantic history of the word). For example, the sublemma *de fik ikke et ben til jorden* 'their feet didn't touch the ground' = 'they didn't have a chance' is followed by the marker *(fig.)*. For the purposes of *Dansk-Engelsk Ordbog*, though, it is best to consider *(fig.)* as semantic, not etymological information.

4.2.6 What emerged from using the taxonomy

As Sections 4.2.4 and 4.2.5 will have shown, not all the main groups and categories of the taxonomy can be used in the description of *Dansk-Engelsk Ordbog*. Certain categories that could have been used are moreover only present in implicit or unspecified form: this is above all true of the category *semantic relations*, as it is never specified whether words are hyponyms, hyperonyms, co-hyponyms or have other semantic relations of the types specified in Chapter 3. In a very few cases antonymy may be indicated. Nor is the grammatical category *word formation* present in anything but rudimentary form, as shown in Section 4.2.4 in connection with the entry on *destillationsapparat*. This is of course explained by the fact that *Dansk-Engelsk Ordbog* is a general translation dictionary, whose main function is to provide equivalents and enable the user to distinguish clearly among them in the easiest and quickest way. Its main function is not to describe the source language or target language as such. The source and target language descriptions used in the dictionary thus in practice almost exclusively have the function of differentiation among equivalents (cf Manley/Jacobsen/Hjørnager Pedersen 1987).

One might perhaps claim that the description of these particular small entries in terms of the taxonomy categories produced some very banal results. One could say that all this was well known to us already as dictionary users, so what do we need such a description for ?

But a different light is cast on the results if we look first and foremost at the markers in Figs. 4.2.4-1 a-d that it was possible to assign to more than one of the general taxonomy categories, those indicated by a + between the general categories.

More than one general taxonomy category per marker (readings of Fig. 4.2.4-1 a-d)

The first instance of this is in the entry on *disparat* (Fig. 4.2.4-1 a) — the graphic information type *orthographical information* + the semantic information type *information on Danish-English equivalence* for the English lexical unit 'disparate'. The same is true of the English lexical units in the other entries. This is not surprising, as we are dealing with a printed dictionary; but with the requirements of a future format in mind one should note that information on Danish-English equivalence is marked by a change to a plain typeface.

The next instance is in the entry *desperation* (Fig. 4.2.4-1 b) — *part of speech* + *subclassification of part of speech* for the Danish *en*. Both categories here deal with grammatical information. Taking our point of departure in the category *part of speech* we find that part-of-speech markers can be combined with the Danish grammatical information type *word formation* + the pragmatic information type *administrative information (internal reference)*, as in the entry on *destillationsanlæg* (Fig. 4.2.4-1 c), with the combination indicated by zero-marking. In the entries *detonere*, *gå* and *afgå* (Fig. 4.2.4-1 d) information on the part of speech can be seen combined with the Danish grammatical information type *syntax*, marked both by *vi* and *vt*. This can provide food for reflection over the suitability of this mode of communication in connection with the future development of a format.

In the entry on *desperation* (Fig. 4.2.4-1 b) we find an example of pragmatic information (contextual) + grammatical information (syntax) in the English example 'do sth in d.'. This combination, where an item of contextual information also gives information on syntax, is not so remarkable in itself, as context information will always implicitly be syntactic information. But the combination should still lead us to consider whether the implicit syntactic information should be supported by explicit syntactic information for the sake of clear communication with the user.

In the entry on *destillationsanlæg* (Fig. 4.2.4-1 c) we find administrative information + English-English equivalence information + Danish-Danish semantic relations: that is, one item of pragmatic information and two different items of semantic information, as well as dual national-language reference distributed over two different taxonomy categories — all marked by one semicolon. In the entry on *detonere* (Fig.4.2.4-1 d) we again find this combination expressed by one semicolon. In developing a future format we should consider whether this punctuation mark is carrying too much information to be properly understood.

Yet another type of combination can be seen in the entry on *detonere* — the two semantic information types Danish and English *content specification* + Danish-Danish information on equivalence marked by *(eksplodere)*. In this case we can note that it is striking that the Danish-Danish equivalence is not made explicit by, for example, an equals sign, but is only implicitly present.

In the entry *detonere* we also find a combination of pragmatic-administrative information + semantic English-English equivalence information, marked both by *(el.)* and (,). This too is worth reconsidering in terms of optimal communication with the user.

Thus even the above readings of Fig. 4.2.4-1 a-d, showing the multiple relations of information types in these entries with the general taxonomy categories, can provide various grounds for reflection. This is especially evident from parts of entries indicating grammatical information, and pragmatic-administrative information on equivalence.

One can then, as shown in Fig. 4.2.6-1, reorganize the results from Fig. 4.2.4-1 a-d according to general taxonomy categories so one can quickly read off how the various general categories are marked in the dictionary. One can also, as shown in Fig. 4.2.6-2, rearrange the results from Fig. 4.2.4-1 a-d on the basis of the markers that occur more than once as separate items in entries — more subdivisions than those made would also have been possible, for example in connection with the administrative information *internal reference* in the entry on *gå* — and this makes it easier to see which general taxonomy category each marker belongs to.

How each general taxonomy category is expressed (readings of Fig. 4.2.6-1, supplemented by readings of Fig. 4.2.6-2)

It seems appropriate to follow up the results of the reading of Fig. 4.2.4-1 a-d with a reading of Fig. 4.2.6-1 and supplement this with a reading of Fig. 4.2.6-2. We will primarily concentrate on grammatical information, then look at pragmatic-administrative information and information on equivalence.

Looking at the various indicators of grammatical information (Fig. 4.2.6-1), we see that this information can be given in three ways. It can be indicated by the absence of explicit information, i.e. by zero-marking: this applies to information on the part of speech of Danish compound nouns (*destillationsapparat*, cf Fig. 4.2.4-1 c); to inflectional information on the lack of a plural form for the lemma and equivalent (*desperation*, cf Fig. 4.2.4-1 b); inflectional information on regular verbal conjugation in Danish simplex verbs (*detonere*, cf Fig. 4.2.4-1 d); on regular synthetic comparison of Danish adjectives (*disparat*, cf Fig. 4.2.4-1 c); and inflectional information on non-irregular English noun inflection (*despot*, cf Fig. 4.2.4-1 b; *destillationsapparat*, cf Fig. 4.2.4-1 c); in addition there is information on word formation, i.e. status as a Danish compound (*destillationsapparat*). Grammatical information can also be given implicitly, packed into or together with another item of grammatical information: this is true of the information *part of speech* and *subclassification of part of speech* given by *en* for the lemma *desperation* (cf Fig. 4.2.4-1 b) and *part of speech + syntax* given by *vi* for the lemmas *detonere*, *gå*, *afgå* (cf Fig. 4.2.4-1) or the

Fig. 4.2.6-1 Reorganization of the results of Figs. 4.2.4-1 a-d according to the general taxonomy categories

General information types	Project-specific information types	Parts of entries
Graphic information:		
- orthographical information	lemma + lexical unit + national language: Danish	*disparat* *desperation* *-apparat* *detonere* *afgå*
	sublemma + lexical unit + national language: Danish	*-nde tandsnor*
	lexical unit + national language: English	disparate desperation despot distilling apparatus still distiller freshwater generator detonate sing false sing out of tune play false play out of tune detonating fuse
Grammatical information		
- part of speech	national language: Danish	*adj* *en* zero marking *vi* *vt*
- subclassification of part of speech	national language: Danish	*en*
- inflectional information	national language: Danish + English	*-er* zero marking
	national language: Danish	*bedre* *bedst* *gik* *gået* zero marking
	national language: English	*pl* anacolutha zero marking
- word formation	national language: Danish	zero marking
- syntax	national language: Danish	*vi* *vt*
	national language: English	do sth in d.

(Fig. 4.2.6-1 continued)

General information types	Project-specific information types	Parts of entries
Pragmatic information:		
- contextual information	national language: English	do sth in d.
- administrative information		,
		,
		;
		&
		( )
		(,)
		(el,)
		(fx)
		(se ogs godeste, godt, I, gode, bedre, bedst)
		zero marking
Semantic information:		
- subject classification	national language: Danish + English	*(mus,)*
		(i skib)
		zero marking
- semantic relations	national language: Danish	;
- content specification	national language: Danish + English	*(eksplodere)*
		zero marking
- equivalence	*Danish-English*	
	lexical unit	plain typeface in:
	+ national language: English	disparate
		desperation
		despot
		distilling apparatus
		still
		distiller
		freshwater generator
		detonate
		sing false
		sing out of tune
		play false
		play out of tune
		detonating fuse
	Danish-Danish	
	national language: Danish	*(eksplodere)*
	English-English	
	national language: English	,
		;
		(el,)
		(,)

implicit information, given by *-er*, that the English equivalent has a plural form (*despot*, cf Fig. 4.2.4-1 b); or the syntactic information in 'do sth in d.' for the English lexical unit 'desperation' (*desperation*, cf Fig. 4.2.4-1 b). And grammatical information can be given explicitly, i.e. as part-of-speech information, like *adj* for the lemma *disparat* (cf Fig. 4.2.4-1 a); like the inflectional information *-er* for the lemma *despot* (cf Fig. 4.2.4-1 b); *bedre, bedst* for the lemma *god*; *gik, gået* for the lemma *gå* (cf Fig. 4.2.4-1 a); and '*pl* anacolutha' for the equivalent 'anacoluthon' (***anakoluti***, cf Fig. 4.2.4-1 a).

It is only when we come to explicit grammatical information that we can say that there is a really adequate form of communication. Neither implicit nor zero-marked specifications of grammatical information are adequate means of communication. The use of both these devices is of course due to considerations of space in the printed dictionary. In a database one would have to make all the information given this way in the printed dictionary explicit, because selective retrieval of data would otherwise result in incorrect information. But it is very likely that many users of the present printed dictionary miss a considerable amount of the information given this way. So in developing a format for a revised printed edition one should take this into consideration. That zero-marking in particular is problematical is evident if one considers Fig. 4.2.6-2. No less than five different general taxonomy categories are indicated this way in this small sample. In these cases it is very likely that the information which is in fact present in the dictionary is not understood — or, worse, misinterpreted.

Looking at the pragmatic-administrative information in Fig. 4.2.6-1, we can see that here too there are several means of communication. Zero-marking is used here for internal reference (*destillationsapparat*, cf Fig. 4.2.4-1 c; ***afgå***, cf Fig. 4.2.4-1 d). In the case of the Danish compound nouns the zero-marked internal reference can be defended on the grounds of space considerations in the printed dictionary, and one could say that it is mentioned in the instructions to the user (see above, 4.2.4 *destillationsapparat*); but there is no such defence for a zero-marked internal

Fig. 4.2.6-2 Reorganization of results from Fig. 4.2.4-1 a-d in terms of markers occurring more than once in the sample material

Recurrent markers	Project-specific information types	General information types
.		administrative information
,	national language: English	administrative information + equivalence
, in (,),	national language: English	administrative information + equivalence
;		administrative information
	national language: English national language: Danish	administrative information + equivalence + semantic relations
( )		administrative information
adj	national language: Danish	part of speech
en	national language: Danish	part of speech + subclassification of part of speech
vi	national language: Danish	part of speech + syntax
zero marking	national language: Danish + English	inflectional information
	national language: Danish	inflectional information
	national language: Danish + English	inflectional information
	national language: Danish	part of speech + word formation + administrative information (internal reference)
		administrative information (internal reference)
	national language: Danish + English	subject classification

reference from *afgå* to *gå* for inflectional information, since it is not explained in the instructions to the user that this information is to be found in the entry on the second element of compound irregular verbs. Anyone unfamiliar with these conventions, for example a non-Danish user, could be led to believe that *afgå* is a regular verb. This zero-marked internal reference is unacceptable, because it assumes knowledge on the part of the user that may not exist.

Among the other types of administrative information, the full stop, *&*, *( )*, *(fx)* and *(se ogs...)* in Fig. 4.2.4-1 a-d have turned out to indicate no more than one taxonomy category at a time in this sample material. Fig. 4.2.6-2 shows that the full stop and *( )*, the only ones in this group that recur in the sample material, are only used to indicate one general category. As far as these markers are concerned, then, this very small sample suggests that they refer uniquely to the categories of the taxonomy. This might not necessarily be so, of course, in a representative sample.

In contrast, Fig. 4.2.4-1 a-d has shown that the comma, semicolon, (,) and *(el.)* can have multiple reference to the general taxonomy categories. Figure 4.2.6-2 shows that the comma moreover functions as both purely administrative information and information on equivalence, while the semicolon also functions as purely administrative information. These markers seem loaded with so much (changing) information that it is doubtful whether the user of the printed dictionary can always be presumed to understand the information correctly. In developing a future format, therefore, efforts should be made to make these markers indicate information unambiguously.

That this is also necessary for data-processing purposes can be illustrated further, in the case of the comma, by the following example from Axelsen's *Dansk-Engelsk Ordbog* (1984), which uses the comma in the same ways as Vinterberg and Bodelsen's *Dansk-Engelsk Ordbog* (1976). The relevant entries are, however, presented differently in *Dansk-Engelsk Ordbog* (1976).

This dictionary is being analysed by the Compulexis company with computers with a view to drawing up a format — with reasonably successful results. As early as the first page the analysis program met these three examples of sublemmas with accompanying equivalents:

(1) **A, a** ...
har man sagt ~, *må man også sige b* in for a penny, in for a pound; ...

(2) **abe** ...
~ *efter* mimic, ape ...

(3) **absolut** ...
~flertal, ~ *majoritet* an absolute majority; ...

In the first case, the comma is included both as part of a sublemma and part of an English lexical unit — an equivalent. In the two last cases the commas separate two synonymous English lexical units (i.e. two equivalents) and two synonymous sublemmas respectively. The program was totally unable to see the difference; and the editors had to acknowledge that the same goes for the user, unless he or she already knows the English expressions in (2), the Danish ones in (3) and in both languages in (1). The conclusion is that a new separation sign must be introduced for synonyms.

The taxonomic description of even these few entries from Vinterberg and Bodelsen's *Dansk-Engelsk Ordbog*, and the example with the commas from Axelsen's *Dansk-Engelsk Ordbog* thus show that there will be a great deal of thinking to do preparatory to the development of a suitable format for the electronic data processing of an existing dictionary like Vinterberg and Bodelsen's *Dansk-Engelsk Ordbog*. A thorough initial taxonomic description of the text of the dictionary would reveal the most important cases of unsuitable or ambiguous editorial practice, so that corrections could be made when drawing up the format itself rather than when trying it out in practice. The initial taxonomic description would also help with decisions on the categories that would be worth introducing into the final format (cf Section 5.4).

A descriptive apparatus like the general taxonomy for lexicographical information could be used for the thorough analysis of existing dictionaries with the electronic processing of their lexicographical data in mind, with all the advantages for the editors and the users that this would bring. Such an analysis can open one's eyes to how compressed the mode of expression in printed dictionaries can be, and to the demands they make on the users' assumed knowledge. It can thus help to clarify in advance the problems that might arise in the format development phase if one neglected the initial description of the existing dictionary. Thus, on the basis of the experience gained from an initial taxonomic description of an existing dictionary, it will become considerably easier to draw up a definitive format for such a dictionary. And when that time comes, one can again use the taxonomy, as demonstrated in Section 4.1.

4.3 Term banks: examples of the description of DANTERM, the Danish Term Bank, with the help of the taxonomy

4.3.1 DANTERM in general

DANTERM, the Danish Term Bank, has been included in this study to show how the taxonomy covers a well-described, detailed descriptive apparatus for specialized language areas. The DANTERM record, the format used to structure data and enter it into the term bank, has already been discussed in Section 2.3.5. Its content and structure reflect on the one hand terminological working methods, and on the other the requirements for using the term bank, as explained in the original, very broadly defined specifications. These were that DANTERM was to provide a service to all Danish users requiring information on the meaning, usage and translation of specialized terms — for example translators, specialists, documentalists, lexicographers, language students and teachers. Specialist translators are regarded as the primary target group. The bank is also meant to serve as a medium for the storage and application of research results. Finally, it should be possible to produce glossaries and dictionaries for a wide range of purposes. A brief account of DANTERM can be found in Engel/Nistrup Madsen (1985).

At present DANTERM is fully-developed as far as the system is concerned, and about 10,000 records have been entered. These deal with two or more languages in specialized areas like water supply and sewerage, ergonomics, worker safety, nuclear energy, forestry and agriculture. The bulk of the data has been collected in co-operative projects among terminological organizations in the Scandinavian countries and the EEC. In addition, a number of student theses on terminology are being edited for entry into the system. Quantitatively speaking, however, the present body of data is not enough for us to be able to offer the service originally planned; so for the moment the bank is primarily used for research and teaching purposes.

In the following the information fields of the DANTERM record will be compared with the categories of the taxonomy. We will be giving particular emphasis to the ways in which DANTERM differs from the two preceding examples, the GLDO and *Dansk-Engelsk Ordbog*.

Figure 4.3.1-1 shows the fields of the DANTERM record with the corresponding taxonomy categories. The slash in "usage/evaluative information" means that in the DANTERM record this field can contain usage and/or evaluative information.

Fig. 4.3.1-1

DANTERM record

Taxonomy category	Field	Content
Administrative information	PROJ	project name
Subject classification	CLASS	DANTERM classification
Language	LANG	the languages covered in the record
Administrative information	NUM	identification number
Orthographical information (+ equivalence)	TERMS	all registered terms
Subject classification	APPL	area of application
Content specification (+ external reference)	DEF	definition
	ADD	additional definition
	EXPL	explanation
	ILL	illustration

Taxonomy category	Field	Content	(DANTERM record, continued)
		ITERATIVE INFORMATION	
Orthographical information (+ equivalence)	TERM	term (including information on suggested translations)	
Part of speech and inflection	GRAM	grammatical information on the term	
Phonetic information	PHON	pronunciation	
Usage	REG	linguistic region	
Orthographical information	ALT	alternative form of term, including:	
		ABBR	abbreviated form
		NONABBR	non-abbreviated form
		ORTGR	orthographic variant
Graphic symbol		SYMB	symbol
Subject classification	SPEC	special usage	
Usage	STYL	style register	
External reference	REF	source reference for term	
Content specification	EX	example(s)	
Contextual information (+ external reference)	TEXT	context(s)	
Contextual information (+ external reference) (+ equivalence)	TEXT (language)	language-pair related parallel texts	
Contextual information (+ external reference)	SYNTAG	syntagm(s)	
Contextual information (+ external reference) (+ equivalence)	SYNTAG (language)	language-pair related parallel syntagms	
Usage/evaluative information	NOTE	notes on the term	
External reference	THES	thesaurus, including:	
Semantic relations		USE	descriptors
		UF	(used for) non-descriptors
		BT	broader term
		NT	narrower term
		RT	related term
		AT	associated term
Usage/evaluative information	COM	comments on several terms or the whole record	
Equivalence (+ external reference)	QUASYN	quasi-synonym(s)	
Usage/evaluative information	QUASYNOTE	notes on quasi-synonyms	
Evaluative information	DEPR	deprecated term	

Taxonomy category	Field	Content	(DANTERM record, continued)
		ITERATIVE INFORMATION	
External reference	SYST	name of conceptual system	
Semantic relations	POS	position number of concept in conceptual system	
	REL	conceptual relations, including:	
		BC-GEN	broader concept (generic relation)
		BC-PART	broader concept (part-whole relation)
		BC	broader concept (no relation type specified)
		NC-GEN	narrower concept (generic relation)
		NC-PART	narrower concept (part-whole relation)
		NC	narrower concept (no relation type specified)
		PREC	preceding concept (successive relations)
		SUCC	succeeding concept (successive relations)
		CAUS	causal relation
		ANTO	antonym
		RC	related concept
Equivalence	EQ <language>	comments on equivalence in language pairs	
	EQADD <language>	additional comments on equivalence in language pairs	
	REV	information on reversibility	
External reference	SUPPL	reference to supplementary information (drawings, tables etc.)	
	FACTS	supplementary factual information	
	FACTS <language>	supplementary factual information, language-pair related	
Administrative information	INST	institution of origin, including:	
Subject classification		CLASSF	non-DANTERM classification
Administrative information		DATE	date of concluding terminological processing
		COPY	copyright
		RESP	terminologist responsible
		METHOD	working method
	ADM	administrative information (for use in sorting etc.)	
		#CLASSA	key for sorting by subject (verbal description)
		#CLASSB	key for sorting by subject (alphanumeric code)
		#NUM	key for sorting by identification number

(DANTERM record, continued)

ITERATIVE INFORMATION

↓

Administrative information	#TERM	key for sorting by term (alphabetical)
	#POS	key for sorting by position (systematic)
	#CLASSF	key for sorting by non-DANTERM classification
	#DATE	key for sorting by processing date
	#INPUT	date of first input
	#UPDAT	information on last and previous updates

4.3.2 DANTERM compared with the project-specific information types of the taxonomy

Language

We have seen that the DANTERM record is meant for the registration of terminological information. Each record can contain information on one, two or more languages. At the moment we are working with the national languages Danish, English, French, German, Italian, Spanish and Swedish. All information fields from TERMS up to and including INST can be repeated for each language, and in order to distinguish between the fields for different languages, the field names are given language codes — for example DA_TERMS, DA_DEF etc. — so that the record is divided into blocks with information on one language. For selection on language there is also a field LANG, containing information on the languages dealt with in a given record.

The DANTERM record does not normally operate with "source language" and "target language": the various languages are dealt with in parallel.

Approach

The record is concept-orientated: its core is the definition of the concept and the terms that represent it (the onomasiological principle).

There are many different ideas and definitions of what a "concept" is. For the definitions that have been used in connection with terminological theory, reference may be made to Wüster (1979), Drozd (1973), DIN 2330 (1979), ISO/R 1087 (1969) and Frandsen (1982). Here we will emphasize the definition found in Dahlberg (1976): "Begriff *=df* die durch eine Bezeichnung fixierte Zusammenfassung (Synthese) zutreffender Aussagen über einen gegebenen Gegenstand". Each true proposition (zutreffende Aussage) identifies a characteristic feature of the concept. The definition of a concept includes the characteristic features necessary for the determination of the content of the concept.

Terms are the expressive manifestation of specialized concepts.

Thus *lexical unit* in the DANTERM record in principle covers the definitions in DEF and the terms registered in TERMS for all the languages in a given record. In practice the definitions may be missing, however, so the field TERMS must be regarded as *lexical unit*.

The fields in the first box in Fig. 4.3.1-1, containing iterative information types, can be called "term-related" fields, since all the fields from TERM up to and including the thesaurus information in THES can be filled out for each of the terms listed in TERMS. All other fields are "concept-related", since they characterize the concept, not the individual terms.

As a rule a terminological project involves working out one or more conceptual systems (cf the remarks below on semantic relations). As one and the same concept can be a member of several conceptual systems, information about them is similarly iterative.

Medium of expression

The medium of expression is writing in the form of stored text. However, we would also like to be able to store and reproduce illustrations in the form of pictures and diagrams. A special field has been reserved for this — ILL — but it cannot be used at present.

4.3.3 DANTERM compared with the general information categories of the taxonomy

The main groups *pragmatic information* and *semantic information* call for special comment, as it is here that one sees the specialized nature of DANTERM compared with the general dictionaries *Dansk-Engelsk Ordbog* (1976) and the GLDO. As will be evident from the description below, the term bank can be seen as something between a dictionary and an encyclopaedia.

Semantic information

Subject classification

The term bank is ordered by subject. Each record is provided with information on the subject area, CLASS, and this information structures the database. CLASS is of course common to all the languages in a record, as this item of information, as mentioned in Chapter 3 in the comments on the taxonomy, helps to define a concept.

In connection with CLASS we should also mention APPL — area of application. APPL can be used to give more details on the information in CLASS; but, unlike CLASS, it is not based on a controlled list of subject names: the terminologist is free to specify an area — for example, it may be stated that a certain component is only used in a certain type of plough. But there can also be information that the concept is from a broader theoretical area: *fusion*, for example, which is classified in the term bank under the subject area *nuclear energy*, is supplied with the information in the field APPL (application) that it is a concept from nuclear physics.

The same concept may thus occur in several parts of the database, but with the emphasis on special aspects in each case. For example, under the subject area "soil preparation" there are terms related to soil conditions, types of plough, components of ploughs, etc. In the part dealing with soil conditions there are both quite specifically agricultural terms and terms from more general or theoretical geology. The advantage of this is that one can base a specialized dictionary on all the concepts (records) in one subject area. So there is no need to select records from different parts of the database. Moreover, various aspects can be treated — for example, in text and notes — without encumbering the user with irrelevant information ("agricultural aspect" under "pure" geology).

Closely connected with this information is information on the project dealing with the concept. A project, PROJ, may deal with one subject in CLASS or extend over several subjects. Conversely, a subject may be dealt with in several projects. The subject "soil preparation" could be subdivided into several projects, for example "ploughs", "harrows". PROJ must, however be regarded as administrative information (cf *pragmatic information*).

Semantic relations

This section is very well-developed in the DANTERM record, since ideally, as mentioned above, one or more conceptual systems are always worked out for a project. For a thesis on Danish-French waste water terminology (Møller 1985), for example, nine conceptual systems were worked out (for sewage types, water analysis, primary treatment, biological purification, secondary treatment and sludge treatment).

If possible, the conceptual systems worked out are common to all the languages covered in a project. In a few cases, though, there are such great differences between the languages that special systems must be worked out for each of them (cf the conceptual systems in Figs. 4.3.3-1 and 4.3.3-2, from the thesis mentioned above). Fig. 4.3.3-3, an example of a completed record for the identification number 4 in the two systems, shows how the information on conceptual system, the position of the concept in the conceptual system, and the closest superordinate/subordinate concepts are stored in relation to the individual concepts in the records of the term bank (fields SYST, POS, REL).

Fig. 4.3.3-1

CONCEPTUAL SYSTEM 1 (DANISH)

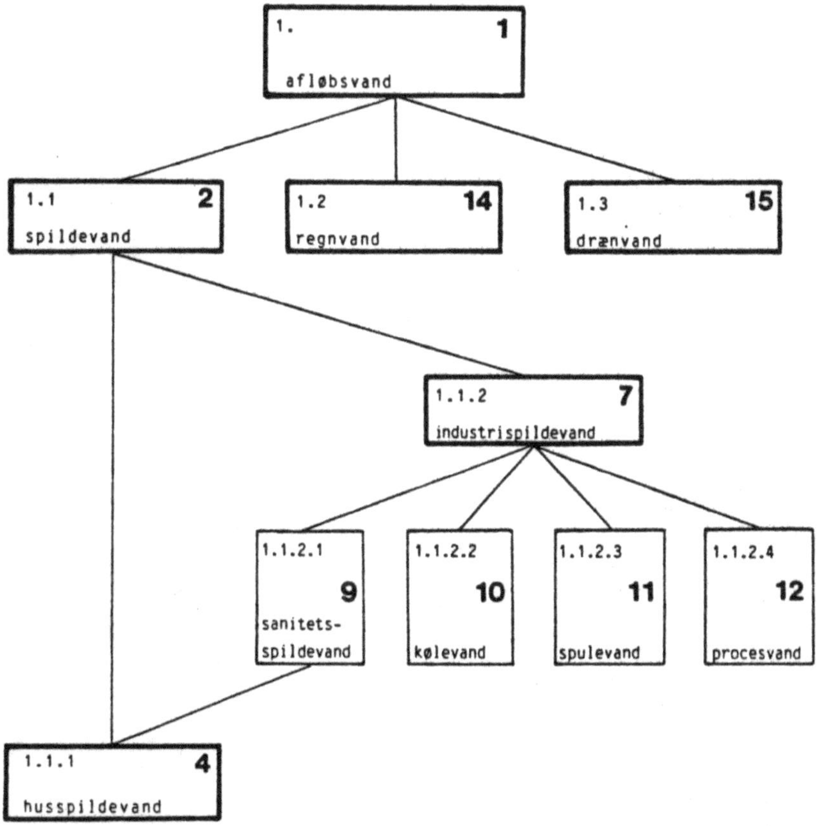

Fig. 4.3.3-2 CONCEPTUAL SYSTEM 2 (FRENCH)

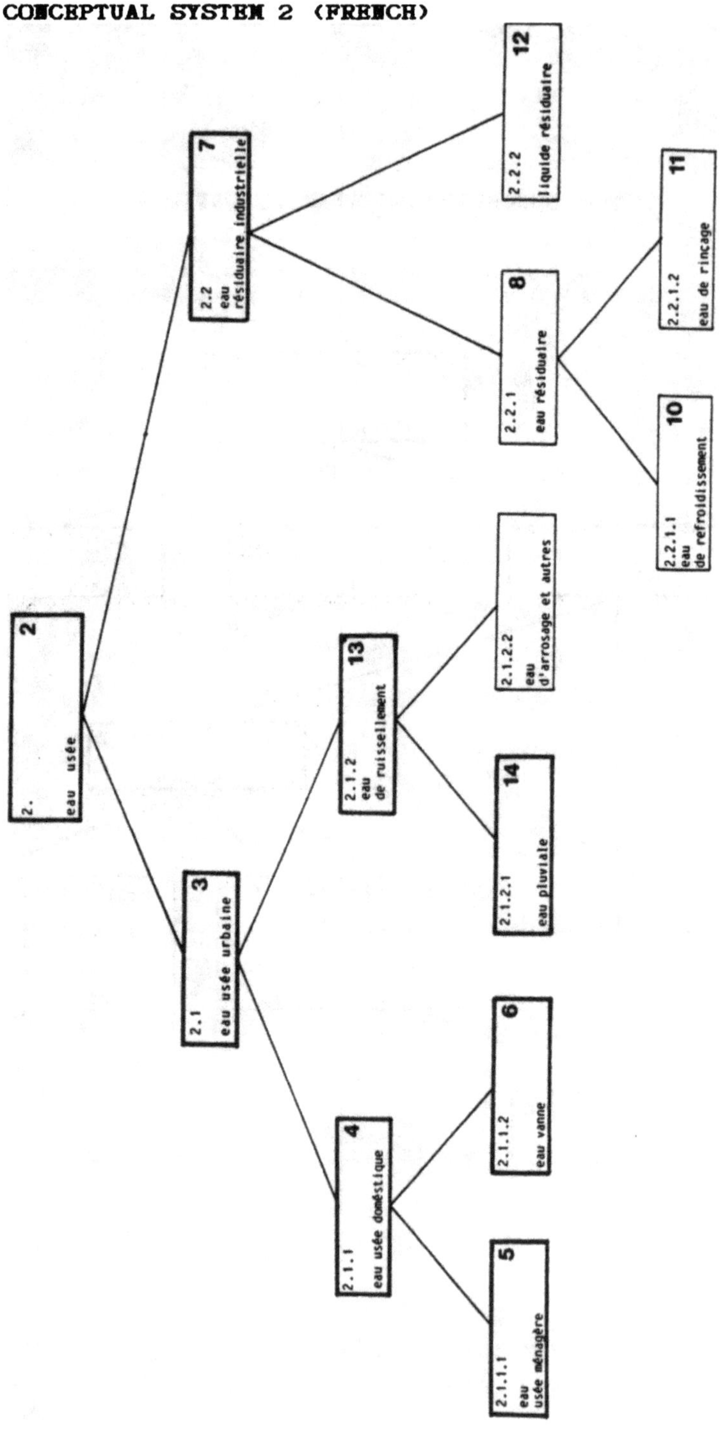

Fig. 4.3.3-3 Completed record

[Danish *terms* left in Danish. As there is no English in the original, everything in English here may be taken as translated from the Danish. French terms and comments have been left in French]

```
PROJ            Danish/French waste water terminology
CLASS           K 8000 Water supply and sewerage
LANG            da fr
NUM             4
DA_TERMS        husspildevand
DA_DEF          Husspildevand includes both domestic waste water and sanitary waste water from industrial
                concerns draining this waste water into the sewers through separate pipes (MilV p. 38)

DA_TERM         husspildevand
DA_GRAM         subst, -et
DA_REF          MilV p. 38
DA_SYST         spildevand system 1
DA_POS          1.1.1
DA_REL
        BC-GEN  spildevand

DA_INST         HHK DATE 1985/09/29
                COPY HHK RESP BM

FR_TERMS        eau usée domestique
FR_DEF          Les eaux usées domestiques comprennent les eaux ménagères (eaux de toilette, de lessive, de
                cuisines) et les eaux vannes (urines et matières fécales). (VaiP p. 21)

FR_TERM         eau usée domestique
FR_GRAM         n.f., usually plur.
FR_REF          VaiP p. 21
FR_SYST         spildevand system 2
FR_POS          2.1.1
FR_REL
        BC-GEN  eau usée urbaine
        NC-GEN  eau usée ménagère, eau vanne

FR_EQDA         The French definition differs from the Danish in not mentioning that sanitary waste water
                from industrial concerns also flows into the domestic sewage system and is purified with it.
                Despite this, there is sufficient equivalence between the two terms for them to be trans-
                lated by one another.

FR_INST         HHK DATE 1985/09/29
                COPY HHK RESP BM

ADM             #CLASSA     (water supply and sewerage)
                #CLASSB     K8000
                #NUM        4
                #DATERM     (husspildevand)
                #DAPOS      0.010101
                #DADATE     1985/09/29
                #DAINPUT    1986/02/27
                #FRTERM     (eau usée domestique)
                #FRPOS      0.020101
                #FRDATE     1985/09/29
                #FRINPUT    1986/02/27
```

Position numbers like 1.1.1 and 2.1.1 are converted to real numbers for sorting under *administrative information*.

Information on relations in a thesaurus used for information retrieval counts as term-related information in the DANTERM record: it is possible, as mentioned in 2.3.5, to mark the presence of a term in a given thesaurus as a descriptor or non-descriptor. Related expressions in the thesaurus can also be listed. For example, in a thesaurus dealing with waste water, *spildevand* might be listed as a descriptor used for *afløbsvand* (cf Fig. 4.3.3-1). In the DANTERM record on *spildevand* the thesaurus fields would look like this:

THES Thesaurus on *spildevand*
USE *spildevand*
UF *afløbsvand*
NT *husspildevand*
RT *regnvand, drænvand*

One use of this type of information in DANTERM is that one can examine the definition of a descriptor and its relations in a terminological conceptual system.

Content specification

Analytic and synthetic definitions (cf Chapter 3) are placed in the DANTERM record under DEF — see for example Fig. 4.3.3-3 above. Other fields related to this are ADD and EXPL. ADD — additional definition — may contain supplementary information not necessary for a unique definition, for example supplementary information on the way a machine works (see Fig. 4.3.3-4 below). As regards subcategories in the taxonomy, ADD is categorized like DEF. EXPL — explanation — is primarily used if the terminologist (so far) has not found or formulated a definition. This may contain the terminologist's own explanation (based on information from documentation material), or an explanatory text from a book (cf Fig. 4.3.3-4). EXPL corresponds most closely to the subcategory *lexical paraphrase* in the taxonomy.

Exemplification (denotative definition) is found in the DANTERM record in EX — example — and a field has been reserved, as mentioned above, for illustrations (ostensive definition).

Fig. 4.3.3-4 (ADM field omitted for reasons of space)

PROJ	*radiatortermostat*
	Danish/German terminology
CLASS	K8900 thermostats
LANG	da de
NUM	19
DA_TERMS	*fjernføler, kapillarrørsføler, løs føler, separat føler*
DA_DEF	Sensor hermetically and inseparably connected with the thermostat element by a capillary tube (NN)
DA_ADD	If, for example, free circulation of room air past the element cannot be expected, and if a certain dependence on the supply-pipe temperature is unacceptable, an element with a remote sensor [*fjernføler*] must be used. This is placed either beneath the radiator or on the wall beside the radiator about 1,5 m above the floor. (VinT p. 13)
DA_TERM	1 *fjernføler*
DA_GRAM	1 subst, *-en, -e*
DA_REF	1 VinT p. 10
DA_NOTE	1 The term *fjernføler* should be used, as it indicates the essential feature that the sensor should be placed at some distance from the radiator thermostat
DA_TERM	2 *kapillarrørsføler*
DA_GRAM	2 subst, *-en, -e*
DA_REF	2 JørR p. 25
DA_TERM	3 *løs føler*
DA_REF	3 JenT p. 30
DA_NOTE	3 *løs føler* [loose sensor] should not be used, as the sensor is neither loose nor detachable
DA_TERM	4 *separat føler*
DA_REF	4 OlsV p. 5
DA_NOTE	4 The sensor is not separate, as the thermostat element and sensor are supplied in one unit
DA_SYST	*radiatortermostat*
DA_POS	3-1-1.2
DA_REL	
BC-GEN	*føler*
NC-PART	*følerpatron, kapillarrør, følerkonsol, følerdæksel*
DA_INST	HHK DATE 1977/08/01
	COPY HHK RESP LA
DE_TERMS	Fernfühler, loser Fühler, getrennter Fühler
DE_EXPL	Der Fernfühler, der durch ein 2 m langes Kapillarrohr mit dem Regler verbunden ist, wird an einem für die Temperaturfassung günstigen Ort an die Wand montiert. (SchH p. 15)
DE_TERM	1 Fernfühler
DE_GRAM	1 m
DE_REF	1 SchH p. 15
DE_NOTE	1 Should be used
DE_TERM	2 loser Fühler
DE_REF	2 HeiZ p. 30
DE_NOTE	2 Should not be used
DE_TERM	3 getrennter Fühler
DE_REF	3 SuhH p. 25
DE_NOTE	3 Should not be used
DE_SYST	Radiatorthermostat
DE_POS	3-1-1.2
DE_REL	
BC-GEN	Fühler
NC-PART	Fühlerbirne, Kapillarrohr, Konsole, Deckel
DE_INST	HHK DATE 1977/08/01
	COPY HHK RESP LA

Equivalence

In Chapter 3 we said that equivalence relations within a language apply to synonyms and quasi-synonyms. It will be noted that the DANTERM record includes no special field for synonyms: all synonymous expressions are listed as terms (in the TERMS field), separated by commas. One reason for this is the difficulty or undesirability of calling one expression the term and the others synonyms. In practice it has emerged that we may wish to append a number of the so-called term-related items of information to an expression: in the DANTERM record these correspond to the boxed fields that can be completed for each of the terms in TERMS (iterative information). See for example Fig. 4.3.3-4 above.

Near-synonyms are to be found in QUASYN. These can be supplemented by source references in brackets and notes in QUASYNOTE.

In principle a DANTERM record stores information on one concept, but in some cases partially equivalent concepts in two languages can be juxtaposed in a record if the differences are such that it is reasonable to use the two concepts to translate one another, if necessary with a footnote. For this to be possible the record must indicate differences and similarities in an equivalence note. This comes in the EQDA field in the relevant foreign-language section of the record (cf Fig. 4.3.3-3). Comments on relations between two foreign languages are possible (in EQEN, EQDE etc.). But these are relatively rare, as a terminologist is usually competent in Danish and one foreign language. It does occur, however, in group projects, that relations between several foreign languages are clarified.

The information that something is a proposed translation is listed in brackets after the information in TERM.

Pragmatic information

Contextual information

Citation corresponds to DANTERM's TEXT, and *possible context* to DANTERM's SYNTAG (cf Fig. 4.3.3-5 below).

Fig. 4.3.3-5 (a number of fields, including ADM, omitted for reasons of space)

PROJ	Danish/German bill-of-exchange terminology
CLASS	E4100 bills of exchange
LANG	da de
NUM	1
DA_TERMS	*den trukne veksel, den trasserede veksel, tratte*
DA_DEF	an order issued in the form of a bill of exchange, whereby the drawer (*trassenten*) requests another person, the drawee (*trassaten*) to pay a certain amount to a third party, the payee (*remittenten*) (JO p. 231)
DA_TERM	1 *den trukne veksel*
DA_REF	1 JO p. 231
DA_TEXT	1 A bill may be drawn on a firm, a joint-stock company, an association etc. (HelV p. 29)
DA_SYNTAGDE	1 *trække veksel på*
DA_TERM	2 *den trasserede veksel*
DA_REF	2 KobJ p. 90
DA_TEXT	2 A drawn bill [*trasseret veksel*], also called a draft [*tratte*] or a drawn bill [*trukket veksel*] ... (KobJ p. 90)
DA_TERM	3 *tratte*
DA_REF	3 KobJ p. 90
DA_COM	Legal texts do not use *tratte*, while legal commentaries and more general works alternate between *den trukne veksel* and *tratte*
DA_INST	HHK DATE 1978/09/01 COPY HHK RESP FV
DE_TERMS	gezogener Wechsel, Tratte
DE_DEF	Gezogener Wechsel, ist ein Wechsel, in dem der Aussteller einen andern anweist, an den durch die Urkunde ausgewiesenen Berechtigten eine bestimmte Geldsumme an einem bestimmten Tag zu zahlen. (BauW p. 38)
DE_TERM	1 gezogener Wechsel
DE_REF	1 BauW p. 38
DE_SYNTAGDA	1 einen Wechsel auf jmdn. ziehen
DE_TERM	2 Tratte
DE_GRAM	2 f
DE_REF	2 CreR p. 1112
DE_TEXT	2 Tratte ist ein gezogener Wechsel (CreR p. 1112)
DE_COM	Legal texts do not use *Tratte*, but legal commentaries and more general works alternate between *gezogener Wechsel* and *Tratte*.
DE_INST	HHK DATE 1978/09/01 COPY HHK RESP FV

Usage

Information on usage is found in the following DANTERM fields:

Temporal dimension	= NOTE, notes on the term
Spatial dimension	= REG, linguistic region
Social dimension	= STYLE, style register
Frequency	= NOTE, notes on the term
	= COM, comments on several terms

External reference

Source references are to be found in REF — the source of the term — and may also be listed in brackets after DEF, ADD, EXPL, TEXT, SYNTAG and QUASYN. Literature references are placed in SUPPL — references to supplementary information.

Evaluative information

Evaluative information may be in DEPR — deprecated term — or in NOTE/COM (cf Fig. 4.3.3-4 above).

Administrative information

Administrative information can be seen at the end of the DANTERM record under INST and ADM (information on collection and processing of data: DATE, COPY, RESP, METHOD, #INPUT and #UPDAT). Information for use in producing sorted lists is repeated under ADM with the special marker "#" (technical information).

Internal references may be found in DEF, ADD, EXPL, NOTE, COM, for example, and thus cannot be separated out.

In addition there is the DANTERM field PROJ, used for information on the project for which a record has been drawn up (cf above under *content specification*).

Factual information

In conclusion, the FACTS field, for factual information, should be mentioned. It has emerged in connection with research projects and theses that there is a need for the storage of extensive reasoned discussion and documentation. This is one of the points at which the encyclopaedic tendency of DANTERM is evident. The FACTS field can contain information corresponding to most categories in the main groups of the taxonomy for pragmatic and semantic information. It is therefore impossible to assign this field to a single taxonomy category.

4.3.4 Summing-up

As will be evident from the above, it is possible to describe the DANTERM record with the help of the categories of the taxonomy. Only in a few cases are several of the taxonomy categories present in a single field. This is true, for example, of TEXT, which contains contextual information as well as external reference (source reference). As a rule these fields can be subdivided on the basis of various characteristic features: in the example given the source reference is listed in brackets. The situation is more difficult with the DANTERM fields NOTE and COM, which may contain information corresponding to the taxonomy categories *usage* (temporal dimension and frequency) and *evaluative information*. The FACTS field, as mentioned before, cannot be assigned to a single taxonomy category — which is hardly surprising, as the information here is of an encyclopaedic rather than lexicographical type.

The exchange of data is very important for term banks, as it is extremely time-consuming to build up a data collection sufficiently large to justify offering it to users for information retrieval. This is why a common taxonomy is so useful. In exchanges between two term banks it is of course best if the transfer of data from the format of one bank to another can be done automatically, i.e. without human categorization of the content. With one exception, DANTERM can supply information to another term bank without this kind of human processing, if the format of the bank in question is subdivided into fields corresponding to the categories of the taxonomy. The only problem is the DANTERM categories NOTE and COM (cf above).

However, the DANTERM format is — especially as regards semantic and pragmatic information — far more detailed than the subclassifications of the taxonomy at the categorial level. The DANTERM subclassifications correspond in many ways to the classification of the taxonomy into subcategories described in Chapter 3. As mentioned before, the content specification information is split up into the fields DEF, ADD (analytic/synthetic definitions), EXPL (lexical paraphrases), ILL (ostensive definitions) and EX (denotative definitions) (cf Fig. 4.3.1-1).

It is therefore impossible for DANTERM to receive information from another term bank without human processing if the field structure of such a term bank corresponds only to the subdivisions of the taxonomy at the *categorial* level, and if it otherwise has the same information types as DANTERM. However, if the field structure of the other term bank corresponds to the *subcategorial* divisions of the taxonomy, automatic exchange is possible.

Term banks can also exchange information with other types of lexicographical data collections: for example, one could exchange individual items of information, like pronunciation information from a pronunciation dictionary to a term bank, or contextual examples from a term bank to a collection of citations. Also conceivable is the transfer of specialized terms with accompanying information (grammatical, content-specifying, contextual) to a general (semasiological) dictionary.

We have noted above that the field structure of the DANTERM record is determined by the planned function of the term bank: information retrieval, research and the production of specialized dictionaries. In this respect the very detailed subdivisions ensure selective retrieval and printouts of terms and related information to cater for all conceivable needs. The same considerations apply to the automatic selection and structuring of term bank data for directional, user-orientated dictionaries.

Both for answering enquiries and producing dictionaries, what we want is a search profile that will select, for example, terms, analytic/synthetic definitions and possible contexts (TERMS, DEF and SYNTAG) — and the field structure of DANTERM makes this possible.

If the field structure corresponded to the divisions of the taxonomy at the categorial rather than the subcategorial level, it would only be possible to specify a search profile for terms, content-specifying and contextual information. This would give a printout of too large a subset from DANTERM, corresponding to the categories TERMS, DEF, ADD, EXPL, ILL, TERM, EX, TEXT and SYNTAG.

In connection with term bank data it is important that one can present the information sorted both alphabetically by term and systematically, i.e. in the order in which it occurs in a conceptual system (cf. Fig. 4.3.4-1 below).

Fig. 4.3.4-1 Systematic list corresponding to the conceptual systems in Figs. 4.3.3-1 and 4.3.3-2 (Types of waste water)

SYSTEMATIC NO.	CONCEPTUAL SYSTEM 1	IDENTIFICATION NO.
1.	afløbsvand	1
1.1	spildevand	2
1.1.1	husspildevand	4
1.1.2	industrispildevand	7
1.1.2.1	sanitetsspildevand	9
1.1.2.2	kølevand	10
1.1.2.3	spulevand	11
1.1.2.4	procesvand	12
1.2	regnvand	14
1.3	dranvand	15
	CONCEPTUAL SYSTEM 2	
2.	eau usée	2
2.1	eau usée urbaine	3
2.1.1	eau usée domestique	4
2.1.1.1	eau usée ménagère	5
2.1.1.2	eau vanne	6
2.1.2	eau de ruissellement	13
2.1.2.1	eau pluviale	14
2.2	eau résiduaire industrielle	7
2.2.1	eau résiduaire	8
2.2.1.1	eau de refroidissement	10
2.2.1.2	eau de rinçage	11
2.2.2	liquide résiduaire	12

Sorting into systematic order is possible in DANTERM because the position of the concept in the conceptual system, POS, is separately marked. This would not be possible if the information was included unmarked among the other items of information on semantic relations.

In the introduction to the section on DANTERM it was stated that the content and structure of the DANTERM record reflect the terminological working method. In conclusion it should be mentioned, however, that work with DANTERM has also had a reciprocal effect on the practical terminological work at the Copenhagen School of Economics and Business Administration, as the use of a detailed format has helped to promote systematic and consistent lexicographical work.

5.1 The description of the structure of dictionaries

The taxonomy classifies individual information types uniquely, but tells us nothing about their interrelations, as these will depend on the specific dictionary. The interrelations are expressed by the *format* of the dictionary, by which we mean the structure in which the information types are arranged, whether described as a database layout or, for example, by means of a set of typographical rules.

Format description, too, should observe uniform rules, although the method of description must to some extent depend on what is to be described — for example, a printed dictionary or a database; and on what the function of the description is — for example, the design of a new dictionary or the analysis of an existing one. At all events it is essential to be aware that automatic data processing presupposes a completely accurate description of the data.

The dictionary as database may, for example, have a network structure and several means of access to the same data, while the printed dictionary must be described on the basis of the linearity of its text: it is a unique sequence of characters, to which certain rules apply. In the following we will concentrate on the latter type of description: this is the essential first step when existing dictionaries are to be described with a view to extracting as much information as possible about the more or less implicitly marked relations between the items of information — relations which then, if required, may be made explicit in a database layout. Similar descriptions will be important again when the contents of the database are to be presented in linear form, whether in a book, on a screen or in some other medium.

The mathematical theory of formal languages provides a tool for the description of structure. According to the theory of automata, various types of automaton correspond to the various types of formal language. The types of automaton have properties that determine how complicated it is to construct a program that emulates the automaton. If one can describe dictionary structures by means of a weak formalism, one knows, by virtue of the parallel with a given type of automaton, that it is feasible to construct a program to deal with the structure.

5.2 Formal languages

Our present experience suggests that the formats of many dictionaries can be described by using concepts from the theory of context-free formal languages as a grammar with a vocabulary and rewriting rules. The grammar stipulates which strings are well-formed, i.e. are in accordance with the editorial rules.

By *vocabulary* or alphabet, this theory means a non-null, finite set of symbols. Some of these are *terminal*: for example, the set of characters called the "alphabet" in normal language would be terminals in a grammar of spelling; the limited set of standard words, including inflectional forms, that are necessary and sufficient to write a weather report would be the terminals of a grammar of weather reports. In the latter case, for example, *rainy* belongs to the terminal vocabulary and cannot be further split up. In other words, the analysis stops at the *terminal symbols*.

By a *string* is meant an ordered sequence of symbols from the vocabulary. If the vocabulary is the Danish alphabet, a grammar might consist of a set of rules stating which sequences of letters form valid Danish monosyllabic words.

Unless the dictionary description is to incorporate a grammar for the natural language or languages dealt with in the dictionary — and this is hardly desirable — it must have two types of terminals: object-language strings not subject to further analysis than "string of Russian letters", or perhaps "string of semibold Russian letters"; and terminals that are reserved character combinations like *vb*, *adj*, *may be rendered* or symbols like "~", "*". We are thus operating with a terminal vocabulary whose elements include *a* and *d* and *j* as well as *adj*. Some of them are permissible elements in strings (unspecified); others help to determine the formal structure of the dictionary.

From a typographical point of view, for example, the non-specified strings could be broken down into sequences of individual characters, and in practical dictionary work it may be very relevant to take this last step — to take the analysis right down to the character set or sets that are actually available in the composing-room or on the computer device — keyboard, screen or printer — or data communication line. In the following, however, we will only take the analysis as far as the *end-categories*. It is assumed that these, in accordance with the rules of the natural language or languages concerned, are made up of terminal symbols proper (for example in the typographical sense).

A *grammar* consists of four components:

1. A (non-terminal) start-symbol for the unit (e.g. text type) to be described — for example *weather report*, *dictionary* or *entry*.

2. A finite number of other non-terminal symbols for permissible subsets of this unit.

3. A finite number of terminal symbols — the terminal vocabulary.

(1, 2, and 3 together constitute the vocabulary).

4. A finite number of rewriting rules (also called productions) of the form:

   A → B (can be read "A is rewritten as B")

— where A is a non-terminal symbol (Point 1 or 2 above) and B is an ordered sequence of symbols, each of which can be terminal or non-terminal.

That only one symbol, A, is placed to the left of the arrow means that this symbol can be rewritten as the symbols placed to the right of the arrow, irrespective of the context of A — i.e. the grammar is *context-free*. In the dictionaries studied (Hjorth 1984, 1985) this is almost, but not quite, the case. For example, the rules for the placing of certain punctuation marks (like the full stop and semicolon) have proved to be context-sensitive, as the characters are not used if the preceding string ends with an exclamation or question mark. Similarly, the full stop as punctuation mark is not placed after a full stop used to mark an abbreviation.

5.2.1 Backus-Naur notation

This formal notation, also known as the Backus Normal Form — BNF — is the classic, and still the most widespread notation for the description of context-free formal languages, especially programming languages. It was developed for the description of the programming language ALGOL60, and was an important aid to our initial analyses of the dictionaries. Two examples of the use of BNF to describe dictionaries (*Retskrivningsordbogen*, the Danish spelling dictionary, and the DANwORD dictionary) can be found in Ruus (1983).

In BNF, category names (non-terminal symbols) are written as an arbitrary word or other symbol surrounded by < >; actual text strings (consisting of terminal symbols) are written as themselves. The symbol ::= is the rewriting symbol. If the same symbol can be rewritten as several different strings, these are separated by a vertical line, "|", which thus stands for the exclusive "or". The sentence

> A translation of a lemma or sublemma consists of a facultative discriminator (for example a specification of the semantic or usage area where the translation is valid) followed by one or more (near-synonymous) equivalents; if there are several of these, they are separated by a comma

can thus be expressed by the notation

a) <Translation> ::= <Equivalents> | <Discriminator><Equivalents>

b) <Equivalents> ::= <Equivalent> | <Equivalent> , <Equivalents>

Recursive definitions like b) above are necessary because BNF in its classical form has no notation for repetition. One is thus often forced to introduce non-terminal symbols (here "Equivalents" — i.e. the plural form) for subsets which there is no special reason to name. In later extensions of BNF the iteration symbol { }* has therefore been introduced to mark an arbitrary number of occurrences (or none at all). Using this extended notation we can combine a) and b) into one rule:

<Translation> ::=
<Equivalent> {, <Equivalent>}* |
<Discriminator> <Equivalent> {, <Equivalent>}*

This way we avoid the rather superfluous category "Equivalents" and its recursive definition.

5.2.2 The ETTO Notation

Several times in this book (for example in Chapter 6 below) we describe formats in what we have called the ETTO Notation. This is a very compact notation which only uses three symbols apart from the category names: facultative brackets, ( ), and iterative brackets, [ ] $^{+}$ and [ ] *.

A category in ( ) can be included or omitted as required.

A category in [ ] $^{+}$ can appear once or several times at the point in question; a category surrounded by [ ] * can be omitted or appear once or several times.

An unbracketed category appears just once.

At this level of description the marking of terminal symbols is less relevant. No convention has therefore been defined for the marking of actual strings and characters, including punctuation marks. The example

> A translation of a lemma or sublemma consists of a facultative discriminator (for example a specification of the semantic or usage area where the translation is valid) followed by one or more (near-synonymous) equivalents; if there are several of these, they are separated by a comma

will therefore be described in the ETTO Notation as follows:

(Discriminator)
[Equivalent] $^{+}$

One advantage of this notation is that it is at once compact and transparent — as long as one does not go into too much detail, entailing too many levels of bracketing, in which case the notation should be explicated by subdivision into more schemata.

The formats for the GLDO and ODSS have been described at about this level to the software supplier we use for experiments with formatted data entry (Chapter 6); and the notation has proved well-suited for this. However, it has been necessary to describe the typographical consequences of the rules separately.

For more precise descriptions, however, the ETTO Notation has certain disadvantages, as there is no provision for:

1) the naming, and thus for the description, of higher-order data structures, for example the category groupings that can be placed in iterative brackets; nor
2) for specifying the structure "selection" (the obligatory choice of one and only one of two or more possibilities), so almost all categories end up notated as facultative.

So, as a consequence of 2) both

Either A or B occurs here

and

AB, A, B or none of these can occur here

are notated thus:

(A)
(B)

5.2.3 Bracket diagrams

A notation for the missing obligatory selection can be found in Warnier & Orr's bracket diagrams (see for example Higgins 1979). These describe hierarchical data structures and classify them into three types, the three basic control structures of data processing, from which all others can be built up:

- Sequence
- Selection
- Iteration

Rewriting rules are marked by brackets that can be regarded as left set-brackets with the right brackets omitted for the sake of clarity. The bracket thus corresponds to the " ::= " in BNF.

Sequence. That the set M (these are always ordered sets) consists of the data elements A, B and C in sequence and that each occurs once only, is written thus:

```
    ┌ A
    │ (1)
    │
    │ B
M  {  (1)
    │
    │ C
    └ (1)
```

Selection. That M is the result of selecting one and only one of these elements is written thus:

$$M \left\{ \begin{array}{c} A \\ (0,1) \\ \oplus \\ B \\ (0,1) \\ \oplus \\ C \\ (0,1) \end{array} \right.$$

where the symbol "⊕" means the exclusive "or" and so corresponds to the vertical line of BNF.

Iteration. Finally, M may be a sequence of at least m and at most n identical elements A:

$$M \left\{ \begin{array}{c} A \\ (m,n) \end{array} \right.$$

with the special cases

$$M \left\{ \begin{array}{c} A \\ (0,n) \end{array} \right. \qquad M \left\{ \begin{array}{c} A \\ (1,n) \end{array} \right. \qquad M \left\{ \begin{array}{c} A \\ (n) \end{array} \right. \text{(exactly } n \text{ times).}$$

Where an element is an actual text string — a string constant — it is written in quotation marks, for example

$$\textbf{Part of speech} \left\{ \begin{array}{c} \text{"sb"} \\ (0,1) \\ \oplus \\ \text{"vb"} \\ (0,1) \\ \oplus \\ \text{"adj"} \\ (0,1). \end{array} \right.$$

One *can* combine the three types in one set of brackets; however, for the sake of clarity we have often kept them separate.

To describe dictionary manifestations (typically printed dictionaries) we have added the *iterative separator* — the constant string used to separate the individual elements of the iteration, if there are more than one. If the elements are also marked in numerical order, the number designator # is written before the separator. Where different iterative separators can occur in the same position, a common name may be written instead, e.g. "connector" in Section 5.8.1, Fig. 5.8.1-5. Our recurring example,

> A translation of a lemma or sublemma consists of a facultative discriminator (for example a specification of the semantic or usage area where the translation is valid) followed by one or more (near-synonymous) equivalents; if there are several of these, they are separated by a comma

can thus be notated:

Translation {
Discriminator
(0,1)
Equivalent
(1,n; ", ")

If the equivalents are also numbered (for n > 1), we write

Equivalent
(1, n;#", ")

5.3 Format description and practical lexicography

The format, as stated above, is a system of rules allowing one to decide whether a given segment of text is a valid part of the dictionary in formal terms.

The criterion for validity is given by the editorial rules of the dictionary, and the format must be a precise statement of the formal component of these. Yet many dictionaries have no written editorial rules, and simply build on tradition. For others, it is true, there are written rules; but they are far from having the degree of detail we need here. The safest source for the editorial rules is frequently the dictionary itself.

The experienced dictionary editor has the rules at her fingertips — or rather in her bones. She writes down the right information in the right order and, with great assurance, places semicolons, various types of brackets, bars, numbers and typographical instructions in the right places. "Right" here means "in accordance with certain broadly consistent rules" — even if these have not been explicitly formulated.

The task of the outside analyst drawing up a format for an existing dictionary is not to describe its structure in all its detail, but, through comparative study of many entries, to arrive at the (ideal) underlying structure. In the closing phases of the work the editor of the dictionary will be of invaluable assistance, for example by commenting on apparent inconsistencies. The result may be that a new rule must be added, or that the editor — perhaps even with pleasure, because it makes the dictionary clearer — changes the editorial principles. An example of this (ambiguous use of commas) was mentioned in Section 4.2.6.

5.4 An example: *Dansk-Engelsk Ordbog*

The technique of format description will be illustrated here by an example. The entries dealt with are taken from Vinterberg and Bodelsen's *Dansk-Engelsk Ordbog* (1976), which was analysed in Section 4.2 with the taxonomy as a point of departure and tool, with the purpose, among others, of preparing a suitable format for use in the (computer-aided) preparation of new editions. The analysis in this section will use the formal apparatus reviewed earlier in the chapter for a top-down analysis of the dictionary entry as a tree-structure.

Fig. 5.4-1 Examples from *Dansk-Engelsk Ordbog*

a 1. **navle** *en -r* 1 *(anat)* navel; *(fagl)* umbilicus; 2 ⚘ hilum; 3 *(på sneglehus)* umbilicus; 4 *(her.)* nombril, navel (of an escutcheon); 5 *(glasnavle)* punty (*el.* pontil) mark; *verdens ~* the hub of the Universe; *stirre på sin egen ~ (fig)* be self-centred, be a narcissist, be narcistic.

b **narkotisere** *vt* anaesthetize, narcotize. **narkotiserende, narkotisk** *adj* 1 narcotic; 2 *(bedøvende)* anaesthetic, *adv* -ally; *~ middel* (1) narcotic, drug (fx a habit-forming drug); (2) anaesthetic. **narkotisør** *en -er* anaesthetist.

c **narre|biskop** *(hist)* boy bishop. **-bjælde** fool's bell. **-briks** bauble. **-hoved** 1 fool's head; 2 ⚓ (deck) quoits. **-hue, -hætte** fool's cap, cap and bells.

d **najs** *adj, se nejs.*

e **nakke|fatning** *(gymn)* neck rest position. **-fistel** *(vet)* poll evil. **-fjer** hackle. **-flade** *(vet, anat)* occipital plane. **-fletning** *se fletning 3.* **-frisure** chignon. **-grube** *(anat)* hollow (*el.* nape) of the neck. **-holder** headrest. **-hud** skin of the back of the head. **-hul** *(anat)* = *-åbning.* **-hule** = *-grube.* **-hår** back hair.

f **detonation** *en -er (eksplosion)* detonation; ♪ false intonation; singing (, playing) out of tune. **detonations|bølge** detonating wave. **-signal** *(jernb)* detonator, fog signal. **detonator** *en* ⚔ detonator. **detonere** *vi (eksplodere)* detonate; ♪ sing (, play) false (*el.* out of tune); *-nde tændsnor* detonating fuse.

g **disparat** *adj* disparate. **disparitet** *en* disparity.

h **desperation** *en* desperation (fx do sth in d.).
despot *en -er* despot. **despoti** *et -er* despotism.

i **destillations|anlæg** distilling plant. **-apparat** distilling apparatus, still, distiller; *(i skib)* freshwater generator. **-kar, -kedel** still. **-kolbe** distilling flask, retort. **-ovn** still. **-rest** (distilling) residuum.

In the first instance no special consideration will be given to the taxonomy, as the guideline for the choice of non-terminals and thus of one of the many possible approaches to such a task is the conceptions of trained dictionary users and of the editors themselves of how the entries are built up. To this we must add an estimate of the information units and groups of information units it will be useful for the editors and/or users to identify later as separate categories. Finally, it has been taken into consideration that the description must be capable of use as a basis for automatic structural analysis (parsing) of the dictionary text; no distinctions have therefore been made over and above those assumed to be determinable by formal criteria. Only then are the results of the analysis compared with the taxonomy, and the adjustments made that are necessary to create agreement between them.

Initially we will analyse a single entry which is reasonably typical of the format of the dictionary, the entry *I. navle* (Fig. 5.4-1 a). Then we will expand and generalize the format description by incorporating other entries (Fig. 5.4-1.b-e).

5.4.1 The ETTO Notation

The description, by means of the ETTO Notation, of the first entry can be seen in Fig. 5.4.1-1. It is read from the top down, and should be self-explanatory.

HOMGR	I.					
LEMMA	navle					
LGRAM	*en -r*					
INDEX +	1		2	3	4	
DISCR +	*(anat)*	*(fagl)*	[illegible]	-	*(her.)*	
EQUIV +	navel	umbilicus	hilum	-	nombril	navel (of ...

SBLEM +	*verdens -*	*stirre på sin egen -*		
(DISCR) +		*(fig)*		
EQUIV +	the hub of the Universe	be selfcentred	be a narcissist	be narcistic

Fig. 5.4.1-1 The ETTO Notation. Description of the entry *I. navle*. Abbreviations used explained below. Meanings 3 and 5 omitted for reasons of space

If one now attempts to fit just a few of the other entries in the dictionary into this model, one quickly realizes that the model must be adjusted if it is to deal with all the entries:

1) The homograph marker (HOMGR) occurs with very few LEMMAs and is thus facultative in the general model.

2) Two synonymous heads, i.e. LEMMAs with accompanying grammatical information (LGRAM) may begin the same entry if they are alphabetically contiguous e.g. *narkotiserende/narkotisk* 'narcotic', *narrel-hue/-hætte* 'fool's cap'. The head can thus be iterative. If LGRAM (for example, inflection) is identical for the two, it is only specified once and thus becomes facultative.

3) Furthermore, LGRAM becomes facultative anyway, inasmuch as it does not appear in principle with compound nouns.

4) The meaning number (INDEX) is also facultative. In many entries there is only one translation, or several translations only separated by semicolons or commas.

5) Discriminators (DISCR) do not always appear with a translation, and are therefore facultative with both lemma and sublemma equivalents.

6) Far from all entries include a section with sublemmas (SBLEM). This section, the "tail", is thus facultative in its entirety.

These observations have been incorporated in Fig. 5.4.1-2, which thus represents a more general description of the dictionary:

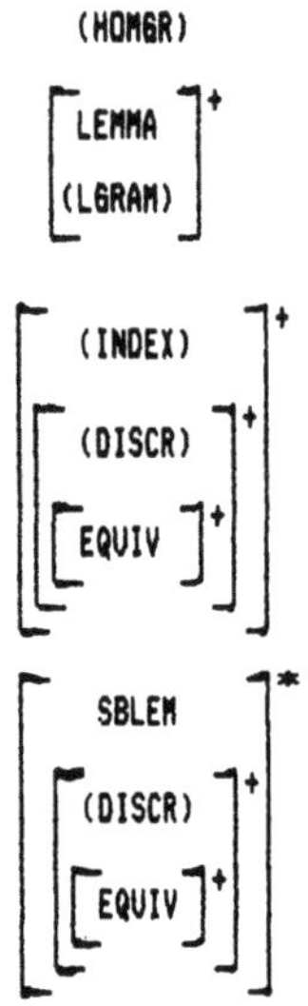

Fig. 5.4.1-2 The ETTO Notation. A more general format description based on the entries in Fig. 5.4-1 a-e.

At this stage it seems that all we can say with certainty is that an entry contains at least one (Danish) LEMMA, and at least one (English) equivalent (EQUIV). But not even this is true: in fact the LEMMA is the only certain element. For instead of an equivalent or equivalents there may be a reference (REFER) to another entry, e.g.

> **nakke|fletning** *se fletning 3.*
> ...-**hul** *(anat) = -åbning.*

Thus everything but the lemma is facultative, and the format now looks as in Fig. 5.4.1-3 (left-hand column).

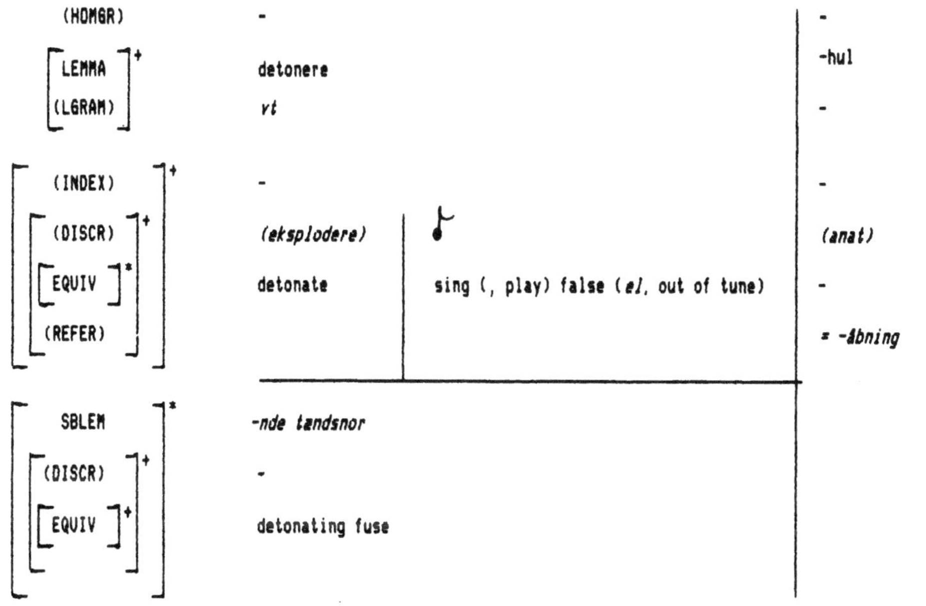

Fig. 5.4.1-2 The ETTO Notation. A further generalization: LEMMA is now the only category occurring with certainty. On the right-hand side the entries *detonere* and *(nakke)-hul* are located in the format.

One of the things we have tried to do in Fig. 5.4.1-3 is to place the example used in Fig. 4.2.2-1 d, *detonere* (see also Fig. 5.4-1 f) in the format. It is evident that it can be done; but also that one of the "equivalents" needs further scrutiny, i.e.

> sing (, play) false (*el.* out of tune)

— an example of what we have called telescoping, here of four equivalents, making up two pairs of synonyms (cf Section 4.2.4).

The description in Fig. 5.4.1-3 is compact and manageable; but for some purposes it is not sufficiently detailed. It gives no indication of the typographical form of the categories used, nor of punctuation marks and numbering, for example. Furthermore, it is too "broad" in the sense that it does not allow for the specification of the structure *selection*: for example, it permits an entry to consist of nothing but a LEMMA.

5.4.2 The bracket diagram

These weak points can be avoided with a bracket diagram of the type shown in Fig 5.4.2-1. Here, too, the hierarchical structure of the entry emerges more clearly. Note, for example, the three levels of semantic grouping (SEGMent), distinguished typographically by numbering (SEGM1), separation with semicolons (SEGM2) and

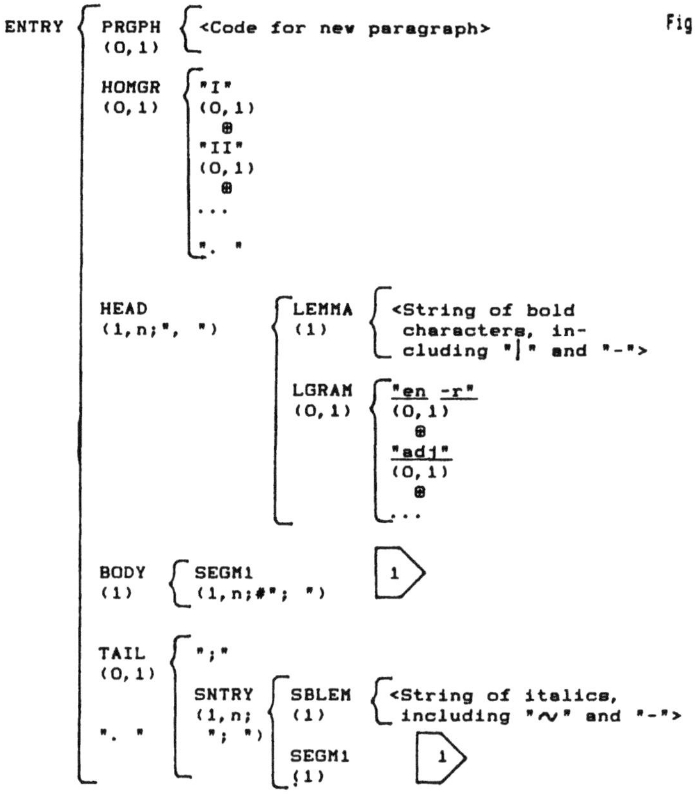

Fig. 5.4.2-1 Bracket diagram

(Fig. 5,4,2-1, continued)

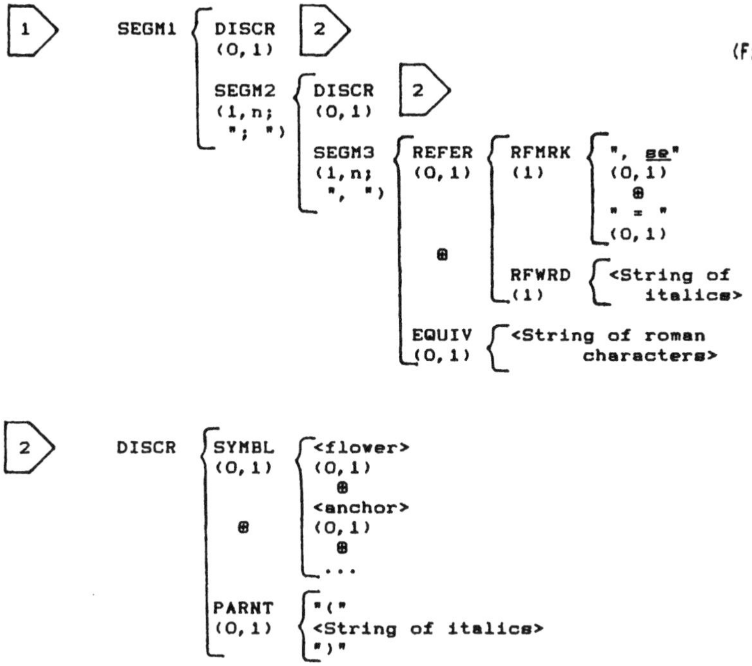

Fig. 5,4,2-1 Bracket diagram, An alternative, and more detailed description of the format from Fig. 5,4,1-2, A number of new (superordinate and subordinate) category names have been introduced; they are explained in more detail in Section 5,5 below.

separation with commas (SEGM3). In terms of content the typographical differences represent a semantic classification going from a top level with quite separate numbered translations to a bottom level with (near-)synonymous translations separated by commas.

5.4.3 Extended BNF

The bracket diagram is clear and therefore well-suited to the actual work of analysis, as well as for heuristic purposes. Yet it is space-consuming, not least when tables have to be set up for terminal symbols like alphabets, part-of-speech abbreviations, specialized usage markers etc. For the final presentation of the analysis results, extended BNF (EBNF) may therefore be preferable. This notation is used in Fig. 5.4.3-1.

Fig. 5.4.3-1 Extended BNF. The same format as in Fig. 5.4.2-1, here notated in Extended Backus-Naur Form (Jensen/Wirth 1985)

```
<ENTRY> ::= <Start> <Rest>. |
            <PRGPH> <Start> <Rest>.

<Rest> ::= <BODY> | <BODY>; <TAIL>

<Start> ::= <HOMGR>. <HEAD> (, <HEAD>)* |
            <HEAD> {, <HEAD>}*

<HOMGR> ::= I | II | ...

<HEAD> ::= <LEMMA> | <LEMMA> <LGRAM>

<LEMMA> ::= <String of bold
             characters, including " " and "-">

<LGRAM> ::= en -r | adj | ...

<BODY> ::= <SEGM1> |
           1 <SEGM1>; 2 <SEGM1> (; <Index> <SEGM1>)*

<Index> ::= 3 | 4 | 5 | ...

<TAIL> ::= <SNTRY> {; <SNTRY>}*

<SNTRY> ::= <SBLEM> <SEGM1>

<SBLEM> ::= <String of italics, including "  " and "-">

<SEGM1> ::= <DISCR> <SEGM2> {; <SEGM2>}* |
            <SEGM2> {; <SEGM2>}*

<SEGM2> ::= <DISCR> <SEGM3> {, <SEGM3>}* |
            <SEGM3> {, <SEGM3>}*

<SEGM3> ::= <REFER> | <EQUIV>

<REFER> ::= <RFMRK> <RFWRD>

<RFMRK> ::= , se | =

<RFWRD> ::= <String of italics>

<EQUIV> ::= <String of roman characters>

<DISCR> ::= <SYMBL> | (<string of italics>)

<SYMBL> ::= <flower> | <anchor> | ...
```

In this, as in the other notations, the same dictionary can be described in many different ways. Finding the best or the right one — the most suitable grouping of non-terminal subsets — is no trivial matter: it is the whole point. Another example of an (exhaustive) formal description of a dictionary entry will demonstrate that the choice of non-terminal subsets is by no means without consequences:

<Entry> ::= {**<Type>**} *.

<Type> ::= **a** | **b** | ... | **ø** | **Å** | **A** | **B** | ... | ~ | ...

5.5 Relationship with the taxonomy

In the above we have outlined how one approaches the format analysis of an existing dictionary, and described an actual example in three different formal notations. It must be emphasized that for the sake of clarity these descriptions have deliberately not been exhaustive: the dictionary contains more information categories and combinations of categories than it has been desirable to account for here. Even in the example entries (Fig. 5.4-1) structural elements occur that have not been included. Among other things, there are some of the space-saving devices mentioned in Section 4.2, and there is a part-of-speech marker (*adv* under *narkotiserende 2*) subordinated to a semantic grouping. In particular, we can mention here the type *(fx ...)* under *narkotisk* and *desperation*; this represents the taxonomy category *possible context*, which for the sake of clarity has not been included in the much reduced version of the format given here.

Several of the "end-categories" we have arrived at must be further subclassified before agreement with the taxonomy is ensured. On the basis of the format categories in Fig. 5.4.2-1 and the introductory taxonomical analysis in Section 4.2 (the entry examples for this have been repeated as Fig. 5.4-1 g-k) this complex of problems will be reviewed below.

5.5.1 The entry

As the inclusive category we have chosen the ENTRY, defined here as the unit beginning with a (semibold) headword and ending with a full stop (or sometimes an abbreviation marker, or a question or exclamation mark, cf Section 5.2 on *context-free*). Certain entries are begun with a new paragraph (PRGPH), but this has no significance in terms of content.

5.5.2 Lexical units

The project-specific information in *Dansk-Engelsk Ordbog* — the lexical units of the work — are Danish words (LEMMA) and phrases (SBLEM = Sublemma) and their equivalents (EQUIV) in the form of English words and phrases.

The two languages are national languages: sociolects, dialects and language stages, if dealt with at all, are treated as usage variants of the national language. The approach is semasiological, and the medium of expression is writing.

The lexical units as such are outside the domain of the taxonomy. However, their written representations convey in the first instance orthographical information, and also information on word formation, among other things. LEMMA moreover has an administrative function, as it is the basis for the alphabetical ordering of the entries. For the purposes of automatic processing these functions should be made explicit: we must extract a complete, unadulterated orthographical form (without vertical separators, missing first elements or other space-saving devices), information on the elements that a compound or derived word consists of (word formation), and a version of the word for alphabetization (administrative information). The latter will often, but not always, be the orthographical form, if necessary supplemented with a homograph marker; but capital/small letters, spaces and accents, for example, will need special treatment, depending on the alphabetization rules we wish to use.

5.5.3 The format categories and the taxonomy

The ENTRY includes the categories PRGPH, HOMGR, HEAD, BODY and TAIL; it ends with a full stop.

PRGPH, marking a new paragraph, begins some, but far from all entries. Taxonomy category: *administrative information*.

HOMGR, the homograph marker, is a Roman number in a plain typeface, followed by a full stop. It occurs in some, but far from all entries. Taxonomy category: *administrative information*.

HEAD, the "head(s)" of the entry, includes LEMMA, followed if required by LGRAM. The entry has at least one HEAD; if there are more they are separated by a comma.

BODY, the "body" of the entry, deals with the lemma itself (as distinct from TAIL). In the entry examples it occurs just once. It consists of one or more segments of the type SEGM1; if there are more, they are numbered with Arabic numerals and separated by semicolons.

TAIL, the "tail" of the entry, deals with the sublemmas, i.e. phrases etc. It does not occur in all entries. It consists of a semicolon followed by one or more sub-entries (SNTRY).

LEMMA, see Section 5.5.2 on lexical units.

LGRAM, Lemma GRAMmar, is information on the part of speech and/or inflection of the lemma. According to the taxonomy this category must be subdivided into *part of speech* (POFSP), *inflectional information* (FLEX) and an item of syntactic information concerning the transitivity of the verb (TRANS).

- **POFSP** can for example be specified as *adj*, *adv*, *en* (i.e. common-gender noun), or *v* in *vi* (verbum intransitivum) or *vt* (verbum transitivum). POFSP is not normally indicated for compound nouns.

- **FLEX** is not specified for compound nouns and verbs, weak verbs or adjectives with regular comparison. For simplex nouns, inflectional plurals (*-er*, *-r*) or indefinite plural forms are given; for strong verbs the simple past and perfect participle; for irregular adjectives, the comparative and superlative forms.

- **TRANS** : *i* or *t* in *vi* or *vt*; cf POFSP above.

SNTRY, the sub-entry, consists of a sublemma (SBLEM) and a segment of the type SEGM1.

SBLEM, sublemma, see Section 5.5.2 on lexical units.

SEGM1, a translation segment at the top level, consists of one or more translations (SEGM2) of the lemma/sublemma which are so close semantically that they can be glossed by the same overall discriminator (DISCR), which may however be omitted. If there are several SEGM2 segments, they are separated by semicolons.

SEGM2, a translation segment at the intermediate level, consisting of one or more near-synonyms, translations (SEGM3) covered by one discriminator, which may however be omitted. If there are several SEGM3 segments, they are separated by commas.

SEGM3, a bottom-level translation segment, usually consisting of one equivalent (EQUIV). But instead of this there may be a reference (REFER) to another entry where the equivalent can be found.

EQUIV, equivalent, consists of an English word or phrase; see Section 5.5.2 on lexical units.

REFER, a dictionary-internal reference to another entry, e.g.

> **(nakke)-fletning**, *se fletning 3;*
> **(nakke)-hul** *(anat) = (nakke)-åbning*,

belongs to the taxonomy category *administrative information*. For automatic checking it is best to subdivide it into:

- **RFMRK**, reference marker, including the markers ", *se*" (Danish: *see!*) and " = ";and

- **RFWRD**, reference word, identifying the word or phrase referred to.

DISCR, the discriminator, is a format category which by its very nature must be expected to contain elements from many different taxonomy categories, inasmuch as the area of applicability of a translation can be indicated in many different ways. Below, however we will restrict the discussion to those discriminators that occur in the entry examples in Fig. 5.4-1. But first a purely typographical subcategorization will be necessary: for DISCR may take the form of a symbol (SYMBL) without brackets or of text printed in italics within brackets.

SYMBL includes (in the entry examples) <anchor> = maritime, <daggers> = military, <flower> = botanical and <note> = musical; in terms of the taxonomy these all belong to the category *subject specification*.

PARNT, discriminator PAReNThesis, sometimes includes free text that neither automatic nor human analysis could assign uniquely to a taxonomy category. In other cases the text could be classified by human intervention, but only with difficulty automatically. We have chosen to call this whole subset of PARNT

- **MISC**, miscellaneous discriminators. Taxonomically, these can be classified with most justification as information on *equivalence*.

There remain a number of frequently occurring, but listed, so easily identifiable, standard discriminators, which can be categorized as semantic/subject classification (SUBJ), or pragmatic information on usage, including for example register (STYLE):

- **SUBJ**, subject, consists of markers like *anat*, *gymn*, *hist* and *vet* (anatomy, gymnastics, history, veterinary medicine).

- **STYLE** is a subdivision (social dimension) of the taxonomy category *use*. The only instance in the entry examples is *fagl* (*fagligt sprog* 'specialized language'); but various other usage markers can be found in the dictionary.

5.5.4 The taxonomy categories and the format

By comparing the above with the overview of the taxonomy in Section 3.3, we can now specify the subset of the taxonomy that has been used:

GENERAL INFORMATION TYPES:

MAIN GROUPS	CATEGORIES	FORMAT CATEGORIES	
Grammatical information	part of speech	POFSP	LGRAM
	inflectional information	FLEX	
	syntactic information/valency	TRANS	
Pragmatic information	administrative information/internal reference	RFMRK	REFER
	/internal reference	RFWRD	
	/homograph number		HOMGR
	/technical information		PRGPH
	use/social dimension	STYLE	DISCR
Semantic information	subject classification	SYMBL	
	subject classification	SUBJ	
	equivalence/two languages	MISC	

PROJECT-SPECIFIC INFORMATION TYPES:

LEMMA	Lexical units
SBLEM	
EQUIV	

Each of the "end-categories" arrived at, the leaves of the tree-structure, has now been assigned to one (sub)category of the taxonomy and one only. However it emerged as expected that the lexical units of the printed dictionary (lemma, sublemma, equivalent) are so complex, taxonomically and in content, that they must be "unpacked" for the purposes of automatic processing (Section 5.5.2, cf Section 4.2).

The punctuation marks, typefaces, etc., classified in Section 4.2 as providing administrative and semantic information, have been ignored here. They are among the criteria for establishing the analysis tree, from which they can be generated again — that is, if one does not choose to generate other indicators instead.

5.6 Mark-up systems

Once the format has been established and described, there must be a method of inserting structural markers in the dictionary text. It seems appropriate here to use methods and notations from the so-called list-processing languages — programming languages like LISP or PROLOG, whose function is precisely to control not only ordered sequences of terminal symbols, but also *ordered sequences of such sequences* at an arbitrary number of levels. The problem is not peculiar to dictionaries: any structured text to be entered into a full-text database needs this type of marking to identify items like authors' names and addresses, abstracts, notes, bibliographies (including separate identification of author, title etc. within these), indices etc.

The ISO (International Organization for Standardization) has drawn up a standard (ISO 8879, 1986) — on the basis of a former IBM standard — for a system of marking text segments according to type (so-called generic marking). This Standard Generalized Mark-up Language (SGML), building on the theory of finite automata, enables one to design programs — parsers — that can process structured documents. Reading the standard itself is heavy going; but it has a number of supplements ("Annexes") with descriptions that are more accessible for non-computer scientists. FORMEX (1985) can be recommended as a good introduction to SGML.

SGML is a general formal system which can be realized with arbitrary symbols, some of which must be reserved for marking purposes. In the following we will observe the conventions (FORMEX, 1985) used by the Office for Official Publications of the European Communities. The reserved symbols here are < 'less than' and *&* 'ampersand' and are used as follows.

The beginning of a given category named *xxx* is written <xxx> and the end of this category is written </xxx>.

Longer expressions that must be repeated frequently, and symbols that are not available in the alphabet used may be indicated by the "stenographical" notation *&yy;* — that is, a name *yy* preceded by *&* and followed by *;*. For example, *&SGML;* could represent *Standard Generalized Mark-up Language*, and *&ag;* could represent lower-case *a* with a grave accent. If one requires symbols for 'less than' or 'and' they must be symbolized by, for example, *≤* and *&an;*.

Although the slash *(/)*, 'greater than' *(>)*, the semicolon *(;)* and several other characters may be used as markers, they are not reserved characters. When they are not part of a marker introduced by < or *&* they have their normal meanings.

The meanings of category names and "stenograms" are stipulated in a document type definition (DTD) giving a precise account of the categories and hierarchies they may be included in, and of the character sets used. In the definition it may also be stipulated that not all categories require markers, as the start of a co-ordinate category or the end of a superordinate one will be sufficient marking. Further simplification can be achieved by defining abbreviated markers for frequently-occurring category names. The codes in word-processing files (control characters etc.) that mark new lines, new paragraphs, tabs, various types of emphasis and the like can also be defined as abbreviated SGML markers. Furthermore, text strings can be defined both as data and as markers. By making full use of these possibilities one can almost completely avoid visible mark-up symbols in a dictionary entry.

For the rules for formulating a DTD reference must be made to ISO 8879 (1986) and FORMEX (1985). It should just be noted here that SGML — apart from the data structures *sequence*, *selection* and *iteration* (cf Section 5.2.3) — permits one more structure: the *and group*. That a category *C* can be rewritten as the sequence *XYZ* is notated *C(X, Y, Z)*; that it can be rewritten as one and only one of the elements *X*, *Y* and *Z* (selection) is notated *(X | Y | Z)*. An *and group* is notated *(X&Y&Z)* and means that all three elements *must* be present, but that their order is arbitrary. *(X&Y&Z)* is thus equivalent to

((X, Y, Z) | (X, Z, Y) | (Y, X, Z) | (Y, Z, X) | (Z, X, Y) | (Z, Y, X))

A notation like this with accompanying computer support could facilitate the description and processing of dictionaries with as much variation in the order of information types as the one described in Section 5.8.1.

The SGML Parser is a program which checks against the document type definition whether a given text complies with the defined structure. In addition, it completes the marking-up of texts with reduced or simplified mark-ups.

The Belgian company SOBEMAP has developed such a parser, called "Mark-it", for the Office for Official Publications of the European Communities: it will be released for sale in 1987. SGML is also being incorporated into leading word-processing products, and broad-application document types are being defined, for example for the usual types of scholarly papers (Smith 1986).

For a dictionary the document type definition would be analogous to the format descriptions we have given above, and the marking-up of a specific entry could look as in Fig. 5.6-1, although in practice one would use even more abbreviated category names and/or word-processing codes, etc. as mentioned above. It is clear that a complete mark-up requires software that automates the work as much as possible. The advantage of using a system of this type is that the dictionary data can be used and re-used in different media, as many different forms of presentation can be derived from the same medium-independent, well-defined structural description.

It can be seen in Fig. 5.6-1 that fonts and meaning numbers, as well as most brackets and punctuation marks, are not listed as such: they are implicit in the general mark-up. These, or other separators etc. required, can be generated from the explicit structural marking. The Roman numbers functioning as homograph markers could also if necessary be dispensed with if the entry itself — like the main text section (SEGM1) in the body of the entry — was defined as an element with a position in a numbered list.

Fig. 5.6-1 Standard Generalized Mark-up Language

```
<ENTRY PRGPH="YES">
  <HOMGR>I</HOMGR>
  <HEAD>
    <LEMMA>navle</LEMMA>
    <LGRAM>en -r</LGRAM>
  </HEAD>
  <BODY>
    <SEGM1>
      <DISCR>anat</DISCR>
      <SEGM2>
        <SEGM3>
          <EQUIV>navel</EQUIV>
        </SEGM3>
      </SEGM2>
      <SEGM2>
        <DISCR>fagl</DISCR>
        <SEGM3>
          <EQUIV>umbilicus</EQUIV>
        </SEGM3>
      </SEGM2>
    </SEGM1>
    <SEGM1>
      <DISCR>&FLOWER;</DISCR>
      <SEGM2>
        <SEGM3>
          <EQUIV>hilum</EQUIV>
        </SEGM3>
      </SEGM2>
    </SEGM1>
    <SEGM1>
      <DISCR>på sneglehus</DISCR>
      <SEGM2>
        <SEGM3>
          <EQUIV>umbilicus</EQUIV>
        </SEGM3>
      </SEGM2>
    </SEGM1>
    <SEGM1>
      <DISCR>her.</DISCR>
      <SEGM2>
        <SEGM3>
          <EQUIV>nombril</EQUIV>
        </SEGM3>
        <SEGM3>
          <EQUIV>navel (of an escutcheon)</EQUIV>
        </SEGM3>
      </SEGM2>
    </SEGM1>
```

(Fig. 5.6-1 continued)

```
    <SEGM1>
      <DISCR>glasnavle</DISCR>
      <SEGM2>
        <SEGM3>
          <EQUIV>punty (el. pontil) mark</EQUIV>
        </SEGM3>
      </SEGM2>
    </SEGM1>
  </BODY>
  <TAIL>
    <SNTRY>
      <SBLEM>verdens &-;</SBLEM>
      <SEGM1>
        <SEGM2>
          <SEGM3>
            <EQUIV>the hub of the Universe</EQUIV>
          </SEGM3>
        </SEGM2>
      </SEGM1>
    </SNTRY>
    <SNTRY>
      <SBLEM>stirre på sin egen &-;</SBLEM>
      <SEGM1>
        <DISCR>fig</DISCR>
        <SEGM2>
          <SEGM3>
            <EQUIV>be self-centred</EQUIV>
          </SEGM3>
          <SEGM3>
            <EQUIV>be a narcissist</EQUIV>
          </SEGM3>
          <SEGM3>
            <EQUIV>be narcistic</EQUIV>
          </SEGM3>
        </SEGM2>
      </SEGM1>
    </SNTRY>
  </TAIL>
</ENTRY>
```

Fig. 5.6-1 Standard Generalized Mark-up Language (SGML). Example of a fully marked-up entry. For the sake of clarity each marker has been placed on a line by itself, and hierarchies are made clearer by indentations. '&FLOWER;' and '&-;' represent respectively the symbol <"flower"> (= botanical) and the swung dash used as a repetition symbol for the lemma.

Fig. 5,6-2 SGML. The same entry with reduced, but still unique, marking-up.

```
<ENTRY PRGPH="YES">
  <HOMGR>I
    <LEMMA>navle
    <LGRAM>en -r
      <DISCR>anat
          <EQUIV>navel
        <DISCR>fagl
          <EQUIV>umbilicus
    <SEGM1>
      <DISCR>&FLOWER;
          <EQUIV>hilum
    <SEGM1>
      <DISCR>på sneglehus
          <EQUIV>umbilicus
    <SEGM1>
      <DISCR>her.
          <EQUIV>nombril
          <EQUIV>navel (of an escutcheon)
    <SEGM1>
      <DISCR>glasnavle
          <EQUIV>punty (el. pontil) mark
      <SBLEM>verdens &-;
            <EQUIV>the hub of the Universe
      <SBLEM>stirre på sin egen &-;
        <DISCR>fig
            <EQUIV>be self-centred
            <EQUIV>be a narcissist
            <EQUIV>be narcistic
</ENTRY>
```

Fig. 5,6-3 SGML; the same entry as in Fig. 5.7.b, but written continuously.

```
<ENTRY    PRGPH="YES">   <HOMGR>I   <LEMMA>navle
<LGRAM>en -r <DISCR>anat <EQUIV>navel <DISCR>fagl
<EQUIV>umbilicus  <SEGM1>  <DISCR>&FLOWER; <EQUIV>hilum
<SEGM1> <DISCR>på sneglehus <EQUIV>umbilicus <SEGM1>
<DISCR>her. <EQUIV>nombril <EQUIV>navel (of an escutcheon)
 <SEGM1> <DISCR>glasnavle <EQUIV>punty (el.  pontil) mark
 <SBLEM>verdens &-; <EQUIV>the hub of  the  Universe
<SBLEM>stirre  på sin egen &-; <DISCR>fig <EQUIV>be
self-centred <EQUIV>be a narcissist <EQUIV>be narcistic
</ENTRY>
```

5.7 *The Oxford English Dictionary* - an example

One of the aims of methods such as those described above is to extract as much structural information as possible from existing dictionary texts and break them down into the categories of the common taxonomy, which can then be further subdivided and if necessary restructured, for example in a database. A further aim is to draw up optimal editorial rules for new dictionary projects, so they can take maximum advantage of computer facilities from the outset. Finally, the methods can be used when new (for example printed) dictionaries — new linear texts — are to be constructed from databases with their more complex data structures.

An interesting example of such a mode of working is the revision of *The Oxford English Dictionary* now being done jointly by the publishers (OUP) and the humanistic computer centre at the University of Waterloo, Ontario. The project has also had considerable support from IBM. The following account is based on Hultin/Logan (1984), Weiner (1985), Simpson (1986) and Weiner (1986).

The project, begun in 1984, is in two phases. The first involves making the main work (twelve volumes, finished in 1928) and the supplement (four volumes, finished in 1986) machine-readable in SGML-coded form, merging them in one database, and finally publishing an 'Integrated OED' in 1989. The main work and supplement have been entered with manually-added marking-up, specifying the broad features of the entry structure. The texts consist of 350 million characters; but with the markers there is a total of 500 million characters. The typographical specifications of various typefaces etc. are preserved during data entry. Parsing will then be done in two stages with slightly different "grammars" for the main work and the supplement, to make the detailed structure explicit. Then the two will be integrated; it is estimated that 80% of this process can be done automatically; the rest involves manual editing of the merged entries. A special editing program, LEXX, has been developed for this. After an entry has been edited it is parsed again to check that the format has been observed. Besides the publication of the printed work, this phase will be concluded with yet another parsing that will further increase the number of identified structural elements.

In the second phase a database will be built up to reflect the structure marked in SGML at the end of the first phase; there is a provisional design for such a database in Hultin/Logan (1984: 191). The database will serve several purposes. It will be a tool for the revision and updating of the Dictionary's contents by lexicographers, a source from which to typeset future printed editions, and a tool for research by a wide range of database users. It is also intended to supplement it with other lexical data. Ultimately, it will be accessible to general users on-line and/or on a CD-ROM compact disc and as both complete and more specialized printed editions.

5.8 Format description and computerized registration of the structure of a printed bilingual dictionary

Blinkenberg and Høybye's Danish-French dictionary *Dansk-Fransk Ordbog* (1975) has been analysed with a view to computerized registration of the structure of the entries and the creation of a database (cf Madsen 1986). The database is primarily to be used in the revision of the dictionary for a new printed edition, but in the longer term the aim is to use the database as an on-line reference work. The printed dictionary has been made machine-readable by means of optical reading, and a program has been developed that automatically analyses the dictionary data and inserts structural markers for the various types of information such as *headword*, *part of speech*, *inflection* etc. necessary for transferring the machine-readable dictionary data to a database. The database system used is DANSTATUS, the Danish version of the English information retrieval system STATUS II. DANSTATUS is used for text corpus, terminological and dictionary databases at the Copenhagen School of Economics and Business Administration.

The analysis and mark-up program developed corresponds to the type of program that will be necessary for automatic insertion of SGML marking-up (cf 5.6 above). Instead of SGML markers, the program used for *Dansk-Fransk Ordbog* inserts the field names (including control characters) used in the database directly. It is not a general-purpose program that can be used without modification for other dictionaries, but to a certain extent the principles can be applied to similar dictionaries.

The program does not check whether a specified entry structure is observed. But it does mark the actual sequence of certain information types (cf 5.8.3) so that irregularities can easily be identified and corrected during revision.

Each dictionary entry is transferred to one record in the database without further marking of the hierarchical structure (for more details, see 5.8.4).

5.8.1 *Dansk-Fransk Ordbog* described with the bracket diagram

This section will show how the printed *Dansk-Fransk Ordbog* can be described by the bracket diagram. As far as possible, the subdivisions and terminology are based on the editors' own description of the dictionary. To provide some background for understanding the principles of the program used to analyse and register the structure of the entries, most of the details and problems have been shown in the bracket diagram. Allowance has thus been made for the great majority of the irregularities and inconsistencies in the printed dictionary. However, the diagram has been simplified in a few instances. Only part of the entry is shown — the first section of the "head" with its homograph number, headword, grammatical features and language markers — while the rest of the "head", with references, style markers, translations etc, and the "tail" with phrases and examples are not discussed here.

Overall view of entry structure

An analysis with the bracket diagram may easily give the impression that the entries are clearly hierarchically structured with many levels. They are not; but because the order of information types is almost free, it has been necessary to introduce a number of "pseudo-levels". There is already an example of this in the first overall view of the entry (cf Fig. 5.8.1-1 below). The homograph number can be placed both before and after the headword, so two extra levels must be used: *headword complex*, and *type a)* or *type b)*.

The diagram also shows that the headword may be missing if the homograph number is II or more (cf Fig. 5.8.1-2 below).

Similarly, two extra levels must be introduced — *grammar/language complex*, and *type a)* or *type b)* — as grammatical information can be placed either before or after a language marker (e.g. *latinsk prp.* or *prp. ital.* — Latin and Italian prepositions) and in either case is facultative. The analysis can be even more difficult, inasmuch as these items of information can appear with or without brackets or in the same set of brackets in the printed dictionary — e.g. *pr. (lt.)* or *(prp. ital.)*.

Fig. 5.8.1-1

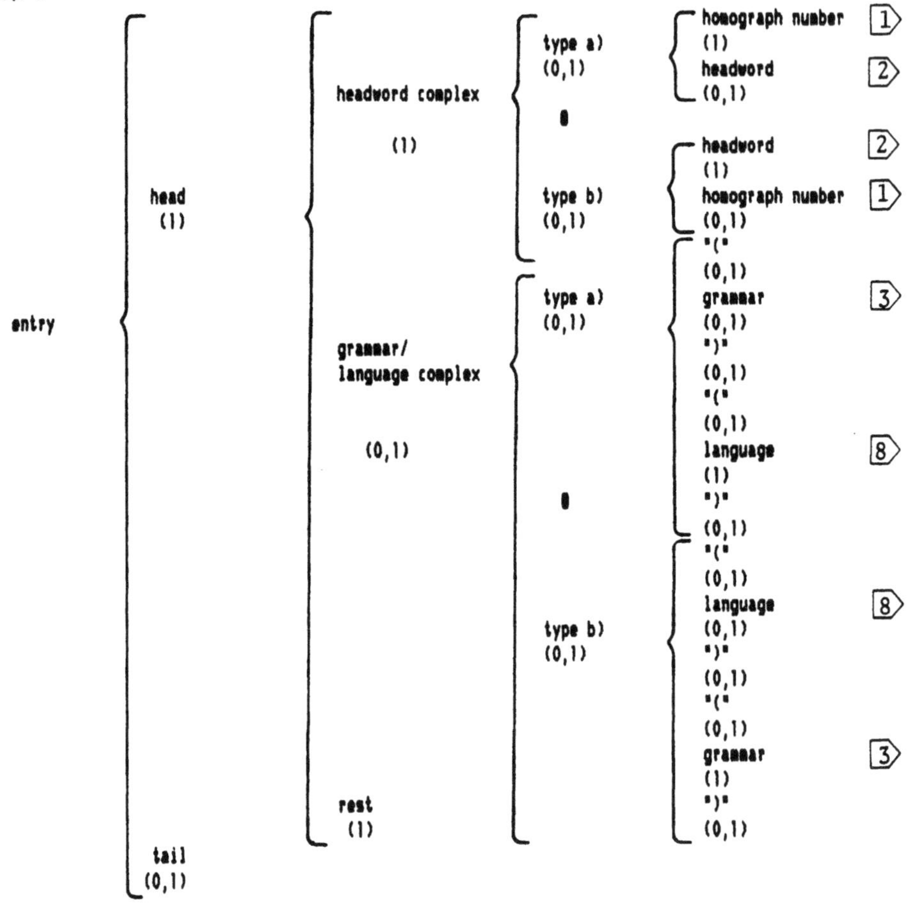

Fig. 5.8.1-2

absolut I. *n (-ter)* absolu; absoluité*; exigence* morale absolue.-
II. *a* **A)** *(Alm.)* (1) absolu *(ogs. pol. = enevældig)*.
B) *(= bestemt, afgørende)* (2) catégorique. (3) péremptoire. (4) décisif; *(undert.)* (5) foncier. (6) [à] cent pour cent.-

Homograph number and headword

The headword is a string of semibold characters which may contain spaces (*a conto*), hyphens (*abe-, A-aktie, disk-jockey*), full stops (*a.c.*), square brackets (*abietin[syre]*), stress markers (*´forfald, for´fald*) or separators (*abdom|en*).

Fig. 5.8.1-3

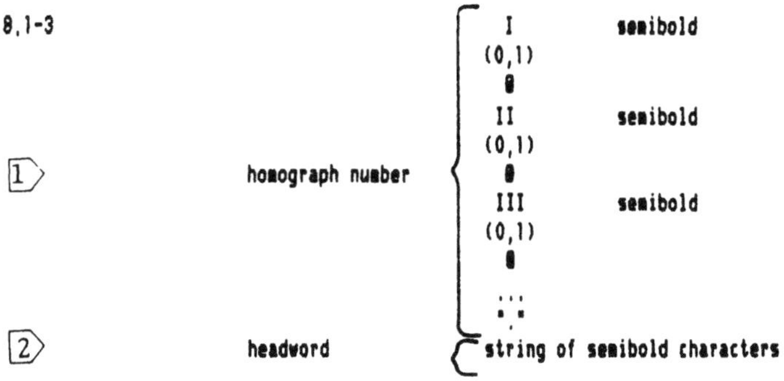

Grammar

Fig. 5.8.1-1 showed that not all entries have grammatical information. Fig. 5.8.1-4 further shows under *type b)* that in accordance with normal lexicographical practice subclassifications (e.g. gender *c* and *n*) can occur without part-of-speech markers. They can also be placed before part-of-speech markers (e.g. *p.p. og a* 'perfect participle and adjective').

Fig. 5.8.1-4

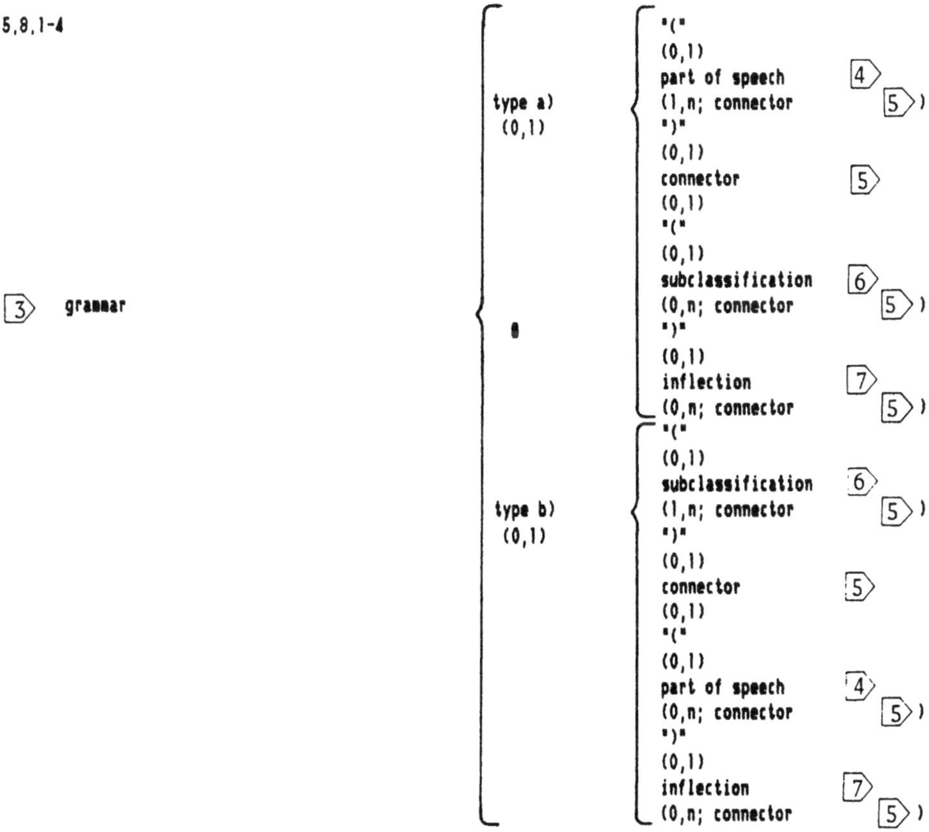

Figure 5,8,1-5

4 part of speech
- "a" italic
- (0,1)
- ●
- "art" italic
- (0,1)
- ●
- "av" italic
- (0,1)
- ...
- "."
- (0,1)

5 connector
- " "
- (0,1)
- ●
- "og"
- (0,1)
- ●
- "el,"
- (0,1)
- ●
- ","
- (0,1)

6 subclassification of part of speech
- "acc" italic
- (0,1)
- ●
- "comp" italic
- (0,1)
- ●
- "cond" italic
- (0,1)
- ...
- "."
- (0,1)

7 inflection
- type a) (0,1)
  - "("
  - (0,1)
  - regular
  - (1,n; connector 5)
  - connector 5
  - (0,1)
  - irregular
  - (0,n; connector 5)
  - ")"
  - (0,1)
- ●
- type b) (0,1)
  - "("
  - (0,1)
  - irregular
  - (1,n; connector 5)
  - connector 5
  - (0,1)
  - regular
  - (0,n; connector 5)
  - ")"
  - (0,1)

Part of speech, connector, subclassification of part of speech and inflection

As can be seen from Fig. 5.8.1-5, various connectors (space, *og* = and, *el.* = or, or a comma) can occur between *part of speech* and *subclassification of part of speech*. One cannot deduce any immediate differences in meaning from the connectors: the variations are more likely to be a result of the practice of different editors.

Both *part of speech* and *subclassification of part of speech* may be ended with a full stop.

Item 7, inflection, is shown in simplified form. When inflection is irregular, a list should be made of all the possible inflectional forms. Examples of this are the irregular plurals *ænder* 'ducks', plural of *and* and *køer* 'cows', plural of *ko*.

Language

With this as with other information types, the same information can be abbreviated in different ways, e.g. *lt.* and *lat.* for Latin. All forms are included in the list of terminals.

Fig, 5,8,1-6

5.8.2 Conclusions on description with the bracket diagram

It is evident from the above that one must go to great pains to represent an entry structure with the bracket diagram if the order of information types varies and there are many facultative items. On the other hand the bracket diagram exposes any irregularities and inconsistencies in the dictionary and is therefore a useful tool, not only in developing the above-mentioned analysis and mark-up program, but also in the editorial formulation of rules for revising existing dictionary entries and compiling new ones. The rules being formulated at present for revision work can afterwards be described in a simpler bracket diagram, which can when the time comes be used as a basis for developing a program for checking whether the new rules have been applied consistently in the revision work.

5.8.3 Computerized analysis and the establishment of a database

Because of the many possible ways of ordering information and the many facultative information types, the analysis and structural registration program is based primarily on the recognition of typographical features (semibold, italics, brackets, semicolons etc.) and content (tables of abbreviations — for example, part of speech, subclassification, language). In a few cases the analysis is also based on sequence.

Here we will give no detailed description of the way the program works; we will, however, cite some examples that illustrate the principles.

The typographical features are present in the machine-readable data in the form of codes. If the program, for example, finds an item of information marked as semibold non-italic, it first checks whether it is some form of tabular information like a homograph number (Roman number with full stop), or a letter marking a semantic subdivision (upper-case letter with right closing bracket — A), B), C) etc.)(cf Fig. 5.8.3-1). If this is not the case, it checks whether the first character is a hyphen, or corresponds to the letter of the alphabet being dealt with in that part of the dictionary (the program is run on one letter of the alphabet at a time). If this is so, the marker for *headword* is inserted; otherwise the information is ignored (i.e. is assigned to another information type, for example *Danish phrases*, where there are words emphasized in semibold type).

Fig. 5.8.3-1

adskille *vt* A) (= *ophæve sammenhæng* el. *forbindelse, danne skel*) (1) séparer (*fra* de, d'avec) (2) désunir (3) disjoindre (4) diviser (5) (= *løsne*) détacher (6) (*to sammenhørende ting*) déparier (7) (*flere sammenhørende ting*) dépareiller; (*phys.*) (8) dissocier (9) scinder; (*chim.*) (10) décomposer (11) réduire (12) ⊕ démonter. B) (= *skelne*) (13) distinguer (14) démêler (15) discerner (16) différencier (17) faire le départ de (18) (*undert.*) disloquer. || *~ sig* différer les uns des autres; *~ sig fra* se différencier de, se distinguer de, différer de (*el.* d'avec), se détacher de, s'opposer à; *~ sig fra de andre derved, at* se différencier des autres en ce que; *derved ~r han sig fra de andre* par là il s'oppose aux autres; *Mk* la crise qui commença en 1929 fut entre toutes singulière et sortit de l'ordre commun; *hvad Gud har sammenføjet, skal mennesket ikke ~* que l'homme ne sépare pas ce que Dieu a uni.

When the program meets italics it similarly checks a series of tables (part of speech, subclassification, language, style, subject etc.). If the item concerned is not listed in the tables, it checks whether the next new typeface is a ~ (the swung dash is defined in the program as a typeface). If this is so, the italicized unit is a Danish phrase; if not, and no translation has yet been found in the entry in question, it is marked *application* .

A large group of italicized information items are bracketed. A left bracket is defined as a typeface, and if the program finds one followed by italics, it checks, for example, whether there is an equals sign, which means that a synonym follows. If the first letter after the bracket is upper-case, it is a Latin plant or animal name (exceptions to this are, for example, the abbreviations *Jfr.* 'cf, compare' and *NB* 'nota bene').

All other non-tabular bracketed information in italics and in front of translations is marked as *application*: it could be non-tabular information on subject (for example, *taxation*), content (explanations), or semantic relations (hyperonyms and hyponyms). It is not possible to separate these information types automatically.

Because of the errors that can arise in optical reading or inconsistencies in the dictionary entries, errors of analysis are of course unavoidable. It will be clear from the above that computerized registration of the structure is to a great extent based on differences in typefaces. The program is therefore particularly vulnerable to errors in the recognition of typefaces by an optical reader. This type of error is unfortunately very common. However, within a reasonable margin of error, the entry is divided up into the following information types, which can be compared with the categories of the taxonomy.

FIELD NAME	INFORMATION TYPE	TAXONOMY CATEGORY
HGNR	homograph number	administrative information
OPSL	headword	orthographical information
LEKS	special lexical type	orthographical/etymological information
VAR	variant	orthographical information
ORDK	part of speech	part of speech
UNDERK	grammatical subcategory	part of speech
FLEKS	inflection	inflectional information
SPROG	language name	origin
HENV	reference to other headword (without translation following)	administrative information
BET	letter indicating semantic group	semantic relations
SYN	Danish synonym	orthographical information and equivalence
NUM	number reference	administrative information
EMNE	subject area	subject classification
STIL	style register	usage
ANV	application	subject classification/content specification/ semantic relations/contextual information/ usage/evaluative information
OVERS	translation	orthographical information + equivalence
LAT	Latin word	parallel
PART	particle collocation	contextual information/syntactic information
SUPPL	supplementary information	subject classification/content specification/ semantic relations/contextual information/ usage/evaluative information
INDD	subdivision marker for phrases	administrative information
RUBR	rubrics	administrative information
DAORDF	Danish phrase	orthographical information/contextual information
FRORDF	French phrase	orthographical information/contextual information/equivalence
DAEKS	Danish example	contextual information
FREKS	French example	contextual information (+ equivalence)
REF	reference to other headword (after translation)	administrative information

In the tail (phrases and examples) the fields SPROG (language), EMNE (subject), ANV (application), STIL (style) and LAT are also marked for the position of the information (before or after a Danish phrase, after a French phrase etc., for example EMNEFDO = *emne før dansk ordforbindelse* 'subject before Danish phrase'). During the revision of the dictionary a fixed order will be specified and then these markers will be removed.

Figure 5.8.3-2 shows the entry from Figure 5.8.3-1 after automatic subdivision.

Fig. 5.8.3-2

OPSL	adskille
ORDK	vt
BET	A
SYN	= ophæve sammenhæng el. forbindelse, danne skel
NUM	1
OVERS	séparer
PART	fra de, d'avec
NUM	2
OVERS	désunir
NUM	3
OVERS	disjoindre
NUM	4
OVERS	diviser
NUM	5
SYN	= løsne
OVERS	détacher
NUM	6
ANV	to sammenhørende ting
OVERS	déparier
NUM	7
ANV	flere sammenhørende ting
OVERS	dépareiller;
EMNE	phys.
NUM	8
OVERS	dissocier
NUM	9
OVERS	scinder;
EMNE	chim.
NUM	10
OVERS	décomposer
NUM	11
OVERS	réduire
NUM	12
EMNE	tech.
OVERS	démonter.
BET	B
SYN	= skelne
NUM	13
OVERS	distinguer
NUM	14
OVERS	démêler
NUM	15
OVERS	discerner
NUM	16
OVERS	différencier
NUM	17
OVERS	faire le départ de
NUM	18
ANV	undert.
OVERS	disloquer.
DAORDF	‖ ~ sig
FRORDF	différer les uns des autres;
DAORDF	~ sig fra
FRORDF	se différencier de, se distinguer de, différer de (el. d'avec), se détacher de, s'opposer à;
DAORDF	~ sig fra de andre derved, at
FRORDF	se différencier des autres en ce que;
DAORDF	derved ~r han sig fra de andre
FRORDF	par là il s'oppose aux autres;
FREKS	Mk la crise qui commença en 1929 fut entre toutes singulière et sortit de l'ordre commun;
DAORDF	‖ hvad Gud har sammenføjet, skal mennesket ikke ~
FRORDF	que l'homme ne sépare pas ce que Dieu a uni.

Because of the primary aim of the database, a fairly detailed structure has been chosen to enable us to restrict searches to a single information type. If the database was only intended for on-line information retrieval, one would not need, for example, to have separate categories for letters indicating semantic groups (BET) and translation number references (NUM).

For use by editors and external users, all information must be retrievable without having to consider typefaces. Most typeface changes are dependent on information types, so they can be reproduced on the basis of the field names (OPSL, ORDK etc.). The codes for such typeface changes will be removed. In a few cases, however, there are typographical changes in the middle of an information type (for example spaced italics in Danish phrases). The abbreviation *el.* 'or' also often appears in italics in plain-type surroundings and vice versa. Here the codes for typeface changes will be kept, but can be suppressed on-screen, and have no influence on the retrieval process.

Out of consideration for the users the hyphens in headwords will be "filled in", i.e. the part of the headword which has been replaced by a hyphen during the editing process will be inserted. All hyphens will be changed to vertical separators, and in those words which in fact *do* have hyphens (*A-aktie* 'A-share' etc.) the hyphens will be inserted manually during the editing. The hyphen will be kept after elements of compounds ending with hyphens (cf Figures 5.8.3-3 and 5.8.3-4).

Fig. 5.8.3-3

II. abo *vt*, ~ *én efter* singer q.
abo- de singe[s], simiesque, simien. **abo-agtig**, *v. abe.* **-ansigt** *n* visage de singe; (*fig. ogs.*) visage de marmouset. **-blomst** *c* ♣ mimulus, mimule (*Mimulus*); herbe* au musc (*Mimulus moschatus Dougl.*). **-brødtræ** *n* ♣ baobab (*Adansonia digitata*). ‖ *frugt af* ~ pain de singe. **-fest** *c* ₣ noce*, orgie*. **-hus** *n* singerie*, ménagerie* de singes; (*stort, i zool. have*) palais des singes.

Fig. 5.8.3-4

HGNR	II.
OPSL	abe
ORDK	vt,
DAORDF	~ én efter
FRORDF	singer q.

OPSL	abe-
OVERS	de singe[s], simiesque, simien.

OPSL	abe|agtig,
HENV	v. abe.

OPSL	abe|ansigt
UNDERK	n
STIL	fig.
ANV	ogs.
OVERS	visage de singe; visage de marmouset.

OPSL	abe|blomst
UNDERK	c
EMNE	bot.
OVERS	mimulus, mimule herbe* au musc
LAT	Mimulus; Mimulus moschatus Dougl.

OPSL	abe|brødtræ
UNDERK	n
EMNE	bot.
OVERS	baobab
LAT	Adansonia digitata
DAORDF	‖ frugt af ~
FRORDF	pain de singe.

OPSL	abe|fest
UNDERK	c
STIL	F
OVERS	noce*, orgie*.

OPSL	abe|hus
UNDERK	n
ANV	stort, i zool. have
OVERS	singerie*, ménagerie* de singes; palais des singes.

To make data entry and editing easier, many brackets will also be removed — for example for the categories BET, NUM, EMNE. These can be inserted automatically when a new printed edition is being produced.

5.8.4 The representation of the entry structure in the database

As mentioned above, there are not as many levels in the entry structure as one would think from reading the bracket diagram. However, there are three levels in the translation component: there is a subdivision into semantic groups using the letters *A)*, *B)*, *C)* etc., and there are translation reference numbers like *(1)*, *(2)*, *(3)* etc. Moreover, some of the translations are grouped by means of semicolons (cf Figs. 5.8.3-1 and 5.8.3-2).

In the computer system used for the database the entry structure is represented by means of the field names OPSL, ORDK etc. The fact that translation *(8)* belongs to meaning *A)* and translation *(13)* to meaning *B)* is only evident when one can see the whole entry or the translation component (= the rest of the head) in context. If, for example, one requests only the meaning and translation fields BET and OVERS of an entry on-screen, the subdivisions are lost (cf Fig. 5.8.4-1, showing the BET and OVERS fields from Fig. 5.8.3-2). The structure could however be reflected by the field names (cf Fig. 5.8.4-2 below).

Figure 5.8.4-3 shows the BET and OVERS fields from Figure 5.8.4-2 after the addition of letters indicating semantic groups and semantic reference numbers to the field names.

This type of naming has not been used, though, as it seems rather unwieldy, and as it is assumed that the user will normally want to see the whole translation section at once.

By using certain programming options built into the so-called macro facilities of the system one can to some extent achieve the same effects as a relational database, so that the hierarchical structure of the entries is better represented in the database. For this the hierarchies in the entries must be identified and marked, which should be relatively easy to do once the information types have been marked as described above. A bracket diagram can be used to plan a program that will insert hierarchy markers.

Figure 5.8.4-1

BET	A
	B
OVERS	séparer
	désunir
	disjoindre
	diviser
	détacher
	déparier
	dépareiller;
	dissocier
	scinder;
	décomposer
	réduire
	démonter.
	distinguer
	démêler
	discerner
	différencier
	faire le départ de
	disloquer.

Figure 5.8.4-2

OPSL	adskille
ORDK	vt
BETA	A
SYNA	= ophæve sammenhæng el. forbindelse, danne skel
NUMA1	1
OVERSA1	séparer
PARTA1	fra de, d'avec
NUMA2	2
OVERSA2	désunir
NUMA3	3
OVERSA3	disjoindre
NUMA4	4
OVERSA4	diviser
NUMA5	5
SYNA5	= løsne
OVERSA5	détacher
NUMA6	6
ANVA6	to sammenhørende ting
OVERSA6	déparier
NUMA7	7
ANVA7	flere sammenhørende ting
OVERSA7	dépareiller;
EMNEA8	phys.
NUMA8	8
OVERSA8	dissocier
NUMA9	9
OVERSA9	scinder;
EMNEA10	chim.
NUMA10	10
OVERSA10	décomposer
NUMA11	11
OVERSA11	réduire
NUMA12	12
EMNEA12	tech.
OVERSA12	démonter.

```
BETB      B
SYNB      = skelne
NUMB13    13
OVERSB13  distinguer
NUMB14    14
OVERSB14  démêler
NUMB15    15
OVERSB15  discerner
NUMB16    16
OVERSB16  différencier
NUMB17    17
OVERSB17  faire le départ de
NUMB18    18
ANVB18    undert.
OVERSB18  disloquer.
DAORDF     || ~ sig
FRORDF     différer les uns des autres;
DAORDF     ~ sig fra
FRORDF     se différencier de, se distinguer  de, différer de
           (el. d'avec), se détacher de, s'opposer à;
DAORDF     ~ sig fra de andre derved, at
FRORDF     se différencier des autres en ce  que;
DAORDF     derved ~r han sig fra de andre
FRORDF     par là il s'oppose aux autres;
FREKS      Mk  la crise qui commença en 1929  fut entre toutes
           singulière et sortit de  l'ordre commun;
DAORDF     ||  hvad Gud har sammenføjet,  skal mennesket ikke ~
FRORDF     que l'homme ne sépare pas ce que  Dieu a uni.
```

Figure 5.8.4-3

```
BETA      A
OVERSA1   séparer
OVERSA2   désunir
OVERSA3   disjoindre
OVERSA4   diviser
OVERSA5   détacher
OVERSA6   déparier
OVERSA7   dépareiller
OVERSA8   dissocier
OVERSA9   scinder
OVERSA10  décomposer
OVERSA11  réduire
OVERSA12  démonter
BETB      B
OVERSB13  distinguer
OVERSB14  démêler
OVERSB15  discerner
OVERSB16  différencier
OVERSB17  faire le départ de
OVERSB18  disloquer
```

6. EXPERIMENTS WITH FORMATTED ENTRY OF DICTIONARY DATA

The editorial treatment of dictionary data is especially concerned with the phase of lexicographical work Kipfer (1984: 162 ff) calls 'Presentation' (cf Section 2.2). In computer terms this involves a combination of word-processing and data management, but with so many special features that very few — if any — commercially available word-processing and database systems designed for office automation etc. can be used without substantial modification.

6.1 System requirements and experimental material

6.1.1 The word-processing component

The general dictionary system must be able to handle a considerably larger number of different characters and typefaces than a normal word-processing system. In return one can give lower priority to many of the more advanced facilities of modern word-processors, especially those concerned with the graphic appearance of the output, like tabulation, centring, reformatting — sometimes in several columns, with or without hyphenation and right justification, different fonts and emphases. For the graphic appearance of dictionaries is so closely connected with the format that it is best controlled from some form of report generator in the administrative component of the system.

Nor is there any particular need for real-time movement or input/output of major amounts of text. Insofar as this needs to be done, it will normally be an element in an overall plan for the whole project, and is best executed in a precisely planned and controlled batch run. Typically, dictionary word-processing will deal with quite small segments of text at a time — a single entry or the contents of one of the individual fields of the format.

On the other hand, a word-processing facility like "boiler-plates" (stored standard phrases) would be useful, for example for frequently recurring source references. Similarly, a spelling-checker facility could ensure editorial consistency in abbreviations and the like.

Finally, it must be required of the word-processing software that each of the necessary characters can be keyed in easily from the keyboard, and that corrections, deletions and insertions can be made on-screen with the usual word-processing commands.

Character set.
A general dictionary system must be able to distinguish between, process and present a wide range of characters. Even the European alphabets include a large number of letters with diacriticals like å, ç, é, ř and ô; ligatures like æ, œ, ĳ and ß, special characters like þ and ð. Dictionaries also use phonetic alphabets like the IPA or Dania, and foreign alphabets like the Greek, Hebrew, Cyrillic, etc. It would be ideal if all of these characters could be keyed in concurrently, stored uniquely in the computer and reproduced correctly on the same display or printout. But here we come up against a number of technical difficulties.

A normal *keyboard* has fewer than 100 keys, and it is hardly desirable to increase this number significantly. Instead, one or more shift keys can be added which will convert the keyboard output from one alphabet to another (like the familiar typewriter shift from lower to upper case), or special keys can be assigned to diacritical signs, so that an accented letter, for example, can be keyed in as a combination of the letter itself plus a "floating accent".

There are also *internal limitations* in the computer. Here it is normal for each character to be represented by a seven-bit (in some systems an eight-bit) code. Seven bits allow $2^7 = 128$, and eight bits $2^8 = 256$ different characters; but at least 33 of these are reserved according to current standards (ASCII, ISO) for so-called control characters. So at best there are 223 different characters available, or only 95 with seven bits; this is far from sufficient. In existing systems the problem is solved in one of three ways or by combinations of the three:

1. The international standards for the bit configurations of characters have a number of empty spaces which each language area can fill with its own special characters. When this system is used, the same seven-bit code represents æ in Danish and Norwegian, ä in Swedish and German, é in French and Spanish, à in Italian (where é has the same code as Danish Å) and the left curly brace { in Holland, England and the USA. This method is very widespread for monolingual word-processing for office use, for example, but is clearly unsuitable when several languages have to be mixed.

2. Besides the standard alphabet, one or more extra alphabets are defined for the same seven-bit codes. Special shift codes are then inserted in the text indicating the alphabet in use until the next shift code. This method is widespread in type-setting systems, but among other disadvantages, it makes searching on particular characters or character combinations difficult.

3. A character is represented by a combination of two or more seven or eight-bit codes: with a total of sixteen bits per character a good 65,000 different characters can be represented uniquely. For dictionary purposes, this type of representation must be considered most suitable. However, one more requirement — by no means a matter of course in existing systems — is that a given character is always represented internally in the same way; i.e., for example, the internal representation of ä is the same, regardless of whether the letter is keyed in as umlaut + a or by a special ä-key.

Requirements of the *screen* and *printer* must be that they can display — in clear text — all the internally represented characters correctly and in arbitrary combinations; and that the keyboard, on-screen and printed characters are completely identical. Terminals with a built-in fixed character set will therefore as a rule be unsuitable for dictionary purposes. Instead terminals must be used where the character set can be defined and redefined by the processor.

6.1.2 Data management

The administrative aspect of the editing system requires data to be classified into category-marked fields in accordance with the format adopted: if it is hierarchically structured this should be reflected by marking at several levels. The insertion of markers should be wholly or partially automatic, both to save working time and to ensure that they always comply with the format requirements. In addition, the system must be able to check data against formal rules for the permissible content of each field and the sequences of fields stipulated by the format.

On the basis of the classification it should be possible to

- search on logical combinations of categories as well as field content;
- present data ("generate reports") on screen and on paper in different printed formats, both schematically (with category marking) and typographically;
- extract specified subsets of the data for both checking and the exchange of information with other dictionary projects.

If the internal structure and consistency of the dictionary — for example the hierarchies illustrated in Chapter 5 — are to be supported and utilized, the data must be stored in a suitably structured database. With network or relational databases, relations not made explicit in the printed dictionaries can be expressed. For example, descriptions of phrases, compounds and derived words can be linked with information about their individual components just as references and semantic relations (for example superordinate and subordinate concepts) between headwords or their different meanings can be registered. This type of database structure will make the editorial work easier and more efficient, and will allow the dictionary to be consulted on the basis of many other criteria than the alphabetical order of the headwords.

Among other administrative functions are the provision of statistics, the recording of the editor, date, internal editorial notes and questions (cf Section 7.3).

6.1.3 Introduction to experiments with formatted input of dictionary data

Various computer systems are commercially available for the production of dictionaries. They are often closely associated with a particular product (e.g. the new *Oxford English Dictionary*, see Section 5.7), or with the production requirements of a given publisher. Among others, the English publisher Longman and the Dutch Kluwer (the Van Dale dictionaries, see for example Sterkenburg/Martin/Al 1982; Al 1986) have such systems. Or they may be included in a package offer to publishers, where a "dictionary entrepreneur" undertakes to supply a finished dictionary or reference work — for example the English Market House Books Ltd., Laurence Urdang; or the German computer firm Siemens, which offers its system TEAM on similar conditions (information from Dr. Otto Vollnhals, cf Vollnhals 1984).

As far as we know there is only one dictionary editing system on the market — Compulexis — that is both general and decentralized. The system is marketed by the firm Compulexis Ltd. in Oxford, a subsidiary of the Danish firm DataSats Informatik A/S.

Generality and decentralization are promising features in a dictionary editing system, and this was why we decided to test the Compulexis system on formatted dictionary data input.

For this experiment we chose what in our opinion is really demanding dictionary data, i.e. sample entry material from the scholarly dictionary of Old Danish, *Gammeldansk Ordbog* (GLDO) (see also Section 6.2) and entry material from the Supplement to *Ordbog over det Danske Sprog* (ODSS) — a supplement to a large academic monolingual dictionary of Danish. These dictionary data are particularly demanding, as they come from dictionaries with a very high degree of complexity in the information types, and because — especially in the case of the GLDO — many fonts and special symbols are required. In the case of the ODSS its nature as a supplement is also particularly interesting. The definitive editorial rules for the GLDO have not yet been established and can therefore be adjusted to the requirements and facilities of the system, while the editorial rules for the ODSS already exist and consideration for the users means that they cannot be deviated from; here it is a question of whether the system is flexible enough to satisfy the editorial requirements and whether the pre-established editorial rules are an obstacle to the use of the system facilities. By choosing these two types of task we think we have obtained material whose confrontation with a general dictionary system will be able to shed light on the advantages and disadvantages of such a system.

6.2 *Gammeldansk Ordbog*

In Section 4.1 the historical, academic dictionary the GLDO was discussed, and an account was given of how the general taxonomy formed a point of departure for the establishment of a format to be used for the definitive formulation of its editorial rules (see the format overview in Section 4.1.3).

At the beginning of the editorial phase it was clear that formatted input of the dictionary entries observing the established editorial rules, using suitable software, would give us many advantages in the editorial, data entry and updating work. However, the Compulexis system, described in more detail in the following sections, has a number of special facilities that we also wanted to take advantage of.

But to make full use of the system it is necessary to split up certain of the information categories of the GLDO format, as described above in Section 4.1.3.

The facilities we wanted to make full use of were

- the ability to assign as far as possible one typographical convention and one only to each information category;
- the ability to check automatically the content of as many of the information categories as possible.

The wish to use and combine these facilities meant that the categories IHEX (administrative information in the word identification section) and SIHX (administrative information in the semantic information section) each had to be split into two categories — IHEO and SIHO for the reference word and IHEN and SIHE for the actual reference (for the field codes used reference may be made to Section 4.1.3 above and Section 6.4.2 below).

This categorization means

- that for each of the four categories there is one and only one typographical convention, i.e. italic for IHEO and SIHO and plain type for IHEN and SIHE;
- that the content of the categories IHEO and SIHO can be checked automatically: a universe of (reference) words can be pre-defined from which the content of the two categories can be taken. In the case of IHEO the universe at the moment consists of *Jf.* 'cf' and *Se også* 'see also'. All other proposals on the part of the editors for the contents of the categories IHEO and SIHO are rejected by the Compulexis system (for more details of this see below, Section 6.4.4.1).

The wish to make use of the other facility mentioned above means that the categories IOVX (the external reference "variant source" in the word identification section), BØKX (the external reference "source for inflectional form" in the inflectional information section), and SBCX (the external reference "meaning citation source" in the semantic information section) can each be split up into two categories, i.e.

IOVX into IOVK "variant source, title" and
IOVV "variant source, locus";
BØKX into BØKK "inflectional form source, title" and
BØKV "inflectional form source, locus";
SBCX into SBCK "meaning citation source, title" and
SBCV "meaning citation source, locus".

With this classification we achieve an enormous advantage: references to the vast number of sources for the whole dictionary can be checked automatically, since the universe for the three categories IOVK, BØKK and SBCK is pre-defined as the sum of the abbreviations for the sources used; and the content of the three categories must belong to this universe. Any attempt to use a source abbreviation that does not belong to the universe is rejected by Compulexis (for particulars see below, Section 6.4.4.1).

The wish to associate one and only one typographical convention with as many of the information categories as possible, and

- the wish to be able to search through and sort the dictionary data in linguistically relevant ways later, and
- the wish to enable GLDO users with widely different fields of interest to look up information of various degrees of specialization in the stored entry data

mean that the categories BFXX (contextual information on "inflectional forms of original texts" in the word identification section), SBCY (contextual information type "meaning citation" in the section with semantic information) and SCKX (contextual information type "meaning citation from original source", also in the semantic information section) are each divided into two categories:

BFXX into BFLC "inflectional form of original citation" and
BFLS "language of original inflectional-form citation";
SBCY into SBCI the actual "meaning citation" and
SBCP "meaning citation parallel";
SCKX into SCKF "original of meaning citation source" and
SCFO "information on original of meaning citation source".

Field code	Information type	Basic font
	I-SECTION	
(IHOM)	Homograph marker	semibold
IOPO	Headword	semibold
(IVDN)	Coverage marker	
IOKA	Part-of-speech marker	italic
[IOPV]*	Variant	plain
(IOVL)	Variant literature reference	italic
[IOVK]*	Variant source, title	italic
[IOVV]+	Variant source, locus	italic
[IHEO]*	Reference word	italic
[IHEN]+	Reference	plain
	B-SECTION	
[(BSUB)]*	Subclassification	italic
BFLE	Inflectional marker	italic
(BØKO)	Remark on inflectional form	italic
(BØFO)	Inflectional form	plain
[BØCI]*	Inflectional form citation	plain
BØKK	Inflectional form source, title	italic
[BØKV]+	Inflectional form source, locus	italic
(BFLC	Original of citation	plain
BFCS)	Language of original	italic
	S-SECTION	
[SOBN]*	Overview, meaning number	semibold
(SOGK)	Overview, syntactic information	italic
SOBB	Overview, meaning specification	italic
[(SBEN)]*	Meaning number	semibold
(SSGK)	Syntactic information	italic
(SORF)	Phrase	plain
(SBEB)	Meaning specification	italic
(SIHO	Cross-reference word	italic
[SIHE]+)	Cross-referencce	plain
(SBCI)	Meaning citation	plain
(SBCP)	Parallel to meaning citation	plain
SBCK	Meaning citation source, title	italic
[SBCV]+	Meaning citation source, locus	italic
[SCKF]*	Meaning citation, original of source	plain
[SKFO]+	Information on original of source	italic
	E-SECTION	
[(ELDK)]*	Loanword/word formation information	italic
[ELPS]*	Donor language/language of parallel	italic
ELPO	Donor/parallel word	plain
(ELPI)	Information on donor/parallel word	italic
(ELPB)	Meaning of donor/parallel word	italic
(ELPG)	Core meaning of donor/parallel word	italic
[EJSA]*	Compare	italic
(EJSS)	Language of analogue	italic
EJSO	Analogous word	plain
(EJSB)	Meaning of analogous word	italic
(EEHL)	Literature reference	italic
(EBRO)	Usage information	italic

Fig. 6.2-1 Overview of the GLDO format

The format for the GLDO now looks as in Fig. 6.2-1 (cf Section 5.2.2), furnished with field codes for facultative and iterative information, information category names, and basic font codes (for more details on font selection, see Section 6.4.4.6).

6.3 The Supplement to *Ordbog over det Danske Sprog*

6.3.1 Short description of the ODS and the ODSS

Ordbog over det Danske Sprog (ODS — "The Dictionary of the Danish Language") appeared in 28 volumes between 1918 and 1956. The ODS explains the meaning of Danish words, documented by extensive citation material, over a period from c. 1700 to 1954; for each word it also provides inflectional, phonetic and historical/etymological information where possible, as well as information on usage restrictions to the extent this is considered necessary.

Det Danske Sprog- og Litteraturselskab (the Danish Society for Language and Literature), the publishers of the ODS, have had work done since the ODS was finished in 1954 on the supplementation of the ODS material. This work is expected to result in the publication of a six-volume supplement to the ODS, *ODS-Supplementet* (the ODSS). The ODSS is to supplement the ODS within the ODS period, c. 1700 - 1955, but will not feature words more recent than 1955. There will be both supplementary material to the existing dictionary entries and supplementary material in the form of new entries on words not included in the ODS.

The overall entry structure of the ODS consists of the entry head with grammatical, phonetic, historical-etymological and usage restriction information on the headword, and of the entry body, primarily with semantic information on the headword, documented by citations. Apart from phonetic information, not given in a phonetic alphabet in the ODSS, this structure is of course preserved in the ODSS, as it is a supplement to the major work.

The structural basis of the body of the entry is five possible citation groupings — the citation material, which represents the language, is the point of departure for the editor. Within each citation group the material is ordered chronologically. These five citation groups are:

1. the whole entry as one main meaning, marked by the headword;
2. main or sub-meanings, marked by meaning numbers;
3. the "plank" section, marked by "planks" (‖);
4. spaced phrase, marked with the phrase as editorial text, as "sub-headword";
5. a commentary citation group, with a marker followed by a colon — for example, *som adv.:* 'as adverb'; *i talem.:* 'as colloquialism'; *billedl.:* 'figuratively'; *jf.:* 'compare'.

These citation groups are part of the hierarchical structure of the entry. At the top level are the headword and head. The lowest-level citation groups are Nos. 4 and 5. No. 3 is subordinate to Nos. 1 and 2. Citation groups of types 1, 2 and 3 normally have a main section and then space for the lower-level types. Of course all the citation groups need not be present in the same entry. Immediately before citation groups 1 - 4 there may be editorial text on the history of the word or of its meaning, usage restrictions and meaning specification. In the space for meaning specification there may be editorial information on grammar: the point of a citation group may be grammatical rather than semantic. The text before a commentary citation group may also concern grammatical rather than semantic matters, as the commentary citation group may be formed on a grammatical basis. This basic entry structure is of course clearest in the new ODSS entries, that is in entries on words not already in the ODS. Such entries are marked in the ODSS with a preceding "+". In ODSS entries on words already in the ODS the headword will indicate the entry to be supplemented; a citation from or summary of information from the ODS will mark where the supplementary material to the ODS belongs in the existing ODS entry; and a "+" will introduce the supplementary text. The basic structure of ODSS entries like these may not be immediately apparent, as they will often be part-entries of the ODS.

The ODS is a dictionary with a very high degree of complexity in the way information types may be given. ODSS entries that supplement existing ODS entries should be read together with the existing ODS entries being supplemented — otherwise the broad view of the entry may be obscured by the degree of complexity.

6.3.2 A format for the ODSS

As stated above, the ODSS is a work in progress, and there are in fact a number of finished entries. One means of speeding up the publication of the ODSS would be the use of a computerized dictionary editing system.

Given the opportunity of experimenting with the computerized dictionary editing system Compulexis, it seemed appropriate for the DANLEX Group to offer the editors of the ODSS an experiment with ODSS material that could result in an editing system that would facilitate further editing of the dictionary. Work on the dictionary had been done up to this point without computers.

To begin with the ODSS editors made a body of entry material available to the DANLEX Group consisting of about 50 very varied entries. On the basis of a detailed analysis of the lexicographical information categories in the entry material the DANLEX Group drew up a proposal for a format for ODSS entries. This proposal was discussed with the ODSS editors and the outcome was the format that can be seen in Fig. 6.3.2-1.

As we have stated, this is a dictionary with a high degree of complexity, so it turned out to be best to subdivide the information categories that were to function as fields in the format into two types: information categories constituting fixed fields, and those that constituted free fields.

The fixed fields are ordered in a sequence designed to represent the basic structure or skeleton of an ODSS entry. The basic entry structure, which of course reflects the structure discussed in Section 6.3.1, is described by means of the ETTO notation (cf Section 5.2.2).

To describe this basic entry structure at all it was necessary to extract a set of information categories as freely locatable fields; this set makes up the free fields that can be placed as required in relation to the basic structure. Among these are a number of fields whose presence in the format has nothing to do with the final appearance of the ODS Supplement as a printed book: they are there for the sake of the absolutely unique identification of all text segments.

Fig. 6.3.2-1 Overview of the ODSS format

Meaning of abbreviations:

(f) bold font (h) semibold font (o) plain font

(k) italic font (s) spaced plain font (u) field content suppressed in column manifestations

Fixed fields

Field codes and structure	Information category names and font codes	
(SEC)	new line for beginning of entry	
(ODS)	ODS text introduction	(u)
(PLUS)	introduction to supplementary material	(o)
(HOMB)	homograph marker	(f)
OPSL	headword	(f)
(SORT)	sort key for exceptions	(u)
ORDK	part of speech	(k)
[SUBK]*	subclassification	(o)
(UDT)	pronunciation	(k)
[SIDF]*	alternative form of headword	(h)
[SUBK]*	subclassification	(o)
(FLEK)*	inflectional marker	(k)
BØJF	inflectional form	(h)
[HIST]*	history	(k)
HHEO *	reference word (historical reference)	(k)
HHEN	word referred to (historical reference)	(o)
[GEO/FAG/TID/STIL/FRE]*	geographical distribution/subject/period/style/frequency	(k)
(ONR/UNR/PL)	superordinate meaning number/subordinate meaning number/"plank"	(h)
[HIST]*		
HHEO *		
HHEN		
[GEO/FAG/TID/STIL/FRE]*		
(BETB)	meaning specification	(k)
(BCIT) +	meaning citation	(o)
BKIL	meaning citation source	(k)
KOLB *	colon meaning	(k)
(BCIT) +		
BKIL		
(PL)		
FORB	spaced phrase	(s)
(FNR)	phrase meaning number	(o)
[HIST]*		
HHEO *		
HHEN		
[GEO/FAG/TID/STIL/FRE]*		
(BETB)		
(BCIT) +		
BKIL		
KOLB *		
(BCIT) +		
BKIL		

(Fig. 6.3.2-1, continued)

Free fields

Field codes	Information categories and font codes	
KOMF	preceding comment	(k)
KOMB	following comment	(k)
HEOB	following reference word (dictionary-internal reference)	(o)
HENB	following word referred to (dictionary-internal reference)	(k)
GEOF	preceding "geographical distribution"	(k)
FAGF	preceding "subject"	(k)
TIDF	preceding "period"	(k)
STIF	preceding "style"	(k)
FREF	preceding "frequency"	(k)
CIT	citation outside meaning section, in head	(o)
KIL	(citation) source outside meaning section, in head	(k)
LITT	literature reference	(k)
SPLI	column-and-line reference to the ODS	(k)
RET	ODS correction beginning	(k)
PLUS	supplementary material beginning	(o)
SEC	entry-internal new line	
PNC	change in automatically generated punctuation	

Free fields suppressed in column manifestations

ODS	ODS text beginning	(u)
KBST	preceding beginning of complex usage restriction	(u)
KBSL	following end of complex usage restriction	(u)
QUE	query (re editing, registration, etc.)	(u)

The fields in question are ODS, for the ODS text introduction, which is there so that the ODS citation or summary can be distinguished from the supplementary text; KBST, for a preceding introduction to complex usage restriction information; and KBSL, for concluding an item on complex usage restrictions. These two fields enclose the complex usage restriction content, the individual parts of which we wish to be able to register separately, to make it easier to find entries containing complex usage restrictions. Without KBST/KBSL separate registration of the parts of complex usage restriction sections could lead to incorrect information when subsets of the ODSS entry material are retrieved.

This is also true of the free query field QUE, reserved for the insertion of queries arising during the entry of dictionary material; it is directly associated with the information category or text segment to which the query applies. What all these fields have in common is that their contents are suppressed automatically in the column manifestation of the dictionary entries (cf Section 6.4.4.4 below). In the format overview one can also see the fields SEC for "new line", SORT for sort keys and PNC for changing automatically generated punctuation (see Section 6.4.4 for more information on this, and Section 6.4.2 for the principles used for naming format fields).

As is evident from consideration of the overview of the fixed and free fields of the format, the dictionary text is split up into a very large number of individually named information categories furnished with field and font codes. This subdivision is partly due to the wish to be able to extract each of these information categories as a subset of the dictionary text when the latter has been made machine-readable; and partly to the wish for as high a degree of automatic printing control as possible, so that during data entry one can give as little thought as possible to typographical appearance (see also Section 6.4.4.6 on this point). The use of field codes allows these wishes to be realized, as any information category can be uniquely identified by its field code. It should be noted that during the drawing-up of a format for a dictionary like the ODSS a conflict may arise between the two wishes: if the extraction of an information category as a subset of the dictionary text is to be meaningful, that category must itself constitute a meaningful whole; and if there is to be automatic control of typography, only one typeface or font must be used for each information category. But there can be cases where one cannot reasonably make any further subdivisions of an item of information without making the item cease to be an independently meaningful part of the dictionary text. This could make a typeface change within a single information category necessary. The conflict of course arises from the fact that out of consideration for the user it would be unreasonable to make typographical changes in a dictionary which supplements an existing dictionary — it would only result in confusion and irritation.

For example, there is a convention in the ODSS of inserting necessary explanatory text in a citation with the explanatory material italicized, unlike the citation itself, which is in a plain typeface. But without the explanatory text — which must be marked as such, as it is not part of the citation — the citation would either be incomprehensible to the user, or so much longer that it would occupy excessive space in the dictionary. Consider for example the BCIT fields in the entries on *autobiografisk* and *Autografalbum* (Fig. 6.3.2-2).

Fig. 6.3.2-2 Print-out of appearance of data entry for the ODSS entries *auto-biografisk* and *Autografalbum*

SEC	s ODS	PLUS +	HOMB	ODS	PLUS
OPSL	auto-biografisk				
ORDK	adj.				
BETB	til Autobiograf(i).				
BCIT	jeg gør opmærksom paa at *(min produktion)* ikke paa noget Punkt er autobiografisk.				
BKIL	JVJens.HH.184.				
BKIL	EFrederiksen.UL.15.				

SEC	ODS	PLUS +	HOMB	ODS	PLUS
OPSL	Autograf|-album				
ORDK	# subst.				
SUBK	et.				
BCIT	de Poesibøger og Autografalbums, som det da *(: i 16.århundrede)* var blevet Mode at føre i adelige Kredse.				
BKIL	CSPet.Litt.200.				

It has thus been necessary to let a reasonable estimate of advantages and disadvantages determine the information categories into which the dictionary text is best subdivided for the purposes of the format.

6.4 Compulexis and the GLDO/ODSS

For the experiments with formatted entry of material from the GLDO and ODSS, we have used, as mentioned in Section 6.1.3, the dictionary editing system Compulexis.

6.4.1 Compulexis

The dictionary editing system Compulexis is based on the use of a microcomputer with either floppy discs — in two disc drives — or a Winchester disc as an external storage medium: for the purposes of the DANLEX Group floppy discs are used. A dot-matrix printer is connected with the microcomputer. The printer's fonts can be controlled by the special Compulexis software. So far it has been possible to use a Victor 9000 (= Sirius 1) microcomputer with at least 256 Kb of internal memory, and an Apricot PC and XI — for our experiments we used the Victor 9000. The machines mentioned are notable for their high-resolution screens and can handle several character sets, including characters freely defined by the system. The keys can also be configured by the software, and both the key definitions and the characters that can be displayed on-screen are determined by the system software. The same is true of the characters that can be produced by the printer: this has to be an NDK P7700 or Printstar 5010. We use the NDK P7700. A full European character set with several typefaces (bold, italic, plain etc.) and the IPA phonetic alphabet is standard; but other alphabets and characters can be freely added.

The use of the microcomputer and dot-matrix printer constitutes the decentralized aspect of the system; some of its functions, like statistical reports and the final preparation of data for typesetting, are not yet present in the end-user component of the system, but are run centrally by the company in Oxford.

The dictionary editing system is a standardized system that can be adapted to the requirements of the individual dictionary project — for example as regards the codes to be used for the names of information categories and the character sets required for such a project. The company thus supplies a special system configuration for each dictionary project, with the field names and alphabets the project needs.

The status of the system as an adaptable standard constitutes its general aspect. The great advantage of this is of course that adapting the system for a specific job is fast compared with the time that would be spent developing a new system for each project. In addition, knowledge of the standard system is a great help to the editors in establishing the special requirements of the task before them.

Compulexis is supplied as a system disc and a utilities disc, while the dictionary entries are written to one or more data discs — the system and data are thus kept physically separate.

The idea of the editing system is that a dictionary editor or secretary keys in draft or finished entries or revises previous input on the microcomputer, reads proofs immediately on a print-out from the matrix printer, keys in the corrections and produces discs with copies of the finished dictionary text. Then final typesetting can be done on the basis of the machine-readable data. The system does not automatically deal with hyphenation at the end of lines: it must be inserted during the final reading of the galley proofs. However, it is now possible at the data entry stage to mark permissible points for division in words where one anticipates that automatic hyphenation could go wrong — this facility did not exist in the system versions used for the GLDO/ODSS experiments.

In practice the editing system works like a sophisticated word-processing system that is particularly easy to use whether the dictionary text is to be corrected or entered for the first time. For example, it is very easy to correct errors: one can overwrite text directly to correct it, or one can insert text by pressing a special key and then writing the required material at precisely the point in the text where it is to be inserted. New fields can be added, several fields can be merged, and one field can be split into several. Deleting text is just as easy: the text segment one wants to delete is located on-screen and then either single characters, parts of lines consisting of all text to the right of the cursor, or whole lines can be deleted by a single keystroke. Whole fields or entries can also be deleted at once by two keystrokes — the second of which is a confirmation of the delete command, so there is always a chance to cancel the command at the last moment!

Figure 6.4.1-1, illustrating a printout of the data entry form for the ODSS and GLDO material, will give a broad impression of the way dictionary data are entered in practice (cf Section 6.4.4 for the more specialized system facilities).

Fig. 6.4.1-1 a Printout of data entry form for ODSS entries *Billedstof* and *I. Auto* to *Autocykel*

SEC	ODS PLUS + HOMB ODS PLUS
OPSL	Billed|stof
ORDK	# subst.
SUBK	et.
HHEO	(jf.
HHEN	-materiale S).
BCIT	et Anhang over det Nye Testamentes Billedstof.
BKIL	BerlTid.15/3 1850.4.sp.2.
BCIT	et omfattende Billedstof.
BKIL	Riget.19/5 1912.3.sp.7.
BCIT	Reklamer med Hensyn til Tekst, Billedstof og Komposition.
BKIL	Lov Nr.149 26/4 1933‡§2.
KOMB	(om forfatterret og kunstnerret).
QUE	Jvf. QUE sub "billedkunstnerisk"
BCIT	Uge-Revyen det moderne ugeblad .. billed-stof fra hele verden.
BKIL	Hjemmet.16/2 1954.29.sp.4.

SEC	s ODS = PLUS HOMB I. ODS PLUS
OPSL	Auto
ORDK	# subst.
SUBK	en.
BETB	automobil.
PLUS	+ *ældre:*
BCIT	Auto - Det kan ikke nytte at stritte mod Fremskridtet.
BKIL	Ekstrabl.1/7 1905.1.sp.4.

SEC	s ODS PLUS + HOMB III. ODS PLUS
OPSL	Auto
ORDK	# subst.
SUBK	en.
STIL	(fagl.)
BETB	d.s.s. Autotypi S.
BCIT	en Margarineannonce med to Dompapper, hvis smaa røde Maver var trykt i Auto.
BKIL	Da.Reklame.1930.marts.5.sp.2.
BKIL	HåndbLokalhist.111.

SEC	s ODS PLUS + HOMB III. ODS PLUS
OPSL	Auto-
ORDK	i ssgr.
HHEO	(jf.
HHEN	Automobil- S, Bil- S, Motor-).

SEC	s ODS PLUS + HOMB ODS PLUS
OPSL	Auto-bane
ORDK	# subst.
SUBK	en.
HIST	(efter ty. autobahn;
HHEO	jf.
HHEN	Autostrada S)
TIDF	ældre
BETB	betegnelse for motorvej.
BCIT	Bygningen af disse Autobaner byder Ingeniøren mange interessante Opgaver ... Disse tyske Strada'er *(osv.).*
BKIL	TeknVidundere.(1933-36).II.606.
BKIL	LSal.I.456.
BCIT	autobane Rødby havn - Nykøbing F.
BKIL	JernbaneT.15/12 1952.1.sp.1.

SEC s ODS PLUS + HOMB ODS PLUS

OPSL	auto-biografisk
ORDK	adj.
BETB	til Autobiograf(i).
BCIT	jeg gør opmærksom paa at *(min produktion)* ikke paa noget Punkt er autobiografisk.
BKIL	JVJens.HH.184.
BKIL	EFrederiksen.UL.15.

SEC s ODS = PLUS HOMB ODS PLUS

OPSL	Auto|-bus
ORDK	# subst.
SUBK	en.
PLUS	+
HHEO	(jf.
HHEN	III.Bus;
KBST	<
FRE	sj.
STIL	i alm. spr.
TID	efter ca. 1940).
KBSL	>
BCIT	Autobussen paa Strøget - En ny Dødsdom over Hestene.
BKIL	Riget.2/1 1913.3.sp.3.
BCIT	Sammenstødet mellem Ekspres og Autobus.
BKIL	Aftenp.24/1 1930.2.sp.2.
BCIT	enhver autobus eller automobil skulle kunne overføres *(: med en ny færge)*.
BKIL	Vingehjulet.1950/51.66.sp.2.

SEC ODS PLUS + HOMB ODS PLUS

OPSL	Auto|coat
ORDK	# subst.
SUBK	en.
ONR	1
BETB	overtræk af presenningstof, plastic ell. lign. til en parkeret bil.
BKIL	Krak.1950.3019.
BKIL	VTFrO.[5](1959).
ONR	2
BETB	kort frakke.
KOMF	se
BKIL	NyeOrd 1955-75.

SEC ODS PLUS + HOMB ODS PLUS

OPSL	Auto|cykel
ORDK	# subst.
SUBK	en.
HIST	(jf. eng. autocycle)
BETB	(mindre) motorcykel.
BCIT	Autocycle, Motorcykel.
BKIL	Meyer.[8](1924).
BCIT	Jeg er lykkelig Indehaver af en Avtocykle *(og føler mig)* foranlediget til at protestere kraftigt og indtrængende mod, at De kalder nævnte Maskineri en Sofacykle.
BKIL	Pol.10/7 1937.9.sp.6.
TIDF	senere
KBST	<
FREF	(især
STIF	fagl.)
KBSL	>
KOLB	om knallert:
BCIT	Mobylette - den elegante, stærke .. autocykel.
BKIL	MagasinNyt.apr.1954.omslag.
BCIT	Wooler Auto-cyklen.
BKIL	Krak.1955.II.2954.

(Fig. 6.4.1-1 a, continued)

Fig. 6.4.1-1 b Printout of data entry form for GLDO entries
duvebloth to *duvelike*

IHOM	IOPO duvebloth
IOKA	sb.
SEC	§
SBEB	blod af en due, dueblod
SBCI	Tac dufu bloth æller palumbis bloth æller turturis bloth oc drøp i the øghæn, thær bloth ær ouer ganget
SBCK	Lægeb. [AM].
SBCV	16,21
SEC	§
ELDK	til I. duve.
EJSA	Jf.
EJSS	vn.
EJSO	dúfublóð,
QUE	Her burde det kunne lade sig gøre at placere ejss efterfulgt af ejso, uden at skulle have været rundt om EJSA først
EJSA	# Jf.
EJSS	fsv.
EJSO	duvoblodh

IHOM	IOPO duvebrøthre
IOKA	sb. pl.
SEC	§
SBEB	betegnelse for personer tilknyttet en godgørende stiftelse i Roskilde (jf. KultLeksM.III.358f.)
SBCI	Erland foghet af delæ *(afskriverfejl for* dwæ*)* brødræ i Roskyld
SBCK	# \D\
SBCV	22/4 1437(DiplKbh.I.161,13, afskr. 1681)
SEC	§
SSGK	i forb.
SORF	duvebrøthre kloster *el. (elliptisk)* duvebrøthre
SBEB	om stiftelse
SBCI	wij .. forstandere i Dwebrøthre closter
SBCK	# \D\
SBCV	27/7 1429(Esrumb.248, Rosk.)
SBCI	A.T., fforstandher j Dwbrødhrekloster hoss Roosskildh
SBCK	# \D\
SBCV	5/7 1497(DiplLund.V.324,15)
SBCI	Jtem fatigæ folck i Dwæbrødræ ij marc
SBCK	# \D\
SBCV	11/5 1501(DiplLund.VI.23,16)
SEC	§
ELDK	til I. duve sb. (i relig. symbolik)

IHOM	IOPO duvehus
IUDN	+
IOKA	sb.
SEC	§
SBEB	hus til tamme duer, duehus, dueslag
SBCI	columbarium .. dwehwss
SBCK	Chr. Ped. Voc. 1510.
SBCV	31ᵛ
SEC	§
ELDK	til I. duve sb.

(Fig. 6.4.1-1 b, continued)

IHOM	IOPO duvelike
IOKA	sb.
SEC	§
SSGK	kun i forb.
SORF	i duvelike
SBEB	i skikkelse af en due
SIHO	Jf.
SIHE	I. duve
SBCI	thet war then Helliand i dwe ligė, oc sagde till Ottwel *(etc.)*
SBCK	KMagn. (RomD. III.
SBCV	136,7)
SCKF	í dúfu líki
SKFO	Vn.
SEC	§
ELDK	til I. duve sb.

The first field codes shown on screen for an entry are those that appear above the horizontal line in the entry printout or data entry form. Thus in the case of the ODSS one begins in the field SEC; this is filled with an arbitrary keystroke if one wishes to begin on a new line after the preceding entry; otherwise one ignores the field and goes on to fill in the subsequent fields according to the requirements of the ODSS entry in question. However, data input is obligatory in the OPSL (headword) field (the IOPO field in the GLDO) — an entry without a headword is rejected by the system. After the horizontal line no more fields automatically appear for data entry. What the screen does show is a form with a separate column on the left-hand side where one can write the name — i.e. the four-character code — of the field required. The system checks that a valid field code has been entered, and it is only possible to continue if this code is accepted by the system. Then one enters the actual field data without having to think about typography (unless extraordinary typeface changes are necessary) or line breaks within the field. The field content is thus normally written in one standard typeface (see also Section 6.4.4.6) and there are no limits to the length of a field. The space grows by a line whenever required. Thus one can select fields as required until the entry is finished.

In configurations for bilingual dictionaries the screen is split into four columns, with the source language in the left and the target language in the right half of the screen.

The printouts in Fig. 6.4.1-1 illustrate how the screen looks after each entry is input; but this clearly does not look like a proper dictionary. It is in fact also possible to see the dictionary entry with its proper dictionary appearance on-screen; this requires the selection of another program from the system disc. Fig. 6.4.1-2 shows how the data appear after the finished entries have been automatically generated and sent to the matrix printer.

This is almost the form in which they appear on-screen, except that the screen only shows one entry or part of an entry (depending on the length of the entry) at a time. In this column-mode printout only text that is to appear in the finished dictionary is shown. Any other text entered or generated, including field names, is suppressed here (see also Section 6.4.4.4).

Fig. 6.4.1-2 a Printout of column form of ODSS entries *Billedstof* and *I. Auto* to *Autocykel*

+ **Billedstof,** et. *(jf.* -materiale S*).* et Anhang over det Nye Testamentes Billedstof. *BerlTid.15/3 1850.4.sp.2.* et omfattende Billedstof. *Riget.19/5 1912.3.sp.7.* Reklamer med Hensyn til Tekst, Billedstof og Komposition. *Lov Nr.149 26/4 1933 (om forfatterret og kunstnerret).§2.* Uge-Revyen det moderne ugeblad .. billed-stof fra hele verden. *Hjemmet.16/2 1954.29.sp.4.*

I. Auto, en. *automobil.* + *ældre:* Auto – Det kan ikke nytte at stritte mod Fremskridtet. *Ekstrabl.1/7 1905.1.sp.4.*

+ **III. Auto,** en. *(fagl.) d.s.s.* Autotypi S. en Margarineannonce med to Dompapper, hvis smaa røde Maver var trykt i Auto. *Da.Reklame.1930.marts.5.sp.2. HåndbLokalhist.111.*

+ **III. Auto-,** *i ssgr. (jf.* Automobil-S, Bil- S, Motor-*).*

+ **Auto-bane,** en. *(efter ty.* autobahn; *jf.* Autostrada S*) ældre betegnelse for motorvej.* Bygningen af disse Autobaner byder Ingeniøren mange interessante Opgaver ... Disse tyske Strada'er *(osv.). TeknVidundere.(1933-36).II.606. LSal.I.456.* autobane Rødby havn – Nykøbing F. *JernbaneT.15/12 1952.1.sp.1.*

+ **auto-biografisk,** *adj. til* Autobiograf(i). jeg gør opmærksom paa at *(min produktion)* ikke paa noget Punkt er autobiografisk. *JVJens.HH.184. EFrederiksen.UL.15.*

Auto-bus, en. + *(jf.* III.Bus; *sj. i alm. spr. efter ca. 1940).* Autobussen paa Strøget – En ny Dødsdom over Hestene. *Riget.2/1 1913.3.sp.3.* Sammenstødet mellem Ekspres og Autobus. *Aftenp.24/1 1930.2.sp.2.* enhver autobus eller automobil skulle kunne overføres *(: med en ny færge). Vingehjulet.1950/51.66.sp.2.* + **-coat,** en. **1)** *overtræk af presenningstof, plastic ell. lign. til en parkeret bil. Krak.1950.3019. VTFrO.^{5}(1959).* **2)** *kort frakke. se NyeOrd 1955-75.* + **-cykel,** en. *(jf. eng.* autocycle*) (mindre) motorcykel.* Autocycle, Motorcykel. *Meyer.^{8}(1924).* Jeg er lykkelig Indehaver af en Avtocykle *(og føler mig)* foranlediget til at protestere kraftigt og indtrængende mod, at De kalder nævnte Maskineri en Sofacykle. *Pol.10/7 1937.9.sp.6. senere (især fagl.) om knallert:* Mobylette – den elegante, stærke .. autocykel. *MagasinNyt.apr.1954.omslag.* Wooler Auto-cyklen. *Krak.1955.II.2954.*

Fig. 6.4.1-2 b Printout of column form of GLDO entries *duvebloth* to *duvelike*

duvebloth *sb.*

blod af en due, dueblod: Tac dufu bloth æller palumbis bloth æller turturis bloth oc drøp i the øghæn, thær bloth ær ouer ganget*Lægeb. [AM]. 15,21.*

[*til* I. duve. *Jf. vn.* dúfublóð, *fsv.* duvoblodh]

duvebrøthre *sb. pl.*

betegnelse for personer tilknyttet en godgørende stiftelse i Roskilde (jf. KultLeksM.III.358f.): Erland foghet af delæ *(afskriverfejl for* dwæ*)* brødræ i Roskyld*22/4 1437(DiplKbh.I.161,13, afskr. 1681).*

i forb. duvebrøthre kloster *el. (elliptisk)* duvebrøthre *om stiftelse:* wij .. forstandere i Dwebrøthre closter*27/7 1429(Esrumb.248, Rosk.)* A.T., fforstandher j Dwbrødhrekloster hoss Roosskildh*5/7 1497(DiplLund.V.324,15)* Jtem fatigæ folck i Dwæbrødræ ij marc*11/5 1501(DiplLund.VI.23,16).*

[*til* I. duve *sb. (i relig. symbolik)*]

duvehus + *sb.*

hus til tamme duer, duehus, dueslag: columbarium .. dwehwss*Chr. Ped. Voc. 1510.31ᵛ.*

[*til* I. duve *sb.*]

duvelike *sb.*

kun i forb. i duvelike *i skikkelse af en due (Jf.* I. duve*):* thet war then Helliand i dwe lige, oc sagde till Ottwel *(etc.)KMagn. (RomD. III.136,7)*(í dúfu líki*Vn.*).

[*til* I. duve *sb.*]

Figures 6.4.1-1 and 6.4.1-2 show printouts of full dictionary entries — it can be seen here that they can be printed out one at a time or continuously; but the system also allows selective printouts of information categories. Selective retrieval of information categories as subsets of the input dictionary text may take the form of printouts of separate information categories for one or more entries at a time, or printouts of freely selected combinations of information categories — also of course for one or more entries at a time. Printouts like these can be used for all kinds of editorial checks on the consistency, completeness, etc. of the dictionary. For instance, critical proof-reading of various types of editorial text like historical information or meaning specifications becomes more manageable; references can be printed out separately for checking, and the risk of missing one or more references when checking (almost inevitable if whole entries are to be read) is avoided. Such printed subsets of entries — whether in data entry or in column form — may also be suitable for exchanging data with other projects: Fig. 6.4.1-3 shows, for example, how one could supply useful information to the editors of a smaller Danish monolingual dictionary with no need for citations etc. For the printout the following fields were selected: SEC, ORDK, SUBK, BETB and FORB; HOMB and OPSL were only printed out if the fields selected were present in a given entry.

Fig. 6.4.1-3 Printout of subsets of ODSS entries *I. Auto* to *Autocykel* in data entry and column form

```
SEC    s ODS   =        PLUS          HOMB  I.   ODS            PLUS
OPSL   Auto
ORDK     # subst.
SUBK     en.
BETB     automobil.
```

```
SEC    s ODS            PLUS   +      HOMB  III. ODS            PLUS
OPSL   Auto
ORDK     # subst.
SUBK     en.
BETB     d.s.s. Autotypi S.
```

```
SEC    s ODS            PLUS   +      HOMB  III. ODS            PLUS
OPSL   Auto-
ORDK     i ssgr.
```

```
SEC    s ODS            PLUS   +      HOMB       ODS            PLUS
OPSL   Auto-bane
ORDK     # subst.
SUBK     en.
BETB     betegnelse for motorvej.
```

```
SEC    s ODS            PLUS   +      HOMB       ODS            PLUS
OPSL   auto-biografisk
ORDK     adj.
BETB     til Autobiograf(i).
```

```
SEC    s ODS   =        PLUS          HOMB       ODS            PLUS
OPSL   Auto|-bus
ORDK     # subst.
SUBK     en.
```

```
SEC      ODS            PLUS   +      HOMB       ODS            PLUS
OPSL   Auto|coat
ORDK     # subst.
SUBK     en.
BETB     overtræk af presenningstof, plastic ell. lign. til en
         parkeret bil.
BETB     kort frakke.
```

```
SEC      ODS            PLUS   +      HOMB       ODS            PLUS
OPSL   Auto|cykel
ORDK     # subst.
SUBK     en.
BETB     (mindre) motorcykel.
```

I. Auto, en. *automobil.*
III. Auto, en. *d.s.s.* Autotypi S.
III. Auto-, *i ssgr.*
Auto-bane, en. *betegnelse for motorvej.*

auto-biografisk, *adj. til* Autobiograf(i).
Auto-bus, en. **-coat,** en. *overtræk af presenningstof, plastic ell. lign. til en parkeret bil. kort frakke.* **-cykel,** en. *(mindre) motorcykel.*

Figure 6.4.1-4 shows how the GLDO could supply information on the sources in which certain words occur, and how one could extract information for a smaller Old Danish dictionary.

Fig. 6.4.1-4 Printout of subsets of GLDO entries *dræg* to *dræng* in data entry and column form

IHOM	IOPO dræg
SBCK	Lægeb. [AM].
SBCK	RimKr.(K41)
SBCK	Vald. Jord.

IHOM	IOPO dræk
SBCK	Suso.
SBCK	Kv Rosg.
SBCK	Suso.
SBCK	Chr. Ped. Voc. 1510.

IHOM	IOPO drægtighhet
SBCK	Hr Mich.
SBCK	# \D\

IHOM	IOPO drælle
SBCK	# \D\

IHOM	IOPO dræng
SBCK	KMagn. (RomD. III.
SBCK	Ryd Årb.
SBCK	Ryd Årb.
SBCK	GldBib.
SBCK	GldBib.
SBCK	GldBib.
SBCK	# \D\
SBCK	Dyrerim.
SBCK	RimKr.(K41)
SBCK	PLaale. nr.
SBCK	# \D\
SBCK	GldBib.
SBCK	RimKr.(K41)
SBCK	Skråer. I.
SBCK	Skråer. I.
SBCK	# \D\
SBCK	Hofregnsk.
SBCK	Hofregnsk.
SBCK	Jesu Barnd B.
SBCK	# \D\
SBCK	# \D\
SBCK	PLaale. nr.
SBCK	Hofregnsk.
SBCK	Hofregnsk.
SBCK	Hr Mich.
SBCK	Skråer. II.
SBCK	Skråer. II.
SBCK	Skråer. I.
SBCK	Skråer. II.
SBCK	# \D\
SBCK	Dyrerim.
SBCK	Suso.
SBCK	KMagn. (RomD. III.
SBCK	Kv Rosg.
SBCK	# \D\

(Fig. 6,4,1-4, continued)

IHOM	IOPO dræg
IOKA	sb.
BSUB	fk.
SBEB	gær el. bærme
SBEB	overf. om stank
SBEB	(?) som tilnavn

IHOM	IOPO dræk
IOKA	sb.
BSUB	n.
SBEB	snavs, smuds, skarn, spec. om ekskrementer
SBEB	overf.
SBEB	måske sammenblandet med dræg

IHOM	IOPO dræktighhet
IOKA	sb.
BSUB	fk.
SBEB	tilbøjelighed til at forhale, sendrægtighed

IHOM	IOPO drælle
IOKA	?
SBEB	som tilnavn

IHOM	IOPO dræng
IOKA	sb.
BSUB	fk.
SBEN	1
SBEB	kriger, helt
SBEB	i tilnavn (jf. oda.drængʀ gor.DaRun.nr.1, goan dræng.DaRun.nr.68 ofl.)
SBEN	2
SBEB	(halv)voksen ung mand, yngling, knøs
SBEN	3
SBEB	person af hankøn i tjenesteforhold til en anden
SBEN	3.1
SBEB	i alm. om tjenestekarl el. tjener
SBEB	overf.
SBEN	3.2
SBEB	om ikke voksen tjenestedreng (jf. bet. 4)
SBEN	3.3
SBEB	spec. om lærling, læredreng
SBEN	4
SBEB	barn af hankøn
SBEN	5
SBEB	som tilnavn

dræg *sb. fk. gær el. bærme overf. om stank (?) som tilnavn.*

dræk *sb. n. snavs, smuds, skarn, spec. om ekskrementer overf. måske sammenblandet med* dræg.

dræktighhet *sb. fk. tilbøjelighed til at forhale, sendrægtighed.*

drælle *? som tilnavn.*

dræng *sb. fk.*

1) *kriger, helt i tilnavn (jf. oda.* drængʀ goþr.*DaRun.nr.1,* goþan dræng.*DaRun.nr.68 ofl.).*

2) *(halv)voksen ung mand, yngling, knøs.*

3) *person af hankøn i tjenesteforhold til en anden.*

3.1) *i alm. om tjenestekarl el. tjener overf.*

3.2) *om ikke voksen tjenestedreng (jf. bet. 4).*

3.3) *spec. om lærling, læredreng.*

4) *barn af hankøn.*

5) *som tilnavn.*

The system version used for the ODSS experiments only allows searches on field content for the OPSL (headword) category: this facility is of course practical for quick retrieval (within seconds) of entries one wishes to edit, but it can also be very necessary to search on the contents of other information categories. The newest version (1986), used for the GLDO experiments, allows searches on the field content of all implemented information categories. The search may be on the specified total content of the field or on a specific part of the content, either arbitrarily positioned within the field or at its beginning or end. The search is really a further development of the selective printout of information categories to the matrix printer, as one specifies one or more information categories by entering their field codes, at the same time specifying the field content to be searched for, and the results of the search take the form of printouts — as yet it is neither possible to get the search results displayed on the screen nor to save them as a separate file; but for editorial checking printed lists are eminently suitable.

Figure 6.4.1-5 shows the newly developed selective search printouts demonstrated on small segments of the GLDO. In the first example the search was on the information category SBCI with the specified field content *israel*. In the second the search was on the information category SBCK with the specified content *Kv Rosg.* — i.e. a search for all the references to the source *Kvinders Rosengård*.

Fig. 6.4.1-5 Selective printouts from the GLDO specifying part of field content and whole field

IHOM **IOPO** dræng

SBCI vnghe drenge, ællær smaswennæ aff israels børnæ

IHOM **IOPO** dræpelse

SBCI fforthy sloghæ the *(ɔ: israelitterne)* .. alt hans folk, vt til fordærffwelsæ, ællær dræbælsæ

IHOM **IOPO** dræng

SBCK Kv Rosg.

IHOM **IOPO** drængebarn

SBCK Kv Rosg.
SBCK Kv Rosg.

Besides the general word-processing and data management facilities described here, the Compulexis system has many more specialized facilities, discussed below in Section 6.4.4.

6.4.2 Field code names for information categories

The names of the information categories in the GLDO and ODSS and the field codes used as rubrics for each information category when inputting dictionary entries by means of the editing system were chosen with due consideration for the names traditionally used by the GLDO and ODSS editorial staff for the components of the dictionary entries, and with mnemonic features to help the person entering the data. Another consideration, however, was the fact that in the Compulexis system there is a maximum of four characters available for each field code name.

Two principles were applied to the choice of field codes for information categories in the GLDO.

- The first character of the field code indicates the main section to which the field belongs:
    - I--- is an information category in the word identification section;
    - B--- is an information category in the inflectional information section;
    - S--- and E--- are information categories in the sections for semantic and etymological information sections respectively.
- The last three characters were fixed in accordance with general rules for abbreviations and thus with mnemonic considerations. For example, the field code BFLC stands for the information category *ForLægsCitat* 'citation of original' in the section for *Bøjningsoplysning* 'inflectional information'; SCKF is the field code for the information category *betydningsCitatKildeForlæg* 'original of source for meaning citation' in the section for semantic information.

The majority of the field codes for fixed fields in the ODSS format are mnemonic abbreviations of the names normally used by the editors for parts of the dictionary text. However, a few of these names require further explanation.

The name "colon meaning", abbreviated to KOLB, was invented for the ODSS format. It designates the editorial text that introduces a group of commentary citations. As was evident from Section 6.3.1, this is often text of a meaning-specifying type and is always closed with a colon: i.e. "colon" as characteristic feature plus "meaning relation" as characteristic feature give "colon meaning". The names BCIT and BKIL — for *citat* 'citation' and *kilde* 'source' respectively — which appear in the entry body in the ODSS format, the "meaning" component of the entry, have the initial B (for *Betydning* 'meaning') so the information categories can be uniquely identified as belonging to the semantic component. This B has thus been introduced to distinguish between citations and sources in the head and those in the body of the entry. Citations and sources in the head are called CIT and KIL and are among the free fields in the ODSS format.

Among the names of the other free fields, KOMF and KOMB should be noted. F and B refer to preceding (*Foransat*) and following (*Bagvedsat*) comments (*Kommentar*) on a given fixed field (it is perhaps easier to think of them as standing for 'in Front of' and 'Behind' in English). The B in the fixed fields HEOB and HENB refers to the fact that such references (*HEnvisninger*) always come after (*Bagved*) a given fixed field, unlike the fixed reference fields HHEO-HHEN dealing with the history of words or of their meanings. The F in GEOF, FAGF, TIDF, STIF and FREF refers both to the fact that these various types of usage restriction are Freely locatable and that they normally appear in Front of a given fixed field. In addition, the F distinguishes freely locatable usage restrictions from those that constitute fixed fields — GEO, FAG, TID, STIL and FRE.

The use of these naming principles has allowed us to identify the various information categories uniquely.

Since the ODSS format in general does not use the first character in the field code to indicate the main section of the entry it has been possible to make use of the system facilities for defining "shorthand" versions of field codes for data entry where the possibility of confusion with other codes is excluded. For example, the field codes BCIT, BKIL, SUBK, BØJF and FLEK can be entered either in full or as BC, BK, SU, BØ and FL respectively.

6.4.3 Use of the general facilities of the Compulexis system in the GLDO and ODSS

The general facilities discussed and exemplified above in Section 6.4.1 are of course all used in the same way in both the GLDO and the ODSS, with the exception of the facility for searching on field content that is not the headword.

6.4.4 Use of the specialized facilities of the Compulexis system in the GLDO and ODSS

The Compulexis system has many specialized facilities whose use in connection with the GLDO and ODSS will be discussed in the following sections.

6.4.4.1 Validity checks

The Compulexis system offers various types of validity checks on the use of field codes and the correctness of field content against a pre-determined checklist encoded in the system.

Checks on the order of fields

The system can be furnished with a table of valid field sequences, making it impossible to use the fields in question in an order that conflicts with the editorial rules adopted. If one attempts to use a field code that may not directly follow another field code, a screen message is displayed saying that the order is incorrect; and data cannot be entered under the incorrectly selected field code.

Field order checks are extensively used for the GLDO. In principle, only the order of information categories that can be read off from the format overview is valid — with due consideration for the iteration rules — but the facultative status of some information categories of course entails considerable flexibility in order-checking in practice.

As an example of a field order that can be checked, SECI must be followed by SBCK, which must in turn be followed by SBCV; only the SBCP category (and no other) may interrupt the fixed sequence SBCI-SBCK. This order check ensures that a citation documenting a particular meaning of a word is always furnished with a reference to its source; nor is it possible to forget the reference to the locus in the source text.

Field order checks are not, however, used for the ODSS, as its status as a supplement makes it impossible to predict which fields may only follow other particular fields; supplementation may be necessary anywhere in an entry.

Checks on the content of fields

With certain types of field content it is possible to pre-define a domain consisting of a complete list of valid contents. This universe of discourse is stored in a table in the system, so that the system, when this type of field content is entered, checks whether it belongs to the specified domain for the field code in question. If it does not, a message is displayed on the screen saying that the content is invalid in this field. It is possible, however, to a limited extent, to add new valid content to such a domain. This is done by entering the new field content three times in succession; the screen will then report that the field content in question has now been added to the domain. If it becomes impossible to add more to the domain or if one wishes to use an ad hoc content without adding it to the permanent store of valid contents, the validity check may be disabled by surrounding the field content with backslashes, "\". This type of unchecked field content can either constitute the whole content of the field or be placed before or after the checked field content.

One thing for which field content checks are eminently suitable is checking the abbreviations one wishes to use in a dictionary, as these must always be used in the same form. This makes it impossible to use non-standard variants of the dictionary's abbreviations unless the backslash rule ("\") is used, which will not be normal practice when entering data.

In the GLDO, field content checks are used as far as possible as described above in Section 6.2, where we mentioned that certain information categories had been specially created to enable parts of information categories to be subjected to automatic field content checks.

As stated in Section 6.2, field content checks are most important for the source reference categories IOVK, BØKK and SBCK. The content of these categories must belong to the domain consisting of all the source designations listed — at the moment about 200.

Compulexis offers a further advantage with this checking facility: two sets of source references are defined — a "working set" of short, mnemonically apt source names used for data entry and displayed on the data entry screen, and a "user set" of longer source references to which the working set is automatically converted by the editing system in the data entry form printout, the column form screen display and the column form printout.

An example of this is the source text *Ingeborg Predbjørnsdatters Tidebog* ("Ingeborg Predbjørnsdatter's Book of Hours"), which can be dated c. 1519, and which is printed in *Middelalderens danske Bønnebøger*, ("Medieval Danish Prayerbooks") Vol. I. This is cited in the dictionary with the following abbreviation: "Ingeb.PredbjørnsdTideb.Ca 1519<Bønneb.I."; while the working abbreviation is the obviously more manageable "IPTid<".

Field content checking is not used for the ODSS, since at the time of drawing up the format there were no finished abbreviation lists for sources used, and because the editors of the ODSS to a great extent work with complex usage restrictions; the usage restriction abbreviations in the ODSS are naturally the same as those of the parent work, the ODS; but the number of possible combinations of these is so large that it was considered counterproductive to specify a domain containing all the possibilities.

A special form of field content check offered as standard by Compulexis is its way of ensuring that meaning numbers are automatically generated in the right order as the entry is written: thus it is impossible, for example, to make meaning 3 follow immediately after meaning 1. This might otherwise happen either if the meaning number had been entered incorrectly or if a meaning had been forgotten in the manuscript.

This facility is not used by the GLDO, first and foremost because the meaning specification of one word within each sub-meaning may or may not be subdivided into different levels.

The status of the ODSS as a supplement excludes automatic checks on the numerical order of meanings, as the supplementation may apply to any part of the entry in the parent work.

6.4.4.2 Automatic generation of field content and codes (data entry screen and data entry form printout)

Here we can distinguish between semiautomatic and fully automatic generation of field content. By semiautomatic generation of field content we mean that a field code is entered on-screen, and in it a field content; in the on-screen data entry form this field content, always an abbreviated form of the final content of the field, will remain exactly as entered, while on the data entry form printout it will be converted to the final field content. By fully automatic generation of field content we mean that a field code is entered on-screen, the field content is automatically generated, and one is prompted for the next field code; both data entry form manifestations here show the same content.

For the GLDO semiautomatic generation of field content is used in connection with the source reference categories IOVK, BØKK and SBCK. As described in Section 6.4.4.1 a "working abbreviation" is entered and reproduced exactly as entered on the screen display, but is automatically changed to the "user abbreviation" on the data entry form printout and on the column form printouts. Figure 6.4.4.2-1 shows the data entry form printout and the column form printout for the information category SBCK, with the user abbreviation "Chr. Ped. Voc. 1510" (= *Christian Pedersens Vocabularium*, 1510), which has been automatically converted from the working abbreviation "CPV" in the on-screen data entry form.

For the GLDO the field codes are also generated automatically in certain cases. If the editorial rules state that a particular information category must follow another information category (see above, Section 6.4.4.1), the second category's field code is generated automatically once the first category has had its field code and content entered. This facility is used for the fields IOVK-IOVV, IHEO-IHEN, BØKK-BØKV, BFLC-BFCS, SOGK-SOBB, SIHO-SIHE, SBCK-SBCV and SCKF-SKFO. Figure 6.4.4.2-1 shows the field code SBCV generated automatically after entering SBCK.

Fully automatic generation of field content is used for the GLDO field SEC: entering this field code generates "§" automatically, which is the code in the GLDO data entry form representing a line break within the dictionary entry (see Fig. 6.4.4.2-1).

For the ODSS there is no semiautomatic — only fully automatic — generation of field content. This applies to the fields SEC (line break within the dictionary entry) and to KBST and KBSL (beginning and end of complex usage restriction), so that entering the field code SEC automatically generates the line break number in the entry in question (see Fig. 6.4.4.2-2, *II felt*); entering the field code KBST automatically generates the symbol "<", and entering the field code KBSL automatically generates the symbol ">" (see Fig. 6.4.4.2-3, *Autobus*).

Fig. 6.4.4.2-1 Semiautomatic generation of field content, automatic generation of field code, and fully automatic generation of field content in the GLDO

IHOM	IOPO duvehus
IUDN	+
IOKA	sb.
SEC	§
SBEB	hus til tamme duer, duehus, dueslag
SBCI	columbarium .. dwehwss
SBCK	Chr. Ped. Voc. 1510.
SBCV	31ᵛ
SEC	§
ELDK	til I. duve sb.

duvehus + *sb.*
hus til tamme duer, duehus, dueslag:
columbarium .. dwehwss*Chr. Ped. Voc. 1510.31ᵛ.*
[*til* I. duve *sb.*]

Fig. 6.4.4.2-2 The ODSS entry *II, Felt* in column form (line breaks within the entry) and in data entry form (the SEC field)

SEC s ODS = PLUS HOMB II. ODS PLUS

OPSL	Felt
ORDK	# subst.
SUBK	et.
FLEK	flt.
BØJF	-er
KOMF	ell.
BØJF	*d.s.*
PLUS	+
KOMF	ell.
TIDF	(ældre spr.)
BØJF	-e

(Fig. 6.4.4.2-2, continued - data entry form)

HEOB	(se
HENB	*ndf.).*
ODS	=
ONR	1
PLUS	+
BCIT	hver af Dørene er deelt i to Felte.
BKIL	Rawert&SGarlieb.Bornholm.(1819).23.
SEC	2
ODS	=
ONR	3
PLUS	+
HHEO	(jf.
HHEN	Kul-, Malm-, Skud-, Skyde-, Synsfelt
KOMB	(jf. 885,38)).
SEC	3
ODS	=
ONR	4
PL	‖
BETB	overf.
PLUS	+
BETB	ogs. om deltagere i andre løb.
BCIT	Københavnerne vil blive præsenteret for det fineste Felt, der endnu har været til Start her i Byen.
BKIL	Pol.19/11 1936.12.sp.6
KOMB	(om cykelryttere til seksdagesløb).
BCIT	Halvdelen af Feltets 24 *(cykel)*Ryttere bliver deciderede Sprintere.
BKIL	NatTid.17/10 1951.9.sp.6.
SEC	4
PLUS	+
ONR	5
HHEO	(jf.
HHEN	*bet.* 4)
KOMF	i forb.
FORB	fart over feltet,
BETB	fart på.
BCIT	Næste Morgen, Lørdag, var der stor Rengøring overalt *(: på skoleskibet)* .. der var Fart over Feltet.
BKIL	Frikvarter.20/9 1946.5.sp.4.
BCIT	Fra Hestesport .. der er ro over feltet, når ingen hest bryder ud fra sin placering .. går det stærkt, er der fart over feltet (de to .. udtryk kan i dagligsproget osse stamme fra cykelsport).
BKIL	Bom.S.131.
BCIT	Fart over Feltet i Folketinget. I Gaar kom man igennem 15 Punkter paa 2 Timer.
BKIL	JyllP.2/6 1954.9.sp.4.

II. Felt, et. *flt.* -er *ell. d.s.* + *ell. (ældre spr.)* -e *(se ndf.).* **1)** + hver af Dørene er deelt i to Felte. *Rawert&SGarlieb.Bornholm.(1819).23.*

3) + *(jf.* Kul-, Malm-, Skud-, Skyde-, Synsfelt *(jf.* 885,38*)).*

4) ‖ *overf.* + *ogs. om deltagere i andre løb.* Københavnerne vil blive præsenteret for det fineste Felt, der endnu har været til Start her i Byen. *Pol.19/11 1936.12.sp.6 (om cykelryttere til seksdagesløb).* Halvdelen af Feltets 24 *(cykel)*Ryttere bliver deciderede Sprintere. *NatTid.17/10 1951.9.sp.6.*

+ **5)** *(jf. bet.* 4) *i forb.* f a r t o v e r f e l t e t, *fart på.* Næste Morgen, Lørdag, var der stor Rengøring overalt *(: på skoleskibet)* .. der var Fart over Feltet. *Frikvarter.20/9 1946.5.sp.4.* Fra Hestesport .. der er ro over feltet, når ingen hest bryder ud fra sin placering .. går det stærkt, er der fart over feltet (de to .. udtryk kan i dagligsproget osse stamme fra cykelsport). *Bom.S.131.* Fart over Feltet i Folketinget. I Gaar kom man igennem 15 Punkter paa 2 Timer. *JyllP.2/6 1954.9.sp.4.*

Fig. 6.4.4.2-3 The ODSS entry *Autobus* in data entry (fields KBST and KBSL) and column form

SEC	s ODS	=	PLUS	HOMB	ODS	PLUS
OPSL	Auto|-bus					
ORDK	# subst.					
SUBK	en.					
PLUS	+					
HHEO	(jf.					
HHEN	Ill.Bus;					
KBST	<					
FRE	sj.					
STIL	i alm. spr.					
TID	efter ca. 1940).					
KBSL	>					
BCIT	Autobussen paa Strøget - En ny Dødsdom over Hestene.					
BKIL	Riget.2/1 1913.3.sp.3.					
BCIT	Sammenstødet mellem Ekspres og Autobus.					
BKIL	Aftenp.24/1 1930.2.sp.2.					
BCIT	enhver autobus eller automobil skulle kunne overføres *(: med en ny færge).*					
BKIL	Vingehjulet.1950/51.66.sp.2.					

Auto-bus, en. + *(jf.* Ill.Bus; *sj. i alm. spr. efter ca. 1940).* Autobussen paa Strøget - En ny Dødsdom over Hestene. *Riget.2/1 1913.3.sp.3.* Sammenstødet mellem Ekspres og Autobus. *Aftenp.24/1 1930.2.sp.2.* enhver autobus eller automobil skulle kunne overføres *(: med en ny færge). Vingehjulet.1950/51.66.sp.2.*

6.4.4.3 Automatic generation of alterations in field content in on-screen and printout column forms on the basis of field content in the on-screen data entry form

This system facility is used for the following different purposes.

Automatic generation of markers and punctuation before and/or after field content is entered

The use of this facility requires of course that one has made a list of punctuation marks and markers to be used between information categories or fields, so the system can assign this punctuation data to the proper field codes. But this is not always possible, as the fields are often at the lowest level of a hierarchical entry structure, while punctuation may refer to higher levels whose demarcation is not normally indicated. In less frequent combinations of field types, therefore, automatic punctuation may not always be correct.

When the GLDO and ODSS formats were established, it was not possible for users of the system to enter exceptions to the standard automatic punctuation. It has since become possible by means of a special field code, PNC, and its associated field content, to enter changes in the automatic punctuation. However, automatic bracketing around the contents of one or more fields cannot be changed from the PNC field.

As standard procedure Compulexis generates spaces between the contents of fields in the column form manifestations; but a version without spaces can be ordered for individual dictionaries.

Automatically generated punctuation only appears in the column form manifestations of the entry.

The GLDO uses generated markers for *standard* beginnings and/or endings of fields, e.g.

- to *begin* a field: the information category IOPV regularly begins with "-Var:" (for "variant"), so this is automatically generated in the column manifestations, on-screen and printed, but does not appear in the on-screen or printed data entry forms (see Fig. 6.4.4.3-1 *duvemyk*). The information category ELPG is similarly regularly introduced by "grundbet:" (= basic meaning).
- to *end* a field: for the first version of the editing system Compulexis for the GLDO there was a wish for a very wide range of automatic punctuation at field endings. But it emerged during the trials of the first version that the high degree of complexity in the GLDO would entail far too many exceptions from the basic rules drawn up for punctuation between fields. Many of the automatic punctuation marks for ending fields were therefore removed again in the second and third versions. But there still remained quite a few instances of automatic punctuation, e.g.

    - closing right bracket ")" for the fields SOBN and SBEN;
    - final colon ":" for the fields SOGK and SBEB;
    - full stop "." for the fields IHOM, IOVV and SOBB.

(An example of an automatically generated final colon in the field SBEB can be seen in Fig. 6.4.4.3-1 illustrating the entry *duveæg*).

- to *begin* and *end* a field:
    - the category IOVL begins with "(jf." 'compare' and ends with ")";
    - the categories BØKO, SBCP and ELPI begin with an automatically generated left bracket, "(", and end with an automatically generated right bracket, ")";
    - the SIHO-SIHE complex begins regularly with a left bracket "(" and ends with a right bracket and colon, "):";
    - the SCKF category begins regularly with a left bracket, "(" and ends with a full stop, ".".

(An example of regular automatic generation of a left bracket, "(", and a right bracket, ")", followed by a colon, ":", is shown in Fig. 6.4.4.3-1 in the fields SIHO and SIHE of the *duvemyk* entry).

- *conditional* ending of a field: in the version of the editing system for the GLDO a number of automatically generated punctuation marks have been incorporated that are conditional on the field that follows:
    - the regular ending of the IHEN category with a full stop, ".", is altered to a comma, ",", if the IHEO-IHEN complex is repeated;
    - the BØKV category ends with an automatically generated full stop, ".", unless the BFLC-BFCS complex follows, in which case no concluding punctuation is generated;
    - the SBEB category ends with a colon, ":", unless the SIHO-SIHE complex follows, in which case no concluding punctuation is generated;
    - no concluding punctuation is generated for the category EEHL unless EBRO follows, in which case a semicolon, ";", is automatically generated.

(An example of the conditional ending of a field with punctuation can be seen in the entry on *duvemyk* in Fig. 6.4.4.3-1, where the colon which normally ends the SBEB category is suspended because the categories SIHO + SIHE follow SBEB).

It should be noted that the description of these facilities has not been exhaustive.

As for automatic punctuation in the ODSS, the entry material used to draw up the ODSS format was analysed; it emerged that it would only be possible to obtain automatic generation of punctuation for very few of the many ODSS information categories, given the high degree of complexity in the dictionary, which allows for so many possible combinations of the information categories that a system of rules for all the possible punctuation marks that can conclude a category would have so many exceptions that it would be unreasonable to implement automatic punctuation to any great extent. The following types, however, proved possible:

- after HOMB (homograph marker) an automatic full stop, ".", is generated; but this full stop already appears in the data entry form (see Fig. 6.4.4.3-2, *I. Auto*);
- after OPSL (headword) an automatic comma is generated, "," (see Fig. 6.4.4.3-2, *I. Auto*);
- after ONR (superordinate meaning number) and UNR (subordinate meaning number), an automatic closing bracket is generated, ")", (see Fig. 6.4.4.3-3 *II. Felt* for ONR).
- after FNR (phrase meaning number) an automatic full stop is generated, ".".

Fig. 6.4.4.3-1 Illustration of automatic punctuation (1) as regular beginning of a field; (2) as regular end of a field; (3) as beginning and end of a field; and (4) as conditional end of a field

IHOM	IOPO duvemyk
IOKA	sb.
IOPV	dufv mych
IOVK	Lægeb. [AM].
IOVV	4,12
SEC	§
SBEB	ekskrementer af due, duemøg
SIHO	Jf.
SIHE	duveskarn
SBCI	Tac .. dufæ mych blandæ mæth oleo .. oc thæt bæthrer al harlech oc tumores
SBCK	Lægeb. [AM].
SBCV	58,25
SBCI	berøg qwynnen vnder tiil met dwe møg
SBCK	Kv Rosg.
SBCV	22,5
SCKF	tauben mist
SKFO	Mnty.; sml. KvRosg.121,13: dwue skarn
SEC	§
ELDK	til I. duve sb.

IHOM	IOPO duveæg
IUDN	+
IOKA	sb. pl.
SEC	§
SBEB	æg af due, dueæg
SBCI	gosæ æg, hønsæ æg, duæ æg oc andræ æg
SBCK	Mandev.
SBCV	24,5
SEC	§
ELDK	til I. duve sb.

duvemyk *sb. -Var.:* dufv mych*Lægeb. [AM].4,12.*
ekskrementer af due, duemøg (Jf. duveskarn*).:* Tac .. dufæ mych blandæ mæth oleo .. oc thæt bæthrer al harlech oc tumores*Lægeb. [AM].58,25* berøg qwynnen vnder tiil met dwe møg*Kv Rosg.22,5*(tauben mist*Mnty.; sml. KvRosg.121,13:* dwue skarn).
[*til* I. duve *sb.*]

duveæg + *sb. pl.*
æg af due, dueæg.: gosæ æg, hønsæ æg, duæ æg oc andræ æg*Mandev.24,5.*
[*til* I. duve *sb.*]

Fig. 6.4.4.3-2 The ODSS entry *I. Auto* in data entry form (the HOMB and OPSL fields) and column form

SEC	s ODS	=	PLUS	HOMB	I.	ODS	PLUS
OPSL	Auto						

ORDK	# subst.
SUBK	en.
BETB	automobil.
PLUS	+ *ældre:*
BCIT	Auto – Det kan ikke nytte at stritte mod Fremskridtet.
BKIL	Ekstrabl.1/7 1905.1.sp.4.

I. Auto, en. *automobil.* + *ældre:* Auto – Det kan ikke nytte at stritte mod Fremskridtet. *Ekstrabl.1/7 1905.1.sp.4.*

Fig. 6.4.4.3-3 The ODSS entry *II. Felt* in data entry form (the ONR field) and column form

SEC	s ODS	=	PLUS	HOMB	II.	ODS	PLUS
OPSL	Felt						

ORDK	# subst.
SUBK	et.
FLEK	flt.
BØJF	-er
KOMF	ell.
BØJF	*d.s.*
PLUS	+
KOMF	ell.
TIDF	(ældre spr.)
BØJF	-e
HEOB	(se
HENB	*ndf.).*
ODS	=
ONR	1
PLUS	+
BCIT	hver af Dørene er deelt i to Felte.
BKIL	Rawert&SGarlieb.Bornholm.(1819).23.
SEC	2
ODS	=
ONR	3
PLUS	+
HHEO	(jf.
HHEN	Kul-, Malm-, Skud-, Skyde-, Synsfelt
KOMB	(jf. 885,38)).
SEC	3
ODS	=
ONR	4
PL	‖
BETB	overf.
PLUS	+
BETB	ogs. om deltagere i andre løb.
BCIT	Københavnerne vil blive præsenteret for det fineste Felt, der endnu har været til Start her i Byen.
BKIL	Pol.19/11 1936.12.sp.6
KOMB	(om cykelryttere til seksdagesløb).
BCIT	Halvdelen af Feltets 24 *(cykel)*Ryttere bliver deciderede Sprintere.
BKIL	NatTid.17/10 1951.9.sp.6.
SEC	4
PLUS	+
ONR	5
HHEO	(jf.
HHEN	*bet.* 4*)*
KOMF	i forb.
FORB	fart over feltet,
BETB	fart på.
BCIT	Næste Morgen, Lørdag, var der stor Rengøring overalt *(: på skoleskibet)* .. der var Fart over Feltet.
BKIL	Frikvarter.20/9 1946.5.sp.4.
BCIT	Fra Hestesport .. der er ro over feltet, når ingen hest bryder ud fra sin placering .. går det stærkt, er der fart over feltet (de to .. udtryk kan i dagligsproget osse stamme fra cykelsport).
BKIL	Bom.S.131.
BCIT	Fart over Feltet i Folketinget. I Gaar kom man igennem 15 Punkter paa 2 Timer.
BKIL	JyllP.2/6 1954.9.sp.4.

(Fig. 6.4.4.3-3, continued)

II. Felt, et. *flt.* -er *ell. d.s.* + *ell. (ældre spr.)* -e *(se ndf.)*. **1)** + hver af Dørene er deelt i to Felte. *Rawert&SGarlieb.Bornholm.(1819).23.*

3) + *(jf.* Kul-, Malm-, Skud-, Skyde-Synsfelt *(jf.* 885,38*))*.

4) || *overf.* + *ogs. om deltagere i andre løb.* Københavnerne vil blive præsenteret for det fineste Felt, der endnu har været til Start her i Byen. *Pol.19/11 1936.12.sp.6 (om cykelryttere til seksdagesløb).* Halvdelen af Feltets 24 *(cykel)*Ryttere bliver deciderede Sprintere. *NatTid.17/10 1951.9.sp.6.*

+ **5)** *(jf. bet. 4) i forb.* fart over feltet, *fart på.* Næste Morgen, Lørdag, var der stor Rengøring overalt *(: på skoleskibet)* .. der var Fart over Feltet. *Frikvarter.20/9 1946.5.sp.4.* Fra Hestesport .. der er ro over feltet, når ingen hest bryder ud fra sin placering .. går det stærkt, er der fart over feltet (de to .. udtryk kan i dagligsproget osse stamme fra cykelsport). *Bom.S.131.* Fart over Feltet i Folketinget. I Gaar kom man igennem 15 Punkter paa 2 Timer. *JyllP.2/6 1954.9.sp.4.*

In practice this means of course that the person entering the data need not think about entering these punctuation marks; but in all other cases the punctuation that ends an information category has to be entered.

Given the optional punctuation facility (PNC) introduced later, it would probably have been possible to obtain a considerably higher degree of automatic punctuation in the ODSS, as categories with rare exceptions to the punctuation rules could have been given automatic punctuation. Incorrect punctuation could then have been localized at the proof-reading stage, and the correct punctuation inserted by means of the PNC facility.

The standard facility providing spaces between each field in the column manifestations has been disabled at a number of points for the GLDO. For example, the constant and variable components of source references — the complexes IOVK-IOVV, BØKK-BØKV and SBCK-SBCV — are compressed, i.e. printed without spaces. Similarly, BØKK, SBCK and SKFO are compressed after BØCI, SBCI and SCKF respectively. In a few cases it may be desirable to reintroduce the standard space facility between the fields IOVK-IOVV, BØKK-BØKV, SBCK-SBCV and SCKF-SKFO. This can be done by entering a so-called "hard" or "fixed" space at the beginning of the information categories IOVV, BØKV, SBCV and SKFO. Figure 6.4.4.3-4 shows an example of how the convention that the SKFO field follows SCKF without a space is suspended by means of a "fixed space", represented by the symbol "□" in the data entry form.

Fig. 6.4.4.3-4 Illustration of the "fixed space" facility as used in the entry *II. drøve*, meaning 4.1

SBEN	4
SSGK	præt. part.
SORF	drøv(e)th
SBEB	som adj.
SBEN	4.1
SBEB	om persons sindstilstand
SBCI	*(hun fik at vide)* at han hafdhe gifvit sek diæfolin i vold for hænna skyld. af hwilkit hon vordh mikit drøfdh
SBCK	SjT.
SBCV	22,22
SCKF	=
SKFO	□ Sv.
SBCI	tha worthe iak bekymmerth och drøffueth
SBCK	Kempis.
SBCV	125,8
SCKF	turbatio
SKFO	Lat.
SBCI	iæc ær drøffder i mynne ænxlo
SBCK	Bonav. Medit.
SBCV	71ʳ,b
SCKF	drøfdhir i minom ængxla
SKFO	Sv.
SBCI	fogher glædhelig sang gør then ther gladh ær mere gladh, oc then ther drøfd ær mere drøfd
SBCK	Suso.
SBCV	93,26
SCKF	tristem tristiorem
SKFO	Lat.
SBCI	Hwi ær thu drøfdh, min siæl, hwi drøfwer thu meg?
SBCK	Suso.
SBCV	156,22
SCKF	Quare tristis es, anima mea, et quare conturbas me?
SKFO	Lat. = Salm.41.6(Vulg.)
SBCI	Karlot sagde: "war icke drøffdher, wij wille hannum snarth igen fange (ɔ: *få tilbage)*
SBCK	KMagn. (RomD. III.
SBCV	30,27)
SCKF	úglaðr
SKFO	Vn.
SEC	§
SBEB	om persons legemlige tilstand (sjæld.): dødtræt, udaset
SBCI	oc spaar ickæ legemæt .. Och nar som thu tha finnær thik at wæræ drøffuæt aff værk oc suedæ owær alt thit legemæt *(sic)*, tha *(etc.)*
SBCK	Kærl St.
SBCV	227ᵛ
SCKF	cum illos senties dolores
SKFO	Lat.

4) *præt. part.* drøv(e)th *som adj.:* **4.1)** *om persons sindstilstand: (hun fik at vide)* at han hafdhe gifvit sek diæfolin i vold for hænna skyld. af hwilkit hon vordh mikit drøfdh*SjT.22,22*(= *Sv.*) tha worthe iak bekymmerth och drøffueth*Kempis. 125,8*(turbatio*Lat.*) iæc ær drøffder i mynne ænxlo*Bonav. Medit.71ʳ,b*(drøfdhir i minom ængxla*Sv.*) fogher glædhelig sang gør then ther gladh ær mere gladh, oc then ther drøfd ær mere drøfd*Suso.93,26*(tristem tristiorem*Lat.*) Hwi ær thu drøfdh, min siæl, hwi drøfwer thu meg?*Suso. 156,22*(Quare tristis es, anima mea, et quare conturbas me?*Lat. = Salm.41.6(Vulg.)*) Karlot sagde: "war icke drøffdher, wij wille hannum snarth igen fange *(ɔ: få tilbage)KMagn. (RomD. III.30,27)*(úglaðr *Vn.*).

om persons legemlige tilstand (sjæld.): dødtræt, udaset: oc spaar ickæ legemæt .. Och nar som thu tha finnær thik at wæræ drøffuæt aff værk oc suedæ owær alt thit legemæt *(sic)*, tha *(etc.)Kærl St.227ᵛ*(cum illos senties dolores*Lat.*).

For the ODSS experiments there were no omissions of spaces between fields in the column manifestations. However, when using the software in future, it could be necessary to omit this space between the contents of BCIT and BKIL and between CIT and KIL, i.e. between citations and citation sources. In other cases, for example before the meaning numbers ONR and UNR, one could consider inserting a double space rather than the present single one.

Conversion of the first element in compounds to "-"

It is a typical feature of many dictionaries that series of entries on compounds with a first element in common are gathered into groups, so only the first of such a series of entries has the first element explicitly represented in the headword, while the subsequent entries in the group have the first element replaced by a hyphen, "-", in the headword. If these headwords were entered exactly as they appear in the traditional printed dictionary, i.e. as *-coat* for *Autocoat*, for example, the editing system's automatic alphabetization facility, based on the alphabetical form of the headword, would yield some highly undesirable results (see below on automatic alphabetization, Section 6.4.4.5).

In the GLDO this issue is not relevant, as the editors have chosen to avoid representing first elements of compounds with hyphens altogether.

But the issue is very relevant for the ODSS. Here the convention has been adopted that cases like *-coat* for *Autocoat* above will be entered with a vertical separator after the part of the word to be replaced with a hyphen. Thus *-coat* is entered as *Auto|coat*. The vertical separator is also inserted into the fully alphabetically-represented first headword in such a series of entries on compounds; the principle is then that the text before the "|" and the "|" itself in the subsequent headwords where "|" has been inserted will be replaced with a hyphen in the column manifestations of the entry, as long as this text is identical to the text before "|" in the first headword. In this identity test the distinction between upper and lower case letters is ignored (see Fig. 6.4.4.3-5 *Autobus - Autocykel*).

Fig. 6.4.4.3-5 The ODSS entries *Autobus* to *Autocykel* in data entry form (field OPSL) and column form

SEC	s ODS =	PLUS	HOMB	ODS	PLUS
OPSL	Auto|-bus				
ORDK	# subst.				
SUBK	en.				
PLUS	+				
HHEO	(jf.				
HHEN	III.Bus;				
KBST	<				
FRE	sj.				
STIL	i alm. spr.				
TID	efter ca. 1940).				
KBSL	>				
BCIT	Autobussen paa Strøget - En ny Dødsdom over Hestene.				
BKIL	Riget.2/1 1913.3.sp.3.				
BCIT	Sammenstødet mellem Ekspres og Autobus.				
BKIL	Aftenp.24/1 1930.2.sp.2.				
BCIT	enhver autobus eller automobil skulle kunne overføres *(: med en ny færge).*				
BKIL	Vingehjulet.1950/51.66.sp.2.				

SEC	ODS	PLUS +	HOMB	ODS	PLUS
OPSL	Auto|coat				
ORDK	# subst.				
SUBK	en.				
ONR	1				
BETB	overtræk af presenningstof, plastic ell. lign. til en parkeret bil.				
BKIL	Krak.1950.3019.				
BKIL	VTFrO.[9](1959).				
ONR	2				
BETB	kort frakke.				
KOMF	se				
BKIL	NyeOrd 1955-75.				

SEC	ODS	PLUS +	HOMB	ODS	PLUS
OPSL	Auto|cykel				
ORDK	# subst.				
SUBK	en.				
HIST	(jf. eng. autocycle)				
BETB	(mindre) motorcykel.				
BCIT	Autocycle, Motorcykel.				
BKIL	Meyer.[8](1924).				
BCIT	Jeg er lykkelig Indehaver af en Avtocykle *(og føler mig)* foranlediget til at protestere kraftigt og indtrængende mod, at De kalder nævnte Maskineri en Sofacykle.				
BKIL	Pol.10/7 1937.9.sp.6.				
TIDF	senere				
KBST	<				
FREF	(især				
STIF	fagl.)				
KBSL	>				
KOLB	om knallert:				
BCIT	Mobylette - den elegante, stærke .. autocykel.				
BKIL	MagasinNyt.apr.1954.omslag.				
BCIT	Wooler Auto-cyklen.				
BKIL	Krak.1955.II.2954.				

(Fig. 6.4.4.3-5, continued)

Auto-bus, en. + *(jf.* III.Bus; *sj. i alm. spr. efter ca. 1940).* Autobussen paa Strøget – En ny Dødsdom over Hestene. *Riget.2/1 1913.3.sp.3.* Sammenstødet mellem Ekspres og Autobus. *Aftenp.24/1 1930.2.sp.2.* enhver autobus eller automobil skulle kunne overføres *(: med en ny færge). Vingehjulet.1950/51.66.sp.2.* + **-coat**, en. 1) *overtræk af presenningstof, plastic ell. lign. til en parkeret bil. Krak.1950.3019. VTFrO.*[3]*(1959).* 2) *kort frakke. se NyeOrd 1955-75.* + **-cykel**, en. *(jf. eng.* autocycle*) (mindre) motorcykel.* Autocycle, Motorcykel. *Meyer.*[3]*(1924).* Jeg er lykkelig Indehaver af en Avtocykle *(og føler mig)* foranlediget til at protestere kraftigt og indtrængende mod, at De kalder nævnte Maskineri en Sofacykle. *Pol.10/7 1937.9.sp.6. senere (især fagl.) om knallert:* Mobylette – den elegante, stærke .. autocykel. *MagasinNyt.apr.1954.omslag.* Wooler Auto-cyklen. *Krak.1955.II.2954.*

The homograph marker entered as an Arabic numeral, but converted to a Roman numeral in the column form

In many dictionaries Roman numerals are used as homograph markers. Since Roman numbers usually consist of more characters than Arabic ones, it eases the data entry process if one can enter an Arabic number as the homograph marker, which is then converted to a Roman number in the column form. Compulexis therefore supplies such a conversion facility as standard.

This facility is used by the GLDO. Arabic numerals only are entered in the category IHOM and are then converted in both column forms to (semibold) Roman numerals (see Fig. 6.4.4.3-6).

The ODSS editors chose to dispense with this facility, so Roman numerals are entered as homograph markers. This is because Roman numerals with many digits often occur in the ODSS and there is a risk that someone entering data from a manuscript with Roman numbers could convert them to incorrect Arabic ones. The insertion of Roman figures rather than Arabic ones allows direct checks on the correctness of the Roman numbers against the manuscript, so the discovery of errors need not be left until the proof-reading of the column form. This is thus a trade-off of the advantages and disadvantages of a facility (easy data entry with a high risk of error and no immediate visual checks) against difficult data entry with less chance of error and immediate visual checks.

Fig. 6.4.4.3-6 Illustration of facilities for automatic conversion of Arabic to Roman numerals and line breaks within entries in the GLDO

IHOM	1 IOPO drøve
IOKA	sb.
SEC	§
SBEB	bedrøvelse, sorg, modgang
SBCI	*J marie heder scullæ i ether øffuæ, / huo andhet gør, hannum tymes drøffuæ
SBCK	Hr Mich.
SBCV	123,4
SEC	§
ELDK	vistnok dannet i gld., substantivering af II. drøve vb.

I. drøve *sb.*
bedrøvelse, sorg, modgang: *J marie heder scullæ i ether øffuæ, / huo andhet gør, hannum tymes drøffuæ*Hr Mich. 123,4.*
[*vistnok dannet i gld., substantivering af* II. drøve *vb.*]

Line breaks

The GLDO's "§", the code for a line break within the entry in the data entry forms, is changed in the column forms so that it simply appears as a line break within an entry (see Fig. 6.4.4.3-6).

The ODSS uses two types of line break, dealt with as follows. An arbitrary keystroke in the initial SEC field of the entry, which appears in both data entry forms as the arbitrary character in question, is changed in the on-screen column forms to a downward-pointing arrow, "↓", so that during on-screen proof-reading, where only one entry can be seen at a time, one can see that there is a line break after the preceding entry. In the column form printout there is simply a line break after the preceding entry when several contiguous entries are printed out (see Fig. 6.4.4.3-7, *Auto-bus*, for example).

Fig. 6.4.4.3-7 The ODSS entries *auto-biografisk* to *Autocykel* in data entry form (the initial field in the entry, SEC) and in column form (line breaks between entries)

SEC s ODS PLUS + HOMB ODS PLUS

OPSL	auto-biografisk
ORDK	adj.
BETB	til Autobiograf(i).
BCIT	jeg gør opmærksom paa at *(min produktion)* ikke paa noget Punkt er autobiografisk.
BKIL	JVJens.HH.184.
BKIL	EFrederiksen.UL.15.

SEC s ODS = PLUS HOMB ODS PLUS

OPSL	Auto|-bus
ORDK	# subst.
SUBK	en.
PLUS	+
HHEO	(jf.
HHEN	III.Bus;
KBST	<
FRE	sj.
STIL	i alm. spr.
TID	efter ca. 1940).
KBSL	>
BCIT	Autobussen paa Strøget - En ny Dødsdom over Hestene.
BKIL	Riget.2/1 1913.3.sp.3.
BCIT	Sammenstødet mellem Ekspres og Autobus.
BKIL	Aftenp.24/1 1930.2.sp.2.
BCIT	enhver autobus eller automobil skulle kunne overføres *(: med en ny færge).*
BKIL	Vingehjulet.1950/51.66.sp.2.

SEC ODS PLUS + HOMB ODS PLUS

OPSL	Auto|coat
ORDK	# subst.
SUBK	en.
ONR	1
BETB	overtræk af presenningstof, plastic ell. lign. til en parkeret bil.
BKIL	Krak.1950.3019.
BKIL	VTFrO.[3](1959).
ONR	2
BETB	kort frakke.
KOMF	se
BKIL	NyeOrd 1955-75.

SEC ODS PLUS + HOMB ODS PLUS

OPSL	Auto|cykel
ORDK	# subst.
SUBK	en.
HIST	(jf. eng. autocycle)
BETB	(mindre) motorcykel.
BCIT	Autocycle, Motorcykel.
BKIL	Meyer.[8](1924).

(Fig. 6.4.4.3-7, continued)

BCIT	Jeg er lykkelig Indehaver af en Avtocykle *(og føler mig)* foranlediget til at protestere kraftigt og indtrængende mod, at De kalder nævnte Maskineri en Sofacykle.
BKIL	Pol.10/7 1937.9.sp.6.
TIDF	senere
KBST	<
FREF	(især
STIF	fagl.)
KBSL	>
KOLB	om knallert:
BCIT	Mobylette - den elegante, stærke .. autocykel.
BKIL	MagasinNyt.apr.1954.omslag.
BCIT	Wooler Auto-cyklen.
BKIL	Krak.1955.II.2954.

\+ **auto-biografisk,** *adj. til* Autobiograf(i). jeg gør opmærksom paa at *(min produktion)* ikke paa noget Punkt er autobiografisk. *JVJens.HH.184. EFrederiksen.UL.15.* **Auto-bus,** en. + *(jf.* III.Bus; *sj. i alm. spr. efter ca. 1940).* Autobussen paa Strøget - En ny Dødsdom over Hestene. *Riget.2/1 1913.3.sp.3.* Sammenstødet mellem Ekspres og Autobus. *Aftenp.24/1 1930.2.sp.2.* enhver autobus eller automobil skulle kunne overføres *(: med en ny færge). Vingehjulet.1950/51.66.sp.2.* + **-coat,** en. 1) *overtræk af presenningstof, plastic ell. lign. til en parkeret bil. Krak.1950.3019. VTFrO.*[3]*(1959).* 2) *kort frakke. se NyeOrd 1955-75.* + **-cykel,** en. *(jf. eng.* autocycle*) (mindre) motorcykel.* Autocycle, Motorcykel. *Meyer.*[6]*(1924).* Jeg er lykkelig Indehaver af en Avtocykle *(og føler mig)* foranlediget til at protestere kraftigt og indtrængende mod, at De kalder nævnte Maskineri en Sofacykle. *Pol.10/7 1937.9.sp.6. senere (især fagl.) om knallert:* Mobylette - den elegante, stærke .. autocykel. *MagasinNyt.apr.1954.omslag.* Wooler Auto-cyklen. *Krak.1955.II.2954.*

The automatically generated field content — the line-break number as specified in the data entry forms — is changed in both column forms to appear simply as line breaks within the entry (see Fig. 6.4.4.3-8, *II. Felt*).

Fig. 6.4.4.3-8 The ODSS entry *II. Felt* in data entry form (SEC fields within entry) and in column form (line breaks within the entry)

SEC	s ODS =	PLUS	HOMB II.	ODS	PLUS
OPSL	Felt				
ORDK	# subst.				
SUBK	et.				
FLEK	flt.				
BØJF	-er				
KOMF	ell.				
BØJF	*d.s.*				
PLUS	+				
KOMF	ell.				
TIDF	(ældre spr.)				

(Fig. 6.4.4.3-8, continued)

BØJF	-e
HEOB	(se
HENB	*ndf.).*
ODS	=
ONR	1
PLUS	+
BCIT	hver af Dørene er deelt i to Felte.
BKIL	Rawert&SGarlieb.Bornholm.(1819).23.
SEC	2
ODS	=
ONR	3
PLUS	+
HHEO	(jf.
HHEN	Kul-, Malm-, Skud-, Skyde-, Synsfelt
KOMB	(jf. 885,38)).
SEC	3
ODS	=
ONR	4
PL	‖
BETB	overf.
PLUS	+
BETB	ogs. om deltagere i andre løb.
BCIT	Københavnerne vil blive præsenteret for det fineste Felt, der endnu har været til Start her i Byen.
BKIL	Pol.19/11 1936.12.sp.6
KOMB	(om cykelryttere til seksdagesløb).
BCIT	Halvdelen af Feltets 24 *(cykel)*Ryttere bliver deciderede Sprintere.
BKIL	NatTid.17/10 1951.9.sp.6.
SEC	4
PLUS	+
ONR	5
HHEO	(jf.
HHEN	*bet. 4)*
KOMF	i forb.
FORB	fart over feltet,
BETB	fart på.
BCIT	Næste Morgen, Lørdag, var der stor Rengøring overalt *(: på skoleskibet)* .. der var Fart over Feltet.
BKIL	Frikvarter.20/9 1946.5.sp.4.
BCIT	Fra Hestesport .. der er ro over feltet, når ingen hest bryder ud fra sin placering .. går det stærkt, er der fart over feltet (de to .. udtryk kan i dagligsproget osse stamme fra cykelsport).
BKIL	Bom.S.131.
BCIT	Fart over Feltet i Folketinget. I Gaar kom man igennem 15 Punkter paa 2 Timer.
BKIL	JyllP.2/6 1954.9.sp.4.

II. Felt, et. *flt.* -er *ell. d.s.* + *ell. (ældre spr.)* -e *(se ndf.).* **1)** + hver af Dørene er deelt i to Felte. *Rawert&SGarlieb.Bornholm.(1819).23.* **3)** + *(jf.* Kul-, Malm-, Skud-, Skyde-, Synsfelt *(jf.* 885,38*)).* **4)** ‖ *overf.* + *ogs. om deltagere i andre løb.* Københavnerne vil blive præsenteret for det fineste Felt, der endnu har været til Start her i Byen. *Pol.19/11 1936.12.sp.6 (om cykelryttere til seksdagesløb).* Halvdelen af Feltets 24 *(cykel)*Ryttere bliver deciderede Sprintere. *NatTid.17/10 1951.9.sp.6.* + **5)** *(jf. bet. 4) i forb.* f a r t o v e r f e l t e t, *fart på.* Næste Morgen, Lørdag, var der stor Rengøring overalt *(: på skoleskibet)* .. der var Fart over Feltet. *Frikvarter.20/9 1946.5.sp.4.* Fra Hestesport .. der er ro over feltet, når ingen hest bryder ud fra sin placering .. går det stærkt, er der fart over feltet (de to .. udtryk kan i dagligsproget osse stamme fra cykelsport). *Bom.S.131.* Fart over Feltet i Folketinget. I Gaar kom man igennem 15 Punkter paa 2 Timer. *JyllP.2/6 1954.9.sp.4.*

The RET field in the ODSS

An arbitrary keystroke as the content of the RET field (e.g. an "r") automatically generates the text *læs:* 'read:' in both column forms (see Fig. 6.4.4.3-9 *II. fem*).

Fig. 6.4.4.3-9 The ODSS entry *II. fem* in data entry form (the RET field) and column form (the text *læs:*)

```
SEC    s ODS   =          PLUS        HOMB  II.  ODS              PLUS
OPSL   fem
ORDK     num.
ONR      2
PL       ||
SPLI     893,60
FORB     de fem sanser,
PLUS     +
HEOB     se ogs.
HENB     I.Sans 1.2.
ODS      =
SPLI     894,2
FORB     have (ell. være ved) sine (fulde) fem sind.
PLUS     +
BCIT     ingen som fem Sinde hafde .. skulde dette for en begyndt Krig
         ansee eller holde.
BKIL     Slange.ChrIV.1324.
BCIT     Jeg var .. uden Tvivl fra mine fem Sind.
BKIL     Bagges.(ABagges.JB.I.126).
ODS      =
PL       ||
SPLI     985,35
FORB     lade fem være lige,
RET      r
FORB     lade fem (ell. fem og syv) være lige,
HEOB     se
HENB     V.lige 4.2.
```

II. fem, *num.* 2) || *893,60* de fem sanser, + *se ogs.* I.Sans 1.2. *894,2* have *(ell.* være ved*)* sine (fulde) fem sind. + ingen som fem Sinde hafde .. skulde dette for en begyndt Krig ansee eller holde. *Slange.ChrIV.1324.* Jeg var .. uden Tvivl fra mine fem Sind. *Bagges.(ABagges.JB.I.126).* || *985,35* lade fem være lige, *læs:* lade fem *(ell.* fem og syv*)* være lige, *se* V.lige 4.2.

6.4.4.4 Field content visible in data entry form but suppressed in column form

There may be several advantages in being able to enter information one does not want to be visible in the final dictionary column. With the Compulexis system it is possible to suppress field content in three ways in the final dictionary column. In a dictionary project aimed only at the compilation of one particular dictionary, one may want to store information in one or more fields reserved for this type of latent information. The content of these fields will never appear in the column form: in other words, there is a need on the one hand for *general* field-code-based suppression of data. On the other hand one may also occasionally want to suppress information stored in a field whose content normally appears in the column form — in other words, ad hoc suppression. If a dictionary project aims at the compilation of several different dictionaries at once, one may want to furnish certain whole entries or certain field codes and contents with an extra code showing which of the dictionaries being edited concurrently the entries and fields in question belong to. One is thus working at several levels at once: to this end Compulexis provides a number of level-coding facilities; one can work at a total of five different levels with distinct numerical (1-5) and/or alphabetical (A-E) codes allowing all conceivable combinations of entries and fields for the different end-products. In addition there is an X code that can be used to suppress whole entries or field codes and contents for all the dictionary levels at once.

General field-code-based suppression

The content of the sorting key field, SORT, which is standard in Compulexis, will always be suppressed in the column manifestations (see Fig. 6.4.4.4-1 for the ODSS entry *Autogen-*).

Fig. 6.4.4.4-1 The ODSS entry *Autogen-* in data entry form (the SORT field) and in column form

SEC	ODS	PLUS +	HOMB	ODS	PLUS
OPSL	Autogen-				
SORT	autogena				
ORDK	i ssgr.				
BETB	til autogen 1 S.				
KOMF	se fx.				
BKIL	DaEngTeknO.				
FORB	**Autogen-boring,**				
FORB	**-brænder,**				
FORB	**-flamme**				
BKIL	(JVJens.A.(1916).63),				
FORB	**-skæreapparat,**				
FORB	**-skærer**				
HHEO	(jf.				
HHEN	Skærebrænder),				
FORB	**-skæring,**				
FORB	**-svejse**				
BKIL	(HHLund.Lørdag.(1933).20.				
BCIT	Autogensvejste Beholdere.				
BKIL	Krak.1917.1445),				
FORB	**-svejseapparat,**				
FORB	**-svejsebrænder,**				

(Fig. 6.4.4.4-1, continued)

FORB	**-svejser**
BETB	(specialarbejder.
BKIL	Socialdem.21/1 1916.9.sp.6),
FORB	**-svejsning**
BETB	(flammesvejsning; gassvejsning.
BCIT	Autogén-Svejsning.
BKIL	Krak.1912.1150.
BKIL	Dansk Standard.Nr.315.(1941).2).

+ **Autogen-**, *i ssgr. til* autogen 1 S. *se fx. DaEngTeknO.* **Autogen-boring, -brænder, -flamme** *(JVJens.A.(1916).63),* **-skæreapparat, -skærer** *(jf.* Skærebrænder*),* **-skæring, -svejse** *(HHLund.Lørdag.(1933).20.* Autogensvejste Beholdere. *Krak.1917.1445),* **-svejseapparat, -svejsebrænder, -svejser** *(specialarbejder. Socialdem.21/1 1916.9.sp.6),* **-svejsning** *(flammesvejsning; gassvejsning.* Autogén-Svejsning. *Krak.1912.1150. Dansk Standard.Nr.315.(1941).2).*

The GLDO only uses this facility with the QUE (query) field (see Fig. 6.4.4.4-2, where the QUE field contains an internal editorial remark).

Fig. 6.4.4.4-2 Illustration of general field-code-based suppression of field content in the GLDO

IHOM	IOPO duvebloth
IOKA	sb.
SEC	§
SBEB	blod af en due, dueblod
SBCI	Tac dufu bloth æller palumbis bloth æller turturis bloth oc drøp i the øghæn, thær bloth ær ouer ganget
SBCK	Lægeb. [AM].
SBCV	16,21
SEC	§
ELDK	til I. duve.
EJSA	Jf.
EJSS	vn.
EJSO	dúfublóð.
QUE	Her burde det kunne lade sig gøre at placere ejss efterfulgt af ejso, uden at skulle have været rundt om EJSA først
EJSA	# Jf.
EJSS	fsv.
EJSO	duvoblodh

duvebloth *sb.*
blod af en due, dueblod: Tac dufu bloth æller palumbis bloth æller turturis bloth oc drøp i the øghæn, thær bloth ær ouer ganget*Lægeb. [AM]. 16,21.*
[*til* I. duve. *Jf. vn.* dúfublóð, *fsv.* duvoblodh]

The ODSS uses general field-code-based suppression of field content for the fields ODS, KBST, KBSL and QUE (see Fig. 6.4.4.4-3) *Autobus*, fields ODS, KBST, KBSL, and Fig. 6.4.4.4-4 *Billedstof*, field QUE).

Fig. 6.4.4.4-3 The ODSS entry *Auto-bus* in data entry form (fields ODS, KBST, KBSL) and in column form

SEC s ODS = PLUS HOMB ODS PLUS

OPSL	Auto|-bus
ORDK	# subst.
SUBK	en.
PLUS	+
HHEO	(jf.
HHEN	III.Bus;
KBST	<
FRE	sj.
STIL	i alm. spr.
TID	efter ca. 1940).
KBSL	>
BCIT	Autobussen paa Strøget - En ny Dødsdom over Hestene.
BKIL	Riget.2/1 1913.3.sp.3.
BCIT	Sammenstødet mellem Ekspres og Autobus.
BKIL	Aftenp.24/1 1930.2.sp.2.
BCIT	enhver autobus eller automobil skulle kunne overføres *(: med en ny færge).*
BKIL	Vingehjulet.1950/51.66.sp.2.

Auto-bus, en. + *(jf.* III.Bus; *sj. i alm. spr. efter ca. 1940).* Autobussen paa Strøget - En ny Dødsdom over Hestene. *Riget.2/1 1913.3.sp.3.* Sammenstødet mellem Ekspres og Autobus. *Aftenp.24/1 1930.2.sp.2.* enhver autobus eller automobil skulle kunne overføres *(: med en ny færge). Vingehjulet.1950/51.66.sp.2.*

Fig. 6.4.4.4-4 The ODSS entry *Billedstof* in data entry form (the QUE field) and column form

SEC ODS PLUS + HOMB ODS PLUS

OPSL	Billed|stof
ORDK	# subst.
SUBK	et.
HHEO	(jf.
HHEN	-materiale *S).*
BCIT	et Anhang over det Nye Testamentes Billedstof.
BKIL	BerlTid.15/3 1850.4.sp.2.
BCIT	et omfattende Billedstof.
BKIL	Riget.19/5 1912.3.sp.7.
BCIT	Reklamer med Hensyn til Tekst, Billedstof og Komposition.
BKIL	Lov Nr.149 26/4 1933‡§2.
KOMB	(om forfatterret og kunstnerret).
QUE	Jvf. QUE sub "billedkunstnerisk"
BCIT	Uge-Revyen det moderne ugeblad .. billed-stof fra hele verden.
BKIL	Hjemmet.16/2 1954.29.sp.4.

(Fig. 6.4.4.4-4, continued)

+ **Billedstof,** et. *(jf. -*materiale S*).* et Anhang over det Nye Testamentes Billedstof. *BerlTid. 15/3 1850. 4. sp. 2.* et omfattende Billedstof. *Riget. 19/5 1912. 3. sp. 7.* Reklamer med Hensyn til Tekst, Billedstof og Komposition. *Lov Nr. 149 26/4 1933 (om forfatterret og kunstnerret). §2.* Uge-Revyen det moderne ugeblad .. billed-stof fra hele verden. *Hjemmet. 16/2 1954. 29. sp. 4.*

Ad hoc suppression of data

Besides the above-mentioned automatic suppression of text in the column printout, the system also allows ad hoc suppression of text in freely-selected fields. This is done after the field code has been selected: a hash symbol and space, "# ", are inserted before the content of the field. This enables one to record field-ordered information as part of the data without the information appearing in the column printout.

The GLDO uses this facility when using the fields IOVK, BØKK and SBCK to record information about a particular source group.

As mentioned above in Sections 6.2, 6.4.4.1 and 6.4.4.2, it is extremely useful to be able to split source references up into a constant component (the abbreviated reference to the title of the source) and a variable one (reference to the actual locus in the source) to obtain automatic checks on the source abbreviations. The division of source references into a constant and a variable part is not, however, suitable for one particular group of sources, i.e. charters, which are normally referred to simply by the date of issue followed by any information on scribal features or where the charter was printed — if it was printed.

So as not to lose the general advantages of splitting source references up for automatic checks on the constant component, and the benefits of automatic field code generation for the variable component, the editors have sacrificed the validity checks and conversion of the working abbreviation to the user abbreviation: these facilities are disabled by inserting backslashes, "\", around the source abbreviation "D" for charter; ad hoc suppression by inserting a "# " at the beginning of the field is otherwise not possible. IOVK, BØKK and SBCK in these cases thus always contain the working abbreviation "D" in the form "# \D\", without conversion to "Dipl." as the user abbreviation, while the normal charter source reference is placed in IOVV, BØKV and SBCV respectively. The content of IOVK, BØKK and SBCK thus becomes part of the data without appearing in the column manifestation. Another great advantage of this is that charter source references remain very easy to retrieve, as one can search on the content "D" under field codes IOVK, BØKK and SBCK (see Fig. 6.4.4.4-5).

Fig. 6.4.4.4-5 Illustration of ad hoc suppression of field content in the GLDO

IHOM	IOPO duvebrøthre
IOKA	sb. pl.
SEC	§
SBEB	betegnelse for personer tilknyttet en godgørende stiftelse i Roskilde (jf. KultLeksM.III.358f.)
SBCI	Erland foghet af delæ *(afskriverfejl for* dwæ*)* brødræ i Roskyld
SBCK	# \D\
SBCV	22/4 1437(DiplKbh.I.161,13, afskr. 1681)
SEC	§
SSGK	i forb.
SORF	duvebrøthre kloster *el. (elliptisk)* duvebrøthre
SBEB	om stiftelse
SBCI	wij .. forstandere i Dwebrøthre closter
SBCK	# \D\
SBCV	27/7 1429(Esrumb.248, Rosk.)
SBCI	A.T., fforstandher j Dwbrødhrekloster hoss Roosskildh
SBCK	# \D\
SBCV	5/7 1497(DiplLund.V.324,15)
SBCI	Jtem fatigæ folck i Dwæbrødræ ij marc
SBCK	# \D\
SBCV	11/5 1501(DiplLund.VI.23,16)
SEC	§
ELDK	til I. duve sb. (i relig. symbolik)

duvebrøthre *sb. pl.*
betegnelse for personer tilknyttet en godgørende stiftelse i Roskilde (jf. KultLeksM.III.358f.): Erland foghet af delæ *(afskriverfejl for* dwæ*)* brødræ i Roskyld*22/4 1437(DiplKbh.I.161,13, afskr. 1681).*
i forb. duvebrøthre kloster *el. (elliptisk)* duvebrøthre *om stiftelse:* wij .. forstandere i Dwebrøthre closter*27/7 1429(Esrumb.248, Rosk.)* A.T., fforstandher j Dwbrødhrekloster hoss Roosskildh*5/7 1497(DiplLund.V.324,15)* Jtem fatigæ folck i Dwæbrødræ ij marc*11/5 1501(DiplLund.VI.23,16).*
[*til* I. duve *sb. (i relig. symbolik)*]

The ODSS makes use of this facility to record *subst.* as the content of the part-of-speech field ORDK for nouns — where the dictionary text does not have *subst.*, but the gender markers *en* or *et*, registered as part-of-speech subclassifications under the information category name *subclassification* with the field code SUBK (see Fig. 6.4.4.4-6 *I. Auto*). For the sake of options like statistical checks on the distribution of various parts of speech throughout the entry material it is also desirable to have information on the part of speech of such nouns recorded.

Fig. 6.4.4.4-6 The ODSS entry *I. Auto* in data entry form (fields ORDK and SUBK) and column form

SEC	s ODS	=	PLUS	HOMB	I.	ODS	PLUS
OPSL	Auto						
ORDK	# subst.						
SUBK	en.						
BETB	automobil.						
PLUS	+ *ældre:*						
BCIT	Auto - Det kan ikke nytte at stritte mod Fremskridtet.						
BKIL	Ekstrabl.1/7 1905.1.sp.4.						

I. Auto, en. *automobil.* + *ældre:* Auto - Det kan ikke nytte at stritte mod Fremskridtet. *Ekstrabl. 1/7 1905. 1.sp. 4.*

Level-coding

Neither the GLDO nor the ODSS use level-coding, as there is no intention of compiling other dictionaries at the same time.

However, the use of the level code X might constitute an alternative to the ad hoc suppression method discussed above. The X code could also be used for ad hoc suppression of whole entries that were not fully edited at the publishing date for the dictionary material, and which the editors wanted to publish in a revised edition. These entries could thus still constitute part of the data, could be fully edited later and after the disablement of the level code could without difficulty be included in a revised edition.

6.4.4.5 Automatic alphabetization of entries

In the versions of the Compulexis system used for the GLDO and ODSS there is automatic alphabetization of the dictionary entries based on the alphabetical form of the headwords. This means that the person entering the data in principle has no need to think about the alphabetical order of the entries, as the system takes care of alphabetization by means of an index of the headwords. There may however be cases where it proves impossible to adapt the alphabetization rules available in the system to the alphabetization conventions of the dictionary. If it is discovered at the proof-reading stage that an entry has been inserted in incorrect alphabetical order, the problem can still be solved by means of the special sorting key field SORT, which is given a content that ensures correct alphabetization of the entry. In the system version used by the GLDO it is also possible to have the entries printed out in chronological rather than alphabetical order.

The GLDO has had no need of the SORT field. But the ODSS has found it necessary in four out of 313 entries to use the SORT field. Every case was a headword beginning with a capital letter and ending with a hyphen, i.e. the first element in a compound, and in every case there was also an entry with an identical headword without the capital and the hyphen, e.g. *Autogen-* and *autogen*. The system alphabetizes words beginning with capitals before words beginning with lower-case letters if the form is otherwise the same. It also ignores the presence of hyphens. Since it is an ODSS convention that words like *Autogen-* are alphabetized after words like *autogen*, automatic alphabetization gives the wrong result, i.e. *Autogen-* alphabetized before *autogen*. The solution was to give SORT the field content *autogena* for the entry with the headword *Autogen-*, i.e. to provide SORT with a word form which does not occur as a headword in the ODSS. The system then uses *autogena* as the basis for the sort, making the order of the entries correct (see Fig. 6.4.4.5-1, *autogen* and *Autogen-*).

Fig. 6.4.4.5-1 The ODSS entries *autogen* and *Autogen-* in data entry (fields OPSL and SORT) and column form

SEC s ODS PLUS + HOMB ODS PLUS

OPSL	autogen
ORDK	adj.
HIST	(ty. autogen, eng. autogenous; af gr. autogen■s, selvfrembragt;
STIL	fagl.).
ONR	1
BETB	vedr. en skære- og svejsemetode hvor smeltevarmen frembringes ved forbrænding af en luftart (brint ell. acetylen), idet der ikke tilføres andre stoffer.
BCIT	K. Kirchhoff.Haandbog i autogen Svejsning.
BKIL	bogtitel.1912.
BCIT	Teknologisk Institut - Kursus i avtogen Svejsning.
BKIL	Riget.26/8 1912.2.sp.6.
BCIT	autogen Skæring eller Flammeskæring.
BKIL	LSal.I.442.
PL	‖
BETB	som afkortning af Autogenskæreapparat olgn.
BCIT	Hvad man før måtte mejsle ud .. skæres nu *(: ca. 1935)* med autogen.
BKIL	Smeden.(1952).242.
PL	‖
FRE	(sj.)
BETB	som farvebetegnelse (vel med tanke på flammen).
BCIT	Blæst glas.Farver: Gule, grønne, blå, signalgrønt, grå, autogen, sort.
BKIL	Glarmesterhåndb.(1949).74.
ONR	2
FAG	(psyk.)
BETB	af egen kraft; selv-
BCIT	Det sidste nye Bidrag til Psykoterapien hedder autogen Træning eller koncentrativ Selvafspænding.
BKIL	CarlJørgensen.Psykoneuroser.(1932).156.
BCIT	Man bør gå frem efter følgende recept, plukket sammen af yoga, J.H. Schultz' "autogene træning" *(og)* andre afslapnings-eksperter.
BKIL	Bedre nerver.(1952).184.

SEC ODS PLUS + HOMB ODS PLUS

OPSL	Autogen-
SORT	autogena
ORDK	i ssgr.
BETB	til autogen 1 S.
KOMF	se fx.
BKIL	DaEngTeknO.
FORB	**Autogen-boring,**
FORB	**-brænder,**
FORB	**-flamme**
BKIL	(JVJens.A.(1916).63),
FORB	**-skæreapparat,**
FORB	**-skærer**
HHEO	(jf.
HHEN	Skærebrænder*)*,
FORB	**-skæring,**
FORB	**-svejse**
BKIL	(HHLund.Lørdag.(1933).20.
BCIT	Autogensvejste Beholdere.
BKIL	Krak.1917.1445),
FORB	**-svejseapparat,**
FORB	**-svejsebrænder,**
FORB	**-svejser**
BETB	(specialarbejder.
BKIL	Socialdem.21/1 1916.9.sp.6),
FORB	**-svejsning**
BETB	(flammesvejsning; gassvejsning.
BCIT	Autogén-Svejsning.
BKIL	Krak.1912.1150.
BKIL	Dansk Standard.Nr.315.(1941).2).

(Fig. 6.4.4.5-1, continued)

+ **autogen**, *adj.* *(ty.* autogen, *eng.* autogenous; *af* *gr.* autogenēs, *selvfrembragt; fagl.).* **1)** *vedr. en skære- og svejsemetode hvor smeltevarmen frembringes ved forbrænding af en luftart (brint ell. acetylen), idet der ikke tilføres andre stoffer.* K. Kirchhoff.Haandbog i autogen Svejsning. *bogtitel.1912.* Teknologisk Institut - Kursus i avtogen Svejsning. *Riget.26/8 1912.2.sp.6.* autogen Skæring eller Flammeskæring. *LSal.I.442.* ‖ *som afkortning af* Autogenskæreapparat *olgn.* Hvad man før måtte mejsle ud .. skæres nu *(: ca. 1935)* med autogen. *Smeden.(1952).242.* ‖ *(sj.) som farvebetegnelse (vel med tanke på flammen).* Blæst glas.Farver: Gule, grønne, blå, signalgrønt, grå, autogen, sort. *Glarmesterhåndb.(1949).74.* **2)** *(psyk.) af egen kraft; selv-* . Det sidste nye Bidrag til Psykoterapien hedder autogen Træning eller koncentrativ Selvafspænding. *CarlJørgensen.Psykoneuroser.(1932).156* . Man bør gå frem efter følgende recept, plukket sammen af yoga, J.H. Schultz' "autogene træning" *(og)* andre afslapnings-eksperter. *Bedre nerver.(1952).184.* + **Autogen-**, *i ssgr. til* autogen 1 S. *se fx. DaEngTeknO.* **Autogen-boring, -brænder, -flamme** *(JVJens.A.(1916).63),* **-skæreapparat, -skærer** *(jf.* Skærebrænder*),* **-skæring, -svejse** *(HHLund.Lørdag.(1933).20.* Autogensvejste Beholdere. *Krak.1917.1445),* **-svejseapparat, -svejsebrænder, -svejser** *(specialarbejder. Socialdem.21/1 1916.9.sp.6),* **-svejsning** *(flammesvejsning; gassvejsning.* Autogén-Svejsning. *Krak.1912.1150. Dansk Standard.Nr.315.(1941).2).*

6.4.4.6 Control of typography

A typical feature of dictionaries is the use of many fonts to distinguish between the different information types. A user would have great difficulty finding her way round a dictionary that used a single typeface for all items of information; such a dictionary would also have to be arranged quite differently from the ones we are used to if the uniformity of the typography were not to confuse the user.

The Compulexis system is supplied as standard with plain, italic and semibold fonts. Other fonts can also be ordered for individual dictionaries.

In principle the code for such a font is tied to a field code, so the choice of field code at the data entry stage produces a column manifestation in the font tied to the code. But cases may arise where it is impossible to split information into fields without font changes being necessary within the fields. For these purposes a single keystroke can change the default font of the field to another font and back again. Such font changes appear in both the data entry forms and the column forms.

In the Compulexis system a font code can also be tied to *combinations* of field codes; this typographical control option was not used in the GLDO/ODSS experiments.

Default fonts assigned to field codes

The format overviews for the GLDO and ODSS list default fonts for each field (see Figs. 6.2-1 and 6.3.2-1). It may be mentioned that the GLDO in particular had to order many extra fonts; but the ODSS also had special requests.

As mentioned above in Section 6.2, the wish to assign a single typographical convention to each information category was a contributory factor in the definition of the information categories in the GLDO. This proved possible for many categories. For information categories requiring typeface changes (cf below) a default type was adopted for use in the great majority of cases.

Field-internal font changes selected from the keyboard

The GLDO needs to have the option of changing or selecting fonts for certain information categories. Font selection is used particularly often in the information category SBCI, which has "plain" as its default font. Often it is necessary — partly to make a citation meaningful, partly to limit the space it takes up — to insert "editorial comments". These are printed in italics (see the first occurrence of the SBCI field in Fig. 6.4.4.6-1). The categories SBEB, SBCP, SKFO, ELDK and ELPI also need to change fonts frequently.

Fig. 6.4.4.6-1 Illustration of field-internal font changes selected from the keyboard in the GLDO

IHOM	IOPO duvebrøthre
IOKA	sb. pl.
SEC	§
SBEB	betegnelse for personer tilknyttet en godgørende stiftelse i Roskilde (jf. KultLeksM.III.358f.)
SBCI	Erland foghet af delæ *(afskriverfejl for* dwæ*)* brødræ i Roskyld
SBCK	# \D\

(Fig. 6.4.4.6-1, continued)

```
SBCV    22/4 1437(DiplKbh.I.161,13, afskr. 1681)
SEC     §
SSGK    i forb.
SORF    duvebrøthre kloster el. (elliptisk) duvebrøthre
SBEB    om stiftelse
SBCI    wij .. forstandere i Dwebrøthre closter
SBCK    # \D\
SBCV    27/7 1429(Esrumb.248, Rosk.)
SBCI    A.T., fforstandher j Dwbrødhrekloster hoss Roosskildh
SBCK    # \D\
SBCV    5/7 1497(DiplLund.V.324,15)
SBCI    Jtem fatigæ folck i Dwæbrødræ ij marc
SBCK    # \D\
SBCV    11/5 1501(DiplLund.VI.23,16)
SEC     §
ELDK    til I. duve sb. (i relig. symbolik)
```

duvebrøthre *sb. pl.*
betegnelse for personer tilknyttet en godgørende stiftelse i Roskilde (jf. KultLeksM.III.358f.): Erland foghet af delæ *(afskriverfejl for* dwæ*)* brødræ i Roskyld*22/4 1437(DiplKbh.I.161,13, afskr. 1681)*.
i forb. duvebrøthre kloster *el. (elliptisk)* duvebrøthre *om stiftelse:* wij .. forstandere i Dwebrøthre closter*27/7 1429(Esrumb.248, Rosk.)* A.T., fforstandher j Dwbrødhrekloster hoss Roosskildh*5/7 1497(DiplLund.V.324,15)* Jtem fatigæ folck i Dwæbrødræ ij marc*11/5 1501(DiplLund.VI.23,16)*.
[*til* I. duve *sb. (i relig. symbolik)*]

It should be noted that the Compulexis system considers features like interlinear letters, upper-case letters at lower-case heights etc. (see below, Section 6.4.4.8, for more details) to be font selection options. In practice it will thus be necessary to use font selection in many more information categories than would be required by a simple alternation between plain and italic type.

In the case of the ODSS, one can change to all the fonts listed in Fig. 6.3.2-1 from the keyboard in any field. Besides the fonts listed in Fig. 6.3.2-1, one can choose superscripts, i.e. raised, reduced-size numbers or letters (as in x^2), wherever required (see also Section 6.3.2).

Manifestations of typographical control in the ODDS can be seen in Figs, 6.4.1-1 a and 6.4.1-2 a.

6.4.4.7 Embedded fields

After the GLDO and ODSS formats had been drawn up, the Compulexis system introduced as standard a facility allowing items like the editorial comments mentioned in Section 6.4.4.6 to be placed in their own fields, with their own font codes, thus obviating the need to change typefaces in the middle of an information category. This facility is called an "embedded field" and involves entering an arrow-symbol where the embedded text is to be inserted in an information category. One then continues to write the text in that category. Then the text to be embedded is entered, furnished with its own field code. Not just one, but several fields in succession can be embedded this way as long as the necessary number of arrow symbols is entered in the field that is to contain the embedded texts. In the data entry forms the arrow symbols can be seen in the field that is to contain the embedded items, while the fields to be embedded are shown as the next field code plus the specified amount of field content. The column forms show the text which was assigned to its own field at the data entry stage inserted in its proper place, i.e. embedded.

The embedded field facility is used by the GLDO in certain cases for the information category SBCP. As described in Section 4.1.3, this category contains information on any variants of a (citation) word (in SBCI) from a parallel manuscript or from any earlier or later version of a text, plus a reference to the parallel manuscript or earlier or later version of the text. This information is best placed directly after the word in SBCI to which it refers. But to place this kind of special information in an editorial comment within SBCI would conflict with the principle that users with different special interests should have a free choice of the information categories they find relevant. A GLDO user who only wants documentation for the meaning of some particular word should be "spared" highly specialized information like which parallel manuscripts to a source have such-and-such a variant word form at the point in question. This is why an arrow symbol is placed after the word in SBCI one wishes to furnish with SBCP information, and the information itself is placed in the SBCP field immediately after SBCI (see Fig. 6.4.4.7-1).

Fig. 6.4.4.7-1 Illustration of the "embedded field" facility: the SBCP field embedded in the SBCI field in the GLDO entry on *dumbe*

IHOM	IOPO dumbe
IOKA	sb.
SEC	§
BSUB	fk.
BØKK	Hr Mich.
BØKV	155,30.
SEC	§
SBEB	(døv)stumt menneske
SBCI	hoo gyuær domæ♦ lam
SBCP	dwmme.1506, 1508, 1515
SBCK	PLaale. nr.
SBCV	26(ms.; jf. Komm.II.18)
SBCI	iæk war dwmbe ællær thighdhe
SBCK	GldBib.
SBCV	ms.211ᵛ,a(Fort. til 1Sam.)
SCKF	obmutui
SKFO	Vulg.
SBCI	han war badhæ blinder ok dumbe.Ok Jhesus gaff hannem badhæ syn ok mal.
SBCK	Sønd Ev.
SBCV	118,2
SCKF	caesus, et mutus
SKFO	Matt.12.22(Vulg.)
SBCI	*(Jesus)* Tigher som dommæ vidh *(under spotten)*
SBCK	Bonav. Medit.
SBCV	77ᵛ,b
SCKF	dumbe
SKFO	Sv.
SBCI	*thet war stort wndher hwn bleff ey død / fuld lenghæ bleff hwn en daamæ / Hwn kwndhæ ey see, ey hælder høræ, ey noghet ledhæmod paa sig røræ
SBCK	Hr Mich.
SBCV	155,30
SEC	§
ELPS	vn.
ELPO	dumbi,
ELPS	fsv.
ELPO	dumbe

dumbe *sb.*
fk. Hr Mich. 155,30.
(døv)stumt menneske: hoo gyuær domæ (dwmme.1506, 1508, 1515) lam*PLaale. nr.26(ms.; jf. Komm.II.18)* iæk war dwmbe ællær thighdhe*GldBib.ms.211ᵛ,a(Fort. til 1Sam.)*(obmutui *Vulg.*) han war badhæ blinder ok dumbe.Ok Jhesus gaff hannem badhæ syn ok mal.*Sønd Ev. 118,2*(caesus, et mutus*Matt.12.22(Vulg.)*) *(Jesus)* Tigher som dommæ vidh *(under spotten)Bonav. Medit.77ᵛ,b*(dumbe*Sv.*) *thet war stort wndher hwn bleff ey død / fuld lenghæ bleff hwn en daamæ / Hwn kwndhæ ey see, ey hælder høræ, ey noghet ledhæmod paa sig røræ*Hr Mich.155,30.*
[*vn.* dumbi, *fsv.* dumbe]

For the ODSS the embedded field option is practical for isolating items like comments, references and usage restrictions that it has hitherto been impossible to extract because of their position in the middle of a meaning specification or source citation or the like. After the supply of a system version with this option, the ODSS data was adjusted and these possibilities provided for (see Fig. 6.4.4.7-2 *Billedstof*, Fig. 6.4.4.7-3 *Feltarbejde* and Fig. 6.4.4.7-4 *Femdagesuge*).

Fig. 6.4.4.7-2 The ODSS entry *Billedstof* in data entry form (field sequence BKIL-KOMB) and column form

SEC	ODS	PLUS +	HOMB	ODS	PLUS
OPSL	Billed|stof				
ORDK	# subst.				
SUBK	et.				
HHEO	(jf.				
HHEN	-materiale S).				
BCIT	et Anhang over det Nye Testamentes Billedstof.				
BKIL	BerlTid.15/3 1850.4.sp.2.				
BCIT	et omfattende Billedstof.				
BKIL	Riget.19/5 1912.3.sp.7.				
BCIT	Reklamer med Hensyn til Tekst, Billedstof og Komposition.				
BKIL	Lov Nr.149 26/4 1933♦§2.				
KOMB	(om forfatterret og kunstnerret).				
QUE	Jvf. QUE sub "billedkunstnerisk"				
BCIT	Uge-Revyen det moderne ugeblad .. billed-stof fra hele verden.				
BKIL	Hjemmet.16/2 1954.29.sp.4.				

+ **Billedstof,** et. *(jf.* -materiale S*).* et Anhang over det Nye Testamentes Billedstof. *BerlTid.15/3 1850.4.sp.2.* et omfattende Billedstof. *Riget.19/5 1912.3.sp.7.* Reklamer med Hensyn til Tekst, Billedstof og Komposition. *Lov Nr.149 26/4 1933 (om forfatterret og kunstnerret).§2.* Uge-Revyen det moderne ugeblad .. billed-stof fra hele verden. *Hjemmet.16/2 1954.29.sp.4.*

Fig. 6.4.4.7-3 The ODSS entry *Feltarbejde* in data entry form (field sequence BETB-HEOB-HENB) and column form

SEC	ODS =	PLUS	HOMB	ODS	PLUS
OPSL	Felt|arbejde				
ORDK	# subst.				
SUBK	et.				
PLUS	+				
PL	||				
HIST	(efter eng. field-work; til I.Felt 1;				
HHEO	jf.				
HHEN	Markarbejde S)				
BETB	betegnelse inden for forskellige videnskaber ♦♦ for undersøgelser i marken (I.3.4.), i det praktiske liv, mods. teoretiske studier, laboratoriearbejde olgn.; indsamling af data.				
HEOB	(jf.				
HENB	Felt- S)				
BCIT	Ansøgeren skal .. forestå organiseringen af feltarbejdet under Grønlands Botaniske Undersøgelse.				
BKIL	Statstidende.28/5 1974.4.sp.2.				
BCIT	en fornyelse af skolernes feltarbejde.				
BKIL	Folkeskolen.17/10 1974.1985.				
BCIT	etnografisk feltarbejde.				
BKIL	Pol.2/11 1974.6.sp.4.				

(Fig. 6.4.4.7-3 continued)

Feltarbejde, et. + ‖ *(efter eng.* field-work; *til* I.Felt 1; *jf.* Markarbejde S*)* *betegnelse inden for forskellige videnskaber (jf.* Felt- S*) for undersøgelser i marken* (I.3.4.), *i det praktiske liv, mods. teoretiske studier, laboratoriearbejde olgn.; indsamling af data.* Ansøgeren skal .. forestå organiseringen af feltarbejdet under Grønlands Botaniske Undersøgelse. *Statstidende.28/5 1974.4.sp.2.* en fornyelse af skolernes feltarbejde. *Folkeskolen.17/10 1974.1985.* etnografisk feltarbejde. *Pol.2/11 1974.6.sp.4.*

Fig. 6.4.4.7-4 The ODSS entry *Femdages-uge* in data entry form (field sequence BETB-KBST-TIDF-FREF-KBSL) and column form

SEC	ODS	PLUS	+	HOMB	ODS	PLUS
OPSL	Fem|dages-uge					
ORDK	# subst.					
SUBK	en.					
BETB	uge bestående af 5 dage; dels om kalenderens ugedage, dels ↓↓↓↓ om arbejdsugen.					
KBST	<					
TIDF	(efter midten af 20.årh.					
FREF	især)					
KBSL	>					
BCIT	Ugens Søndage *(er)* afskaffet og erstattet med en 5 Dages Uge *(i Rusland, som led i kampen mod kirken).*					
BKIL	Finanstidende.1929/30.4.					
BCIT	5-Dages Ugen i de engelske Kulminer.					
BKIL	Information.3/5 1947.1.sp.5.					

+ **Femdages-uge**, en. *uge bestående af 5 dage; dels om kalenderens ugedage, dels (efter midten af 20.årh. især) om arbejdsugen.* Ugens Søndage *(er)* afskaffet og erstattet med en 5 Dages Uge *(i Rusland, som led i kampen mod kirken).* *Finanstidende.1929/30.4.* 5-Dages Ugen i de engelske Kulminer. *Information.3/5 1947.1.sp.5.*

However, in some cases it would have been useful to have some more field code names precisely for naming and thus uniquely identifying embedded text segments. For instance there is a practice in the ODSS of bracketing, within Bible citations in BCIT, references to any variants of a (citation) word found in other Bible versions. A BCIT from the entry on *Billedskærer* (Fig. 6.4.4.7-5) may be used to exemplify this.

Fig. 6.4.4.7-5 BCIT field with Bible variant information from the ODSS entry *Billedskærer*

```
SEC     ODS   =        PLUS        HOMB       ODS           PLUS
OPSL  Billed|skærer
BCIT    Hvad gavner det skaarne Billed, at en Billedskærer (1871:
        den, som dannede det) skærer det ud.
BKIL    Hab.2.18(1931).
```

It is conceivable that there could be practical reasons for recording this variant information as an embedded field; but for the sake of unique identification of this type of variant information *as such*, it would be good to have an independent field code for it, for example BIVA for Bible variant information; none of the existing field codes in the ODSS format can be used for this purpose without loss of a unique means of identifying the information, so it was necessary to give up the idea of using embedded fields in such cases.

6.4.4.8 Additions to the Compulexis standard character set

It is well known that dictionaries use many special characters — both alphabetical and other types. As standard, Compulexis is supplied with all the alphabetical characters necessary for the modern Germanic and Romance languages; in addition there are the characters found on a normal typewriter keyboard and the special characters that are most widely used in dictionaries. The system can also include the IPA alphabet for use in a special phonetics program. Over and above this, special characters may be ordered for use in the systems for specific dictionaries.

The GLDO required the following special characters:

- the possibility of placing a single point over a vowel (in order to observe palaeographical conventions for texts of the period the GLDO deals with);
- the possibility of placing a single point under a letter (to indicate that the reading of the letter in question is uncertain);
- the possibility of placing a "˚" above other letters than "a" (i.e. the Danish "å")(to observe palaeographical conventions);
- the possibility of indicating the ellipsis of nasals with a "~" above the preceding vowel;

- the use of the character "½" (because of its frequent use in measurements and prices in accounts and charters).

For the ODSS it proved necessary to introduce "ē" and "ō" for Latin transcriptions of Greek words in the HIST field (historical information). These characters have since become standard in the system. It was pondered whether an "e" should be ordered with both a macron and acute accent (also for Greek words). But since this character would only be used in very few cases, it was decided not to order it for the purposes of the experiment.

6.5 Conclusions on the data entry experiments

6.5.1 The GLDO

For the DANLEX experiment about seventy dictionary entries were input from the GLDO, representing various entry types in terms of

- size (short and long entries)
- parts of speech (nouns, verbs, adjectives etc.)
- types of words (concrete and abstract)

As far as the GLDO was concerned it was in an ideal position for using a dictionary editing system like Compulexis. At the beginning of the project a body of sample entries was available which had been compiled without any form of data processing in mind. These sample entries were at such a reasonably finished and well-thought-out stage that they could form the point of departure for reflections and decisions about the types of information an entry in the GLDO could or should contain. On the other hand the quantity of the sample entries was not so great that it was impossible to make changes in their structure for the sake of using as many of the facilities of the Compulexis system as possible.

As will be evident from this detailed review of the general and specialized facilities of the Compulexis system, the GLDO will benefit from using most of these facilities. From the GLDO's point of view it is

- the checks on field content, and
- the typographical control

that seem most likely to facilitate the editorial work. The GLDO operates with extremely unwieldy source abbreviations (typically containing references to works, editions, scribal features and dates) and the checking facilities for these (described above in 6.4.4.1) constitute a substantial labour-saving factor which will also lead to a more user-friendly documentation system. The wide-spread use in the GLDO of different typefaces for user-orientated distinctions among the different information categories in the entries will be simple to deal with (cf above, 6.4.4.4), while the field-internal font changes selected from the keyboard are a potential easy-to-use facility.

At the GLDO further work is being done with the Compulexis system aiming at

- more general experience of the system;
- possibly more advanced use of automatic punctuation;
- possibly more advanced use of field sequence checking.

This further work is being done with a view to the continued use of Compulexis in editorial work on the GLDO.

6.5.2 The ODSS

For the DANLEX experiment a total of 313 entries from the ODSS have been entered as data by means of the Compulexis system, and it has emerged in practice that the format drawn up was well-suited for containing this dictionary material, As mentioned in 6.1.3, the editorial rules for the ODSS already exist and have not been modified to suit the system. The system has proved flexible enough to absorb the complex ODSS data: this is primarily a matter of the possibility of using field-internal font changes selected from the keyboard, and of using embedded fields; but the system's automatic alphabetization facility has also proved very flexible. As will be clear from Sections 6.4.4.1 and 6.4.4.3, the ODSS has been unable to make use of all the options of the system, but this is due to the very specialized nature of the data and the supplementary status of the work — not to shortcomings in the system as such.

There have of course been doubtful cases as regards the way to record certain parts of the text; it has been possible to place questions about these in the immediate vicinity of the problematical points by means of the QUE (query) field, so that the ODSS editors have been able to decide on the solutions to the problems after being sent printouts of the data. A typical question has concerned the editorial presentation of the dictionary text; the use of the system to enter data with the format as model has mercilessly exposed the points where there has been editorial inconsistency in the order of the information types. This could have been done automatically, of course, if the ODSS had been able to make use of the facility for field order checking. But the system has helped greatly with the observance of editorial rules.

The column printouts represent the dictionary entries in their more or less completed form (cf Section 6.4.4.3) — although still with the exception of hyphenation. But the column printouts are particularly well-suited for letter proofs and critical proof-reading of the content.

In fact it cannot be said that there have been any disadvantages in the use of the system, compared with the previous non-computer-aided editing and drawing-up of the ODSS manuscript — only advantages: much improved data-checking facilities based on the use of the format and selective printouts of fields; less time spent producing and correcting the manuscript. The word-processing facilities have been a great advantage, and the extra work involved in data management requirements — the entering of field names and complete headwords with "|" separators in articles on compounds — is at least fully compensated in terms of time and toil by the advantage that the various text segments only in exceptional cases have to be marked for typographical features by means of field-internal font changes selected from the keyboard.

At present the ODSS editorial staff is continuing to work with great satisfaction with the available software, and is planning a sample fascicle of the ODSS containing about 550 entries, to be published in 1987.

6.5.3 The Compulexis system

It will be evident that the Compulexis system fulfils many of the requirements we stipulated in Sections 6.1.1 and 6.1.2. But the possibility of marking entry-internal hierarchies is still only at a rudimentary stage. It is true that the system has field types that can number text segments at several levels (cf Section 6.4.4.4 on level-coding); but basically a Compulexis text is simply a sequence of named fields without any indication of the beginnings and ends of higher-order structures. With printed dictionaries — for which the system is primarily designed — this is hardly of any great significance. Yet it often requires such complex rules for the generation of correct punctuation etc. (cf Section 6.4.4.3) that in practice the user has no clear conception of — and therefore cannot formulate — these rules. Here, however, the trial-and-error method can be used, since the proofreading of a column printout after implementing a set of trial punctuation rules can indicate the points where problems arise — and these can either be corrected generally in a new system version created for the job or by means of the PNC field.

But if dictionary data are to be stored in electronic information systems so as to provide other means of access than by headwords, a multi-level structure will be necessary. A text mark-up system observing the SGML standard (see Chapter 5) would be suitable for this.

7. COMPLEX DICTIONARY DATA IN DATABASE SYSTEMS

7.1 Introduction

In the preceding chapter we saw how a dedicated system for computerizing dictionary data satisfies the word-processing demands one can reasonably put to it. But the Compulexis system was developed with the production of printed dictionaries in mind, and therefore has limited scope for data management as such. The system only has search facilities designed for the control of data entered for a printed dictionary. Another characteristic feature of this system is that the entry structure of the dictionary must be completely predefined.

If one wishes to store dictionary data in a form that not only reflects the logical relationships between different types of information (and is not directly concerned with the form of presentation) but also allows experiments with different structures for different applications and provides facilities for retrieving various subsets of the stored information, one must have access to software that satisfies the general data management requirements of professional database systems.

In the following we first show how a taxonomy and formal description of dictionary data can be used to design a data structure suitable for storing the body of information in a dictionary in a database system. We then review a number of data management requirements and indicate their relevance to lexicographical work.

7.2 The structuring of data

7.2.1 The bracket diagram

To store lexicographical data in database systems one needs a rigorously structured description of the data. Such a description is a precondition for storing data in a way that yields the full benefit of a database management system's facilities for linking related information types in many different ways.

In Chapter 5 we arrived at the conclusion that a bracket diagram is useful for describing the interrelations in traditional dictionary entries. Here we will show how a bracket diagram for a given dictionary can be used as a starting-point for the work of structuring data to be stored in a database system.

As a specific example we use the entry structure required for *Gammeldansk Ordbog*. In Chapter 4 we demonstrated how the taxonomy has been used to describe information types in *Gammeldansk Ordbog* (the GLDO); and in Chapter 6 we used a format drawn up for working with the Compulexis system. Fig. 7.2.1-1 shows a bracket diagram of the entry structure worked out on the basis of this format (cf Section 6.2).

Fig. 7.2.1-1 Entry structure for *Gammeldansk Ordbog*

- Homograph marker (0,1)
- Headword (1)
- Coverage marker (0,1)
- Part-of-speech marker (0,1)
- Variant information (0,n)
  - Variant (1)
  - Variant literature reference (0,1)
  - Source information (0,n)
    - Variant source, title (1)
    - Variant source, locus (1,n)
- Reference (0,1)
  - Reference word (1)
  - Reference (1,n)
- Inflectional information (0,n)
  - Subclassification (0,1)
  - Inflectional marker (1)
  - Inflectional documentation (1)
    - Remark on inflectional form (0,1)
    - Inflectional form (0,1)
    - Inflection citations (0,n) [1>]

(Fig. 7.2.1-1, continued)

- Semantic information (0,n)
  - Overview meaning (0,n)
    - Overview, meaning number (1)
    - Overview, syntactic information (0,1)
    - Overview, meaning specification (1)
  - Full meaning (1,n)
    - Descriptive meaning (0,1)
      - Meaning number (0,1)
      - Syntactic information (0,1)
      - Phrase (0,1)
      - Meaning specification (1)
      - Reference (0,1) [2>
      - Documentation (1,n)
    - 0
    - Phrase meaning (0,1)
      - Meaning number (0,1)
      - Syntactic information (0,1)
      - Phrase (1)
      - Reference (0,1) [2>
      - Documentation (1,n) [3>
- Etymology (0,1)
  - Origin (1)
    - Loanword/word formation (0,1)
    - 0
    - Cognate words (0,1)
      - Cognates (1,n) [4>
  - Analogues (0,n)
    - Compare (1)
    - Language of analogue (0,1)
    - Analogous word (1)
    - Meaning of analogous word (0,1)
  - Literature reference (0,1)
  - Usage information (0,1)

- [1> Inflection citations
  - Inflection citation (1)
  - Source information (1)
    - Inflection citation, title (1)
    - Inflection citation, locus (1,n)
  - Original of citation (0,1)
    - Citation of original (1)
    - Language of original (1)
- [2> Reference
  - Cross-reference word (1)
  - Cross-reference (1,n)
- [3> Documentation
  - Meaning citation (0,1)
  - Parallel to meaning citation (0,1)
  - Meaning citation source, title (1)
  - Meaning citation source, locus (1,n)
  - Original of citation (0,1)
    - Original of meaning citation source (1)
    - Comments on original of meaning citation source (1,n)
- [4> Cognates
  - Language of cognate (1)
  - Cognate word (1)
  - Information on cognate word (0,1)
  - Meaning of cognate word (0,1)
  - Core meaning of cognate word (0,1)

In the diagram the hierarchical structure of the entry emerges clearly. We may further note that "selection" is necessary at two points (notated ⊕). In the meaning specification section one must either select a full meaning (with meaning specification) or a meaning illustrated by a phrase. In the section on etymology the origin of the word is indicated either by means of cognate words or information on loanword status or word formation.

7.2.2 Entity/relationship diagrams

Over the years, in connection with the work of structuring data for databases, various diagram types have been proposed for the representation of data in databases. Hierarchical databases use a tree-structure diagram, network databases an "owner-member diagram" (Maegaard/Ruus 1980); and for relational databases one may work with entity/relationship diagrams (Date 1986: 610-615).

Several lexicographical projects have now begun to use relational databases (CELEX 1986; Widell 1986; *The Oxford English Dictionary*, cf Section 5.7). Relational database systems often offer powerful tools (so-called "fourth-generation languages") for creating, updating and searching in databases. With this type of software it becomes possible for lexicographers to experiment on their own with various structures for their dictionary data. With a system incorporating a powerful high-level language for building up and using associative databases (Janning/Nachmens/Berild 1979) it has proved possible, for example, to teach students in the humanities without any previous knowledge of computing to create databases of linguistic material within the framework of a two-term course of three lectures a week.

As a basis for the construction of a relational database, one often makes an "infological" model of the universe one wishes to deal with in the database (Sundgren 1981). The model is represented by an entity/relationship diagram. Here one describes the various types of entities in the given universe in terms of their properties or attributes (Biedassek/Blumenthal/Lemnitzer/Storrer 1987). The links between the entities are called relations.

Fig. 7.2.2-1

				Taxonomy category
Headword (1)				Lemma
Inflectional information (0,n)	Sublassification (0,1)			Syntactic information
	Inflectional marker (1)			Inflectional information
	Documentation of inflection (1)	Remarks on inflectional form (0,1)		Administrative information
		Inflectional form (0,1)		Inflectional information
		Inflection citations (0,n) [1]		
Semantic information (0,n)	Overview meaning (0,n)	Overview, meaning number (1)		Semantic relation
		Overview, syntactic information (0,1)		Syntactic information
		Overview, meaning specification (1)		Content specification
	Full meaning (1,n)	Descriptive meaning (0,1)	Meaning number (0,1)	Semantic relation
			Syntactic information (0,1)	Syntactic information
			Phrase (0,1)	Possible context
			Meaning specification (1)	Content specification
			Reference (0,1) [2]	
			Documentation (1,n) [3]	
		Phrase meaning (0,1)	Meaning number (0,1)	Semantic relation
			Syntactic information (0,1)	Syntactic information
			Phrase (1)	Possible context
			Reference (0,1) [2]	
			Documentation (1,n) [3]	
[1] Inflection citations	Inflectional form citation (1)			Citation
	Source information (1)	Inflection citation source, title (1)		Source reference
		Inflection citation source, locus (1,n)		Source reference
	Original of citation (0,1)	Citation of original (1)		Citation
		Language of original (1)		Administrative information
[2] Reference	Cross-reference word (1)			Administrative information
	Cross-reference (1,n)			Administrative information
[3] Documentation	Meaning citation (0,1)			Citation
	Parallel to meaning citation (0,1)			Citation
	Meaning citation source, title (1)			Source reference
	Meaning citation source, locus (1,n)			Source reference
	Original of citation (0,1)	Original of meaning citation source (1)		Administrative information
		Information on original of meaning citation (1,n)		Administrative information

Fig. 7.2.2-2 Entity/relationship diagram of part of *Gammeldansk Ordbog* entry

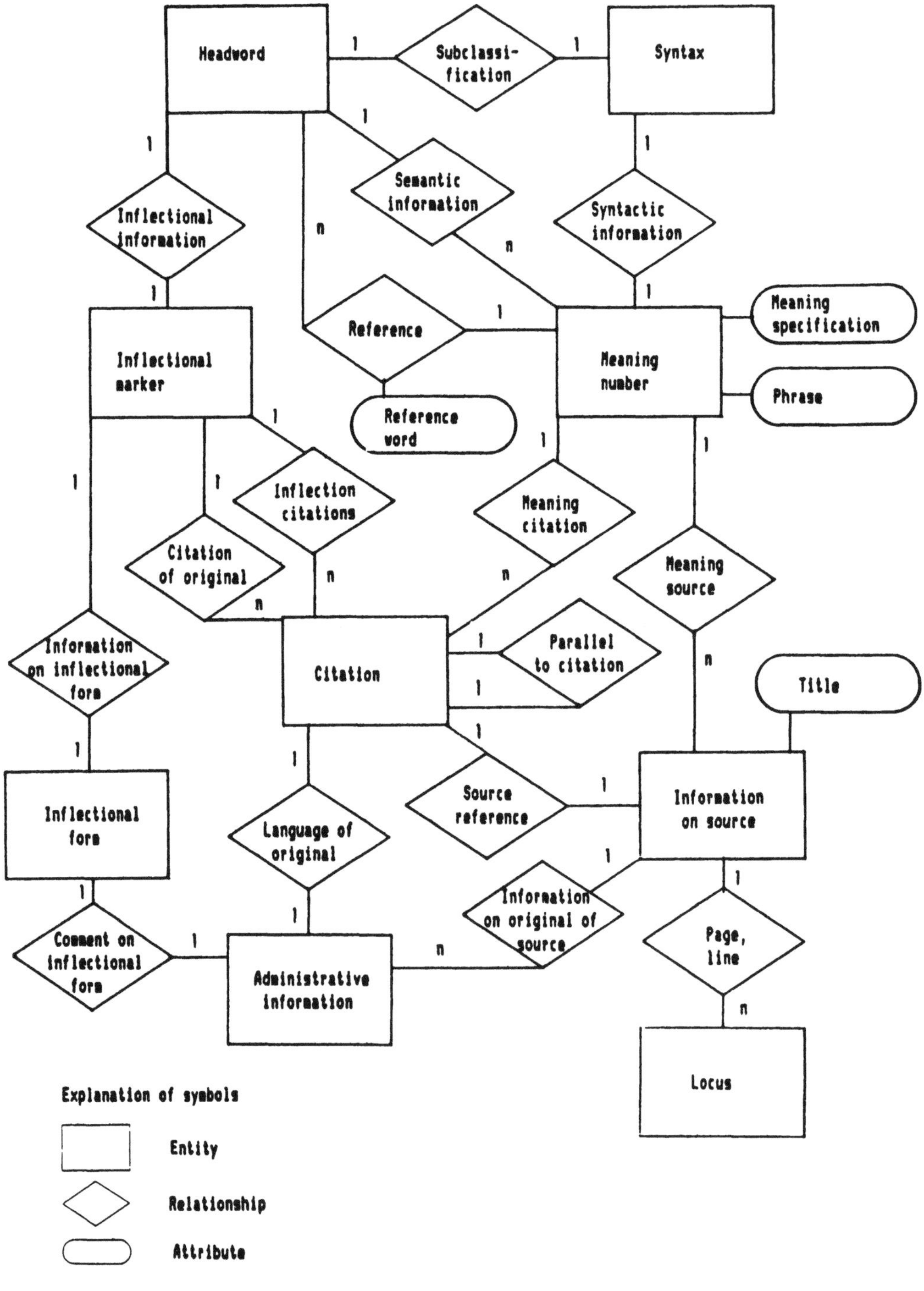

Figure 7.2.2-2 shows a model of part of the *Gammeldansk Ordbog* universe. This section consists of the headword, inflectional information and semantic information, as this part of the dictionary's universe is suitable for illustrating how one can use the taxonomy classification and the formal description in the bracket diagram to build the infological model. For convenience in comparing the bracket diagram and the entity/relationship diagram, the part of the bracket diagram used is reproduced as Fig. 7.2.2-1.

Grouping together information types belonging to the same taxonomy category (cf Section 3.3) tells us which entities we have and which properties exist in this universe. The subclassification of the categories and their localization in the bracket diagram structure show the relations between the various entities. In cases where the dictionary further subdivides a taxonomy subcategory, it may be useful to use the taxonomy subcategory as an entity. Examples of this are the entities *citation* and *information on source*. One of the things one wants to be able to see in an infological model of a scholarly dictionary is how citations and sources are treated in the dictionary.

Information on whether items are facultative, marked in the bracket diagram with (0,1) or (0,n), can be used to determine the entities the relations should originate in: a facultative information type cannot be the point of origin for a relation to an obligatory information type.

From the diagram one can also see the types of relations that occur, i.e. whether they are 1:1 relations or 1:n relations. The third type of relation — n:m relations — cannot occur in a bracket diagram, which is a tree-structure.

Fig. 7.2.2-1 shows the taxonomy category for every item in the bracket diagram. In the E/R diagram one can see that in many cases it is possible to combine information types from the same category in one entity. In the E/R diagram all the citations are collected in one entity: the function of each citation can be seen from the relations into which it enters. An inflectional form citation will be linked with the relevant inflectional marker through the inflectional citation relationship. A meaning citation (in "citation") will be linked with a meaning number through the meaning citation relationship, and to parallel citations through the parallel citation relationship. All citations are linked with source names and page/line references through the source reference relationship.

Similarly, syntactic information is collected in an entity linked to the headword through the subclassification relationship and to the meaning number through the syntactic information relationship.

Comparing the semantic information in the bracket diagram with the information on meaning in the E/R diagram, one can see that there has been some simplification: the overview of meanings and their related numbers, syntactic information and meaning specification do not appear in the E/R diagram. This is because this information is redundant. It can be extracted from the "full meanings" and located in the printed entry as a kind of user's guide to entries with many meanings and sub-meanings. When the information is stored in a database such overviews can be generated on the basis of a profiled search.

When describing the full meanings in the E/R diagram, one has the problem that *descriptive meaning* and *phrase meaning* have no obligatory information type in common that the other information can be related to. In Fig. 7.2.2-2 the meaning number has been made obligatory, and the other semantic information has been related to this number. If one wishes to keep the meaning number facultative one can use a model like the one in Fig. 7.2.2-3.

Fig. 7.2.2-3

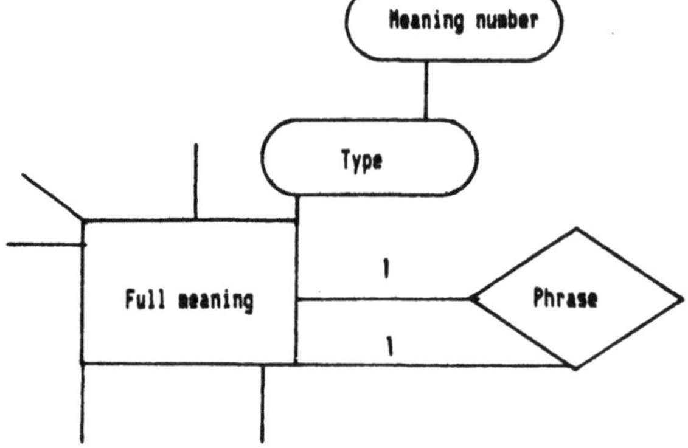

Here an entity — "full meaning" — has been introduced, involving both meaning specification and phrases. The property labelled "type" here can then indicate which. A "phrase" relationship has also been introduced for phrases occurring with a meaning specification.

The E/R diagram provides an overview of an important segment of the universe of *Gammeldansk Ordbog*. For future work on this dictionary with a view to storage in a relational database, the E/R diagram will have to be supplemented with etymological information and the rest of the "head". It will then be possible to use the E/R diagram as a basis for establishing tables in accordance with the conventions of the database system selected.

It will be essential when choosing any database system to have a clear idea of the requirements such a system must fulfil in order to be suitable for storing lexicographical data.

7.3 Lexicographical data management requirements

One overall requirement for any database software is that it should be easy to use, and that it should be possible to design special applications and facilities with as little professional programming assistance as possible. This is particularly true of database software for lexicographical data, as technicians with lexicographical expertise or lexicographers with technical expertise are rarely attached to dictionary projects.

Below we review a number of general requirements for lexicographical data management. The review is not exhaustive; it focuses on the facilities that are of special importance for dictionary work.

7.3.1 Data structure

(a) Reflection of relations between information types

Logical connections between different types of information stored in the database should be reflected, so that the relations can be used in the retrieval and presentation of data.

Example

Dictionary articles are often hierarchically structured; the structure must be represented in such a way that it is possible, for example, to present whole branches or parts of branches in the tree-structure together. Fig. 7.3.1-1 (from Vestergaard 1987) shows part of a tree-structure for an entry in the GLDO.

Fig. 7.3.1-1

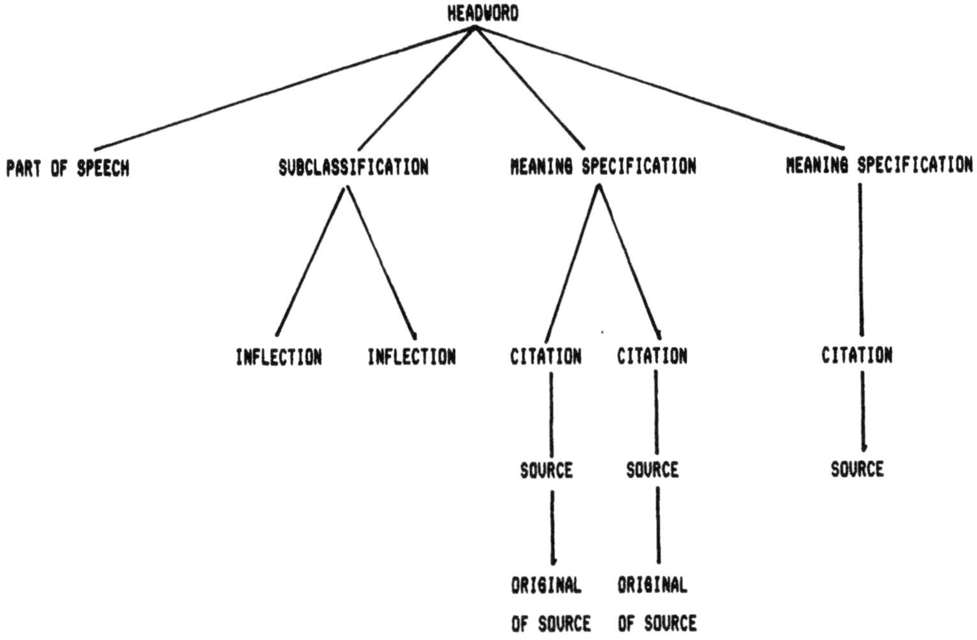

In screen displays and printouts the links between meanings and their related citations and sources should be clear.

(b) Modifications of data structure

Although in principle the entry structure will be fixed before data entry begins, there should be facilities for making changes in the data structure at any time. For example, it should be possible to add an extra level in a hierarchical structure.

There should also be facilities for:

- changing the order of fields;
- subdividing/merging fields;

- changing field names;
- changing the data types of field.

As an example of a change in the data type of a field we can mention changing from an integer field to a date field.

(c) No restrictions on quantity

Most database systems have quantitative restrictions, which have no great significance for address or customer registers etc. For dictionary work, however, the following demands must be made:

- no limit to the number of dictionary entries represented in the database (in practice a maximum of about a million will often be sufficient);
- no limit to the number of fields (information types) per entry;
- no limit to the number of characters per field (field length);
- no fixed field length (if a maximum field length must be specified, the maximum must not be reserved for each field regardless of how much of the field is used — similarly, space must not be reserved in the system for unused fields).

Dictionary data often include facultative information types (cf Fig. 7.2.1-1, the bracket diagram for the GLDO — information types marked 0,1). If the last requirement cannot be met (and it rarely can) one has a great deal of wasted space and problems with storage capacity.

7.3.2 Data entry and changes in the data entered

(a) Word-processing facilities

There should be word-processing facilities corresponding to those offered by Compulexis. These will not be reviewed again here, as reference may be made to Section 6.4.

(b) Checking facilities

Validity checks are needed in connection with data entry and modifications (for example, checks on field names, field content and field order, cf 6.4.4).

(c) (Semi)automatic generation or modification of field content

Cf 6.4.4.

7.3.3 Character set and fonts

(a) Open-ended character set
Ideally, additions to the character set should be possible at any stage.

For most dictionary projects special characters not in the ASCII character set are necessary. Special characters should be directly accessible, uniquely stored and capable of appearing on-screen and in printouts without special coding (cf 6.1).

(b) Facility for marking fonts
Ideally, the data should be structured so that font changes can be field-based. However, this is not the best solution in all cases, so there should be an option for marking text for font changes within a field (cf 6.4.4).

It should be possible to suppress font codes on screen, and they should not affect data retrieval. It should be possible to print out data in different typefaces.

7.3.4 Data transfer

(a) Importation of data from external files
It should be possible to "import" external data in machine-readable, structured form into the database. This might be data extracted from another database (created with the same or another database system); or data stored in files with information types marked by means of a system like Compulexis or an ordinary word-processing system. Ideally it should be possible to feed in both whole entries and parts of entries.

Example
This could be necessary when data exchanges are required or when hardware/software has to be replaced.

The greater the similarity between the data structuring principles in the file to be imported and the importing database system, the easier, of course, the transfer will be.

Without special programming, for example, it is impossible to transfer files from Compulexis to a database in which the structure is reflected.

(b) Transferring data to data files
It should be possible to copy the whole database or parts of it to external files, so that the data can be transferred, for example, to another database.

Example
The extraction of terms and citations from all records pertaining to a particular specialized area in a terminology base for transfer into a dictionary.

7.3.5 Searches

(a) Facility for searching on all information stored
Searches should not be restricted to a specified number of fields.

Example
During the editing process the editor will want to search on information types that a dictionary user normally does not need access to.

(b) Facility for specifying that certain information types are not accessible for searching
Although in principle everything should be retrievable, it is best in practice to be able to specify that some fields are not accessible for searching.

Example
It should be possible to display and print out internal editorial notes, but it may not be necessary to search for individual words in the notes.

Purpose
Savings on storage space and reduced response time.

(c) Facility for specifying that certain information types should not be retrievable by certain types of user

This possibility is especially relevant if the database is made available for on-line data retrieval by external users. This makes for differentiated access to data, depending on the user category, and can be realized by means of read/write protection facilities (cf 7.3.8, on data protection).

(d) Facility for defining a "stop-word" list

Depending on the nature of the dictionary, it may be desirable to draw up a list of "trivial" words not subject to search.

Example

In a terminology base it is not necessary to search for words like *of*, *for* or *on* as such — only if they are combined with other words.

Purpose

Storage space savings and reduced response time.

Ideally, it should be possible to define "stop-word" lists for particular fields. This would obviate the problem of "homography" between languages in translation dictionaries. (Normally, defining the English word *and* as a stop-word throughout the database would make it impossible to search for Danish *and* 'duck' alone).

(e) Browsing

It should be possible to browse through the database without searching for anything in particular.

(f) Facility for limiting search to one or more fields

For precise searches, it should be possible to define search profiles, i.e. specify that the search is to be restricted to one or more fields.

Examples

- Searching on *vi* (intransitive verb) in the part-of-speech field (*vi* is also the Danish 1st person plural pronoun).
- Searching on *mus* (abbreviation for 'musical') in the subject field (*mus* is also the Danish word for 'mouse').
- Searching on *mar* 'maritime' in the subject field (*mar* is also an English verb).

(g) Facility for searching on part of field content
By this we mean searching on one or more words in a field containing more than the word(s) searched for.

Example
Searching on one or more words in a citation field.

(h) Facility for searching on groups of words
(Either in a specified order, whether contiguous or not, or in random order).

Example

When searching on a multiword term like *separate system* one also wants phrases like *separate sewer system*, where the words specified for the search are separated in the text. In a search for *information retrieval*, responses are also required where the words are both separated and in reverse order, e.g. *retrieval of information*.

As a supplement to this it should be possible to specify how far the words may be from one another — to avoid "noise" in the form of irrelevant responses.

(i) Searches on parts of words
Searches on the first, last or a randomly-positioned element in a word (right/left truncation or masking).

Example
Searches on first elements in compounds, endings or a particular derivational form (for example, all words containing *tion* — not only as the last element).

(j) Searches on field names
Retrieval of all entries containing one or more given information types.

Example
Retrieval of headwords with definitions, internal editorial notes, etc.

(k) Searches with several criteria using logical operators (AND, OR, NOT)

Example

Retrieval of all headwords with a particular subject classification, but with no definition.

(l) Indifference to upper/lower case in searches

This facility is necessary for searches in texts, as it is otherwise impossible to search on words irrespective of whether they begin with capitals or small letters. But the opposite facility, the ability to distinguish when searching between upper and lower case, should also be available.

(m) Information on the number of responses to a search

This is really a statistical information type and possibly of most interest to the dictionary user wanting to limit further searching.

Example

In a term bank a search on *charge* or *absorption* could turn up many responses, as there is homography both within and between several languages.

If one is told, for example, that there are fifty responses to *absorption*, one can decide not to look at all the responses. Instead one can request the subset relevant to a particular subject classification.

(n) Further searches in the response list

This could be for limiting the search as described above.

Instead of starting a new search with several criteria, for example with *absorption* as headword and *nuclear energy* as subject, one could search on *nuclear energy* in the first fifty responses received (reduced search time).

(o) Storage and re-use of search profiles in a user-friendly command language

It should be possible to save frequently used and complex search commands as simple commands, where the object(s) of the search can be re-specified each time (macros with parameters), preferably with prompts (i.e. cue texts) to the user.

Example
Search commands using several criteria (see Item *k*) can be long and complex. By defining a macro they can be abbreviated to a simple command and the user need not be familiar with the syntax of the database query language.

Examples of commands in two different systems for retrieving the headword *absorption*.

Ex. 1

QUESTION absorption @ HEADW + nuclear energy @ SUBJ ?

Ex. 2

SELECT HEADW FOR HEADW = "absorption" AND SUBJ = "nuclear energy"

By defining macros one can abbreviate/reformulate the two commands and if required supplement them with a prompt to the user. The framed texts are the instructions from the user, the other texts are the system responses/prompts:

Ex. 1

Without prompts:

| HEADWSUBJ absorption; nuclear energy |

With prompts:

| HEADWSUBJ |

enter headword

| absorption |

enter subject

| nuclear energy |

Ex. 2

| FIND HEADW "absorption" IN SUBJ "nuclear energy". |

(p) Possible option of using a standard menu system or creating a customized menu system

Many database systems today offer the possibility of searching by choosing from a menu. A menu system presents the user with a number of search and presentation options. This facility is convenient for inexperienced users. Expert users as a rule tire of this rather slow form of search: so the system should allow for both "menu-driven" and "command-driven" searches.

A menu system for a term bank, for example, could be built up so that one is presented with the following options:

- subject
- source language
- target language
- area of search
- search with truncation/masking
  etc.

Search facilities in Compulexis

Many of the search facilities mentioned exist already in Compulexis (cf Section 6.4). The following of the facilities listed are available:

(a) Searching in all information stored
(e) Browsing
(f) Limiting search area
(g) Search on part of field content
(i) Search on elements of words
(j) Search on field name
(k) Indifference to upper/lower case

Apart from searches on "main entry", however, searches can only be done as time-consuming batch runs, where all the data are searched through sequentially and the result of the search is printed out on paper.

7.3.6 Sorting

(a) Sorting on all information types

In order to sort the responses to a search in a given order and produce sorted printouts it should in principle be possible to sort on the content of all information types.

In practice it is rarely relevant to sort items like internal editorial notes.

Example

Sorting on headword; producing a sorted list of all subjects dealt with (where each subject used only occurs once).

(b) *Sorting on several criteria*

Example

Producing a list of headwords sorted, first by subject, then (within each subject) alphabetically by headword.

(c) Definition of alternative sorting orders

When working with multilingual data, one needs to be able to define different sorting orders.

Example

German and Swedish ä are not alphabetized the same way:

German	*Swedish*
.	.
.	.
.	.
Ahne	hydrofor
ähneln	hårdhet
ahnen	hävert
.	högzon
.	.
.	.

7.3.7 Presentation

Presentation includes both on-screen display and printouts on paper.

(a) Presentation of one or more entries retrieved by searching

(b) Presentation of selected fields

Just as complex search profiles can be defined, it should be possible to define presentation profiles involving one or more fields (selective presentation).

(c) Storage and re-use of presentation profiles in a user-friendly command language

(Cf 7.3.5, Item *o*). Using the macro facilities of a system one can often define special user commands, so that the user has no need to know the system syntax for presenting responses.

(d) Facilities for varying presentation layout

Presentation with/without printed/displayed field names. For example, it should be possible to present data in the typographical form it will have in the printed dictionary.

(e) Presentation of response lists with new profile or new layout without renewed searching

In many systems, search and presentation profiles are specified at the same time, i.e. presentation with a new profile requires a new search, and this is time-consuming.

Example

A first presentation could show headword and subject. Then one might want entries dealing with a particular subject displayed/printed with all their fields.

(f) Reproduction of structure in printouts of selected fields

(Cf data structure, 7.3.1, Item *a*).

(g) Possibility of specifying that certain fields must only be presented along with one or more other fields

Example

- One might not want a citation presented without a meaning and headword.
- One might not want the original of a source presented without source, citation, meaning and headword.

7.3.8 Data protection

(a) Read/write protection

It should be possible to define differentiated access types for different users (cf 7.3.5, Item *c*).

Ideally, it should be possible to establish user-differentiated read/write protection at the

- database access level
- record level
- field level
- character level

Examples

Database access level:	Only users who know the password for the database can gain access.
Record level:	Certain users (e.g. external users) should not have access to records still in the process of revision; some users should be allowed to use, but not alter, the data.
Field level:	External users should not have access to fields with internal editorial notes.
Character level:	Typographical codes should be suppressed if the database is used for on-line retrieval by external users.

(b) Copy-protection
Certain users must not be able to extract the whole database or parts of it to a file that can be transferred to another system.

7.3.9 Statistical functions

(a) Printouts of frequency information
(Either for the database as a whole, parts of the database or for specific text segments).

Example
In order to define a "stop-word" list it might be desirable to have a frequency or rank list for words in the whole database or certain fields in the database.

7.3.10 Conclusion

The generally available database systems we have experience with satisfy these requirements to varying extents. DANSTATUS, the version of the STATUS II information retrieval system mentioned in Section 5.8, has been supplemented in particular in the character-handling area and thus meets most of the requirements. Of course other systems can similarly be supplemented in areas where they fall short of requirements. As yet we have not encountered a generally available database system with overall suitability for lexicographical work. The above list of requirements can be seen as an aid in evaluating the applicability of database systems to lexicographical work.

REFERENCES

Al, B. Ordinateur et Lexicographie. Université Libre d'Amsterdam, CNRS, UA Silex 382. Sept. 1985. À paraître dans: A. Zampolli (red.): Scritti in Onore di Roberto Busa S.J. (mimeographed).

Allén, Sture. 1981. SPRÅKDATA Lexibase System, An Integrated View of a Lexical Project. Preprint: European Science Foundation Workshop on the possibilities and limits of the computer in producing and publishing dictionaries, Pisa, May 19-22, 1981.

Amsler, Robert A. 1984. Machine-Readable Dictionaries. Annual Review of Information Science and Technology (ARIST) 19, ed. by Martha E. Williams. Published for the American Society for Information Science. Knowledge Industry Publications.

Biedassek, Thomas, Andreas Blumenthal, Lothar Lemnitzer, Angelika Storrer. 1987. Wörterbücher: Ihre Struktur und deren Modellierung. Lesebuch. Eine Sammlung schriftlicher Materialien für das Tutorial. Tutorial Maschinelle Lexikographie 9.3. bis 12.3.1987. Gesellschaft für Linguistische Datenverarbeitung e.V., Arbeitskreis Lexikographie. Bonn. (mimeographed).

Bock, A. 1979. Cykelterminologi. En terminologisk undersøgelse af en cykels hoveddele. Specialeafhandling. Handelshøjskolen i København.

Brustkern, J., K. Hess. 1982. The Bonnlex Lexicon System. In Goetschalckx/Rolling 1982:33-40.

CELEX Newsletter No. 1. 1986. Interfaculty Research Unit for Language and Speech. University of Nijmegen, The Netherlands.

Compulexis™. 1983. System Guide. "Moor's Edge", Charlton-on-Otmoor, Oxford.

Dahlberg, Ingetraut. 1976. Über Gegenstände, Begriffe, Definitionen und Benennungen. Zur möglichen Neufassung von DIN 2330. Muttersprache 2/1976. 81-117.

Dansk-Engelsk Ordbog. 1984. Jens Axelsen. Niende udgave. (Gyldendals Røde Ordbøger). København, Gyldendal.

Dansk-Engelsk Ordbog. ³1976. Hermann Vinterberg og C.A. Bodelsen. Anden reviderede og udvidede udgave ved C.A. Bodelsen. Tredje oplag med tillæg. I. A-Måttevæver, II. N-Åsyn og tillæg. Første udgave 1954-56. Anden udgave 1966. København, Gyldendal.

Dansk Etymologisk Ordbog. [3]1976. Niels Åge Nielsen. 3. reviderede udgave med et tillæg. København, Gyldendal.

Dansk-Fransk Ordbog. [3]1976-77. Andreas Blinkenberg og Poul Høybye. Tredje reviderede og forøgede udgave. I. A-L, II. M-Å. København, Nyt Nordisk Forlag Arnold Busck.

DANSTATUS. The Danish version of STATUS II, information retrieval system, Atomic Energy Research Establishment. Harwell, UK.

Date, C.J. 1986. An Introduction to Database Systems. Volume I. Fourth Edition. (Addison-Wesley Systems Programming Series). United States of America, Addison-Wesley Publishing Company, Inc.

Deutsches Wörterbuch 1-16. 1854-1960. Jacob Grimm und Wilhelm Grimm et al. Leipzig, Verlag von S. Hirzel.

DIN 2330. 1979. Begriffe und Benennungen. Allgemeine Grundsätze. Berlin, Beuth Verlag GmbH.

DIN 2331. 1976. Begriffssysteme und ihre Darstellung, Vornorm. Berlin, Beuth Verlag GmbH.

Dixon, J.E.G. 1983. A Rabelais Thesaurus. The Conceptual Glossary, the Principles of Taxonomy, and the Relations between Language and External Reality. ALLC Journal Vol. 4, nr. 2, 49-55.

Drozd, L., W. Seibicke. 1973. Deutsche Fach- und Wissenschaftssprache. Bestandsaufnahme - Theorie - Geschichte. Wiesbaden. Oscar Brandstetter Verlag KG.

DS/ISO 1703. 1980. Spændeværktøjer til skruer og møtrikker - Terminologi. Assembly Tools for Screws and Nuts - Nomenclature. København, Dansk Standardiseringsråd.

DSNA-Newsletter. 1983. Questionnaire: A Terminological Note: Multiword Lexical Unit, ed. The Committee on Lexicographic Terminology of The Dictionary Society of North America. Enclosed with the DSNA-Newsletter, Fall 1983.

EDB-ordbogen. [4]1979. Bjørn Eriksen, Hans Jørgen Helms, Mogens D. Rømer. Dataserien DS 2049. København, Jul. Gjellerups Forlag a-s.

Engel, Gert, Bodil Nistrup Madsen. 1985. DANTERM. TermNet News 12-1985. Journal of the International Network for Terminology (TermNet). Special Issue on the Nordic Countries, ed. Heribert Picht, Jennifer Draskau. 8-10. Wien, Infoterm.

Felber, H. 1984. Terminology Manual. General Information Programme and UNISIST. International Information Centre for Terminology. Paris, Unesco, Infoterm.

FORMEX. 1985. Formalized Exchange of Electronic Publications: Standard generalized mark-up language (SGLM) as described in Appendix B of the FORMEX manual. Luxembourg, Office for Official Publications of the European Communities.

Frandsen, Lene. 1982. Definition. Objekter, metoder og regler, med terminologisk inventar for ventilation og luftkonditionering. ARK 15. Det erhvervssproglige Fakultet, Handelshøjskolen i København.

Gammeldansk Ordbog. In preparation by Det danske Sprog- og Litteraturselskab, København.

GLDO = Gammeldansk Ordbog.

Goetschalckx, J., L. Rolling (ed.). 1982. Lexicography in the Electronic Age. Proceedings of a Symposium held in Luxembourg, 7-9 July 1981. Amsterdam, New York, Oxford, North-Holland Publishing Company.

Grolier's Encyclopedia. 1986. Bamburg, Connecticut, USA, Grolier Incorporated.

Grundt, Lars Otto. 1983. En større norsk-fransk ordbok. Nordisk Forskersymposium i datamatunderstøttet leksikografi, aug. 1982. SOM 3, Sprog og Mennesker, ed. by Henrik Holmboe. Aarhus Universitet, Institut for Lingvistik.

Hartmann, R.R.K. (ed.). 1983. Lexicography: Principles and Practice. London, New York, Academic Press.

Hartmann, R.R.K. (ed.). 1984. LEXeter '83 Proceedings. Papers from the International Conference on Lexicography at Exeter, 9-12 September 1983. (Lexicographica. Series Maior 1). Tübingen, Max Niemeyer Verlag.

Hausmann, F.J., O. Reichmann, H.E. Wiegand, L. Zgusta. 1984. Konzeption zu einem internationalen Handbuch der Lexikographie. Studien zur neuhochdeutschen Lexikographie IV, hg. von H.E. Wiegand, 487-506. (Germanistische Linguistik 1-3/83). Hildesheim, Zürich, New York, Georg Olms Verlag.

Hess, K., J. Brustkern, W. Lenders. 1983. Maschinenlesbare deutsche Wörterbücher. Dokumentation, Vergleich, Integration. (Sprache und Information. Beiträge zur philologischen und linguistischen Datenverarbeitung, Informatik und Informationswissenschaft 6, hg. von István Bátori, Walther von Hahn, Rainer Kuhlen, Winfried Lenders, Wolfgang Putschke, Hans Jochen Schneider, Harald Zimmermann). Tübingen, Max Niemeyer Verlag.

Higgins, David A. 1979. Program Design and Construction. Englewood NJ, Prentice-Hall.

Hjorth, Ebba. 1984. Rapport til Statens Humanistiske Forskningsråd over Projektet "Analyse af informationerne indeholdt i danske ordbogsartikler og udarbejdelse af et standardformat egnet til elektronisk databehandling". Journal nr. 5.25.35.00 (mimeographed).

Hjorth, Ebba. 1985. Ordbogsarbejde og EDB. Humaniora 6, ed. by Sven T. Achen. 71-76. Copenhagen, Forskningssekretariatet.

Hjorth, Ebba. 1986. Leksikografisk onomastik og onomastisk leksikografi. Mange bække små, ed. by Vibeke Dalberg, Gillian Fellows-Jensen, 95-109. (Navnestudier Nr. 27). København. C.A. Reitzels Forlag.

Hultin, Neil C., Harry M. Logan. 1984. The New Oxford English Dictionary Project at Waterloo. Dictionaries. Journal of the Dictionary Society of North America 6. 128, 183-198.

ISO 8879. 1986. International Standard: Information Processing - Text and office systems - Standard Generalized Markup Language (SGML). Geneva, International Organization for Standardization.

ISO/R 1087. 1969. Vocabulary of terminology. Switzerland, International Organization for Standardization.

Jacobsen, Jane Rosenkilde. 1984. Rapport til Statens Humanistiske Forskningsråd over det videre arbejde med projektet "Analyse af informationerne indeholdt i danske ordbogsartikler og udarbejdelse af et standardformat egnet til elektronisk databehandling". Journal nr. 5.25.35.00 (mimeographed).

Janning, Marianne, Sam Nachmens, Stig Berild. 1979. CS4, Introduktion til associativa databaser och CS4-systemet. Lund, Studentlitteratur.

Jensen, K., N. Wirth. 1985. Pascal User Manual and Report. New York, Berlin, Heidelberg, Tokyo. Springer Verlag.

Jysk Ordbog. In preparation by Aarhus Universitets Institut for jysk Sprog- og Kulturforskning.

Kipfer, Barbara Ann. 1983. Computer Applications in Lexicography: A Bibliography. Dictionaries. Journal of the Dictionary Society of North America 4. 202-237.

Kipfer, Barbara Ann. 1984. Workbook on Lexicography. A Course for Dictionary Users with a Glossary of English Lexicographical Terms by Jennifer Robinson. (Exeter Linguistic Studies 8). Exeter, University of Exeter.

Knowles, F.E. 1983. Towards the machine dictionary. In Hartmann 1983: 181-194.

Kocourek, R. 1979. Lexical phrases in terminology. Travaux de Terminologie. Quebec, GIRSTERM, Université Laval.

Landau, Sidney I. 1984. Dictionaries. The Art and Craft of Lexicography. New York, the Scribner Press.

LDOCE = Longman Dictionary of Contemporary English.

Lenoch, H. 1971-72. Klassifikationssystem. Verzeichnis der Haupt- und Untergruppen, erstellt für das Terminologiebüro der Kommission der europäischen Gemeinschaften. Ergänzt 1974/75. Luxembourg.

Longman Dictionary of Contemporary English. 1978. Comp. by P. Procter et al. Harlow, London, Longman.

Lyons, John. 1977. Semantics. Cambridge, London, New York, Melbourne, Cambridge University Press.

Madsen, Bodil Nistrup. 1986. Danish Projects within the Field of Computational Lexicography. In Proceedings of the Workshop "On Automating the Lexicon", 19-23 May 1986, Marina di Grosseto, Italy.

Maegaard, Bente, Hanne Ruus. 1980. A Linguistic Data Base for Frequency Studies in Modern Danish. Nordic Journal of Linguistics 3. 131-146.

Manley, James, Jane Jacobsen, Viggo Hjørnager Pedersen. Forthcoming 1987. Telling Lies Efficiently: Terminology and the Microstructure in the Bilingual Dictionary. Symposium on Lexicography III. Proceedings of the Third International Symposium on Lexicography May 14-16, 1986 at the University of Copenhagen, ed. by Karl Hyldgaard-Jensen, Arne Zettersten. (Lexicographica. Series Maior 19). Tübingen, Max Niemeyer Verlag.

MATER. 1980. DIN-Vornorm 2341: Magnetband-Austauschformat für terminologische/lexikographische Daten - MATER.

MATER. 1982. Draft Proposal ISO/DP 6156 E (4th DP): Magnetic Tape Exchange Format for Terminological/Lexicographical Records (MATER).

MATER. 1984. Draft International Standard ISO/DIS 6156: Magnetic Tape Exchange Format for Terminological/Lexicographical Records (MATER).

MATER. 1985. Draft International Standard ISO/DIS 6156: Magnetic Tape Exchange Format for Terminological/Lexicographical Records (MATER).

Michiels, A., J. Noël. 1984. The pro's and con's of a controlled defining vocabulary in a learner's dictionary. In Hartmann 1984: 385-394.

Midtvedt, Rune. 1983. STRILEK-Format for leksikalsk database. Seminar om datamaskinstøtta leksikografi og terminologi, Uppsala, 5. og 6. oktober 1983. NOTED, Norske terminologidata. Rapportserie 3. Universitetet i Bergen, Norges Handelshøyskole. Bergen.

Møller, Birte. 1985. Dansk/fransk spildevandsterminologi. EK-speciale. København, Handelshøjskolen.

The (New) Collins Concise Dictionary of the English Language. 1982. Comp. by W.T. McLeod. London, Glasgow, Collins.

Norling-Christensen, Ole. 1982. Commercial Lexicography in the Electronic Age. In Goetschalckx/Rolling 1982: 211-219.

Norling-Christensen, Ole. 1983. Røde Ordbøger i Skolerne. Upubliceret spørgeskemaundersøgelse af folkeskolens og gymnasiets brug af engelske, tyske og franske ordbøger.

Nudansk Ordbog. ^{12}1984. 12. reviderede og forøgede udgave ved Chr. Becker-Christensen, Lars Heltoft, Carol Henriksen, Pia Riber Petersen, Peter Widell. I. A-K, II. L-Å. København, Politikens Forlag A/S.

ODS = Ordbog over det danske sprog.

ODSS = Supplement til Ordbog over det danske Sprog.

Ømålsordbogen. In preparation by Københavns Universitets Institut for Dansk Dialektforskning.

Ordbog over det danske Sprog, 1-28. 1918-1956. Udgivet af Det danske Sprog- og Litteraturselskab. [4]1981-1983. København, Gyldendal.

The Oxford English Dictionary. 1933. Being a Corrected Re-Issue with an Introduction, Supplement, and Bibliography of A New English Dictionary on Historical Principles. I-XII. Edited by James A.H. Murray, Henry Bradley, W.A. Craigie, C.T. Onions. Oxford, Clarendon Press. A Supplement to the Oxford English Dictionary. 1972-1986. I-IV. Edited by R.W. Burchfield. Oxford, Clarendon Press.

Picht, H. 1983. Terminologiens principper og metoder. Språk i Norden, redigert av Else Bojsen, Mikael Reuter, Ståle Løland, Catharina Grünbaum, 51-69. (Nordisk Språksekretariats Skrifter 2). Arlöv, J.W. Cappelens Forlag A.S., Esselte Studium, Gyldendal.

Proceedings of the ESF/IAI-Conference on "Standardization in Computerized Lexicography", Saarbrücken, 15th-17th October 1986. Forthcoming. Sprache und Datenverarbeitung (SDV). (Exact title, editor and volume as yet unknown).

Proceedings of the Workshop "On Automating the Lexicon", 19-23 May 1986, Marina di Grosseto, Italy. Forthcoming. (Exact title, editor and publisher as yet unknown).

Retskrivningsordbogen. 1986. Dansk Sprognævn. Copenhagen, Gyldendal.

Robinson, R. 1962. Definition. Oxford, Clarendon Press.

Roget's Thesaurus of English Words and Phrases. 1974. New Edition Completely Revised, Modernized and Abridged by Robert A. Dutch. Harmondsworth, Penguin Books.

Ruus, Hanne. 1981. Ordbøger for fremtiden. De nordiske datalingvistikkdagene 1981. Foredrag fra en konferanse på Universitetssentret på Dragvoll, 22.-23. oktober 1981, utgitt av Eirik Lien, 149-153.

Ruus, Hanne. 1983. A case for Formal Descriptions of Dictionary Data. Nordisk Forskersymposium i datamatunderstøttet leksikografi, aug. 1982. SOM 3, Sprog og Mennesker, ed. by Henrik Holmboe. Aarhus Universitet, Institut for Lingvistik.

Schaeder, B. 1981. Lexikographie als Theorie und Praxis. (Reihe Germanistische Linguistik 34, hg. von Helmut Henne, Horst Sitta, H.E. Wiegand). Tübingen, Max Niemeyer Verlag.

Sherman, D. 1974. A New Computer Format for Webster's Seventh Collegiate Dictionary. Computers and the Humanities 8. 21-26.

Simpson, J.A. 1986. The New Oxford English Dictionary Project: A New Dimension in Lexicography. Paper to 13th International ALLC Conference, Norwich UK.

Smith, Joan M. 1986. The Standard Generalized Markup Language. Paper to 13th International ALLC Conference, Norwich UK.

Sterkenburg, P. van, W. Martin, B. Al. 1982. A New Van Dale Project: Bilingual Dictionaries on One and the Same Monolingual Basis. In Goetschalckx/Rolling 1982: 221-237.

Sundgren, Bo. 1981. Databaser och datamodeller. Lund, Studentlitteratur.

Supplement til Ordbog over det danske Sprog. In preparation by Det danske Sprog- og Litteraturselskab, København.

Urdang, Laurence. 1984. A Lexicographer's adventures in computing. Dictionaries. Journal of the Dictionary Society of North America 6. 150-165.

Vestergaard, Bodil. 1987. Undersøgelse af databasesystemer til ordbøger. LAMBDA Nr 2. Institut for Datalingvistik, Handelshøjskolen i København.

Vollnhals, Otto. 1984. Utilization of a commercial linguistic data-basesystem for electronic storage and automated production of dictionaries. In Hartmann 1984: 430-434.

Webster's Third New International Dictionary. 1961/1976. Comp. by P.B. Gove. Springfield/Massachusetts, Merriam.

Weinberger, Ota. 1970. Definition. Rechtslogik. Forschungen aus Staat und Recht 13. 249-273.

Weiner, Edmund. 1985. The New Oxford English Dictionary. ALLC Bulletin Vol. 13, nr. 2. 8-10.

Weiner, Edmund. 1986. Standardization and The New Oxford English Dictionary. Paper to the ESF/IAI Conference on Standardization in Computerized Lexicography, Saarbrücken 15th-17th October 1986. Forthcoming. (Exact title, editor and volume as yet unknown).

Widell, Peter. 1986. Semantisk strukturering af definerende ordforråd. Bilag til ansøgning til Statens Humanistiske Forskningsråd.

Wiegand, H.E. 1981. Pragmatische Informationen in neuhochdeutschen Wörterbüchern. Ein Beitrag zur praktischen Lexikologie. Studien zur neuhochdeutschen Lexikographie I, hg. von H.E. Wiegand. 139-271. (Germanistische Linguistik 3-4/79). Hildesheim, Zürich, New York, Georg Olms Verlag.

Wiegand, H.E. 1985. Eine neue Auffassung der sog. lexikographischen Definition. Symposium on Lexicography II. Proceedings of the Second International Symposium on Lexicography May 16-17, 1984 at the University of Copenhagen, ed. by Karl Hyldgaard-Jensen, Arne Zettersten. 15-99. (Lexicographica. Series Maior 5). Tübingen, Max Niemeyer Verlag.

Wilton, Murray T. 1978. The Canadian Dictionary: An Experiment in Automated Lexicography. Vingt-cinq ans de linguistique au Canada: Hommage à Jean-Paul Vinay par ses anciens élèves, publication dirigée par G. Rondeau, G. Bibeau, G. Gagné, G. Taggart. 399-414. Montréal, Centre Educatif et Culturel.

Wüster, Eugen. 1985. Einführung in die Allgemeine Terminologielehre und Terminologische Lexikographie. Hersg. von Univ.-Prof. Dipl.-Ing. Dr. L. Bauer. 2. edition. Copenhagen, The LSP Centre, UNESCO ALSED LSP NETWORK, The Copenhagen School of Economics.

Zgusta, Ladislav. 1971. A Manual of Lexicography. The Hague, Mouton.

ZüriLEX '86 Proceedings. Forthcoming. EURALEX International Congress, 9-14 September 1986, Zürich, Switzerland. Tübingen, A. Francke. (Exact title and editor as yet unknown).

RESUME FRANÇAIS

Le début du 1er chapitre (pp. 1-3) est un compte rendu de la manière dont l'emploi d'ordinateurs a donné des possibilités nouvelles au travail lexicographique: la collaboration et l'échange de données entre divers projets lexicographiques, entre les rédactions lexicographiques et les maisons d'édition et entre les auteurs et les utilisateurs des dictionnaires. Les auteurs du présent ouvrage, le groupe interprofessionnel et interinstitutionnel DANLEX, ont voulu améliorer ces possibilités. Les outils descriptifs présentés peuvent contribuer au développement d'un système informatique pour le travail lexicographique, système qui sera à la fois flexible et général.

L'échange de données lexicographiques ne peut se faire que si celles-ci sont décrites d'une manière homogène. A cet effet, il nous faut un système de classification, une typologie, applicable à toutes sortes de dictionnaires, ainsi que des méthodes qui permettent une description formelle de la structure de chaque oeuvre lexicographique.

Beaucoup d'autres chercheurs ont déjà décrit et classé des dictionnaires en vue de traitement des données par ordinateur. Cependant, le présent travail a un but plus large et plus profond. Nous généralisons les catégories dans une <u>taxinomie</u>, qui comprendra une vaste gamme de dictionnaires, et nous vérifions la valeur descriptive de cette taxinomie en l'appliquant à des types de dictionnaires très différents. Ensuite, nous examinons des méthodes destinées à la description du <u>format</u> d'un dictionnaire, c'est-à-dire la partie formelle de ses règles de rédaction, présentée sous la forme d'un sous-ensemble structuré des catégories de la taxinomie; de telles descriptions pourront notamment servir à la conversion des dictionnaires imprimés en structures de base de données et vice versa. Enfin, dans deux chapitres, nous montrons comment des données lexicographiques, après description et structuration, peuvent être enregistrées et stockées par ordinateur, et nous discutons des conditions à imposer au logiciel destiné au traitement des données lexicographiques.

Le 2ᵉ chapitre (pp. 4-28) a pour sujet les outils descriptifs métalexicographiques. La métalexicographie (théorie et méthodologie de la lexicographie) souffre de problèmes terminologiques. Il arrive que la même notion s'exprime par des termes différents, et inversement, que différents auteurs utilisent le même terme pour des notions qui ne sont que partiellement identiques. Cet état des choses s'explique par le fait que les notions et les termes de la lexicographie nous viennent d'un nombre toujours croissant d'écoles et de disciplines linguistiques, y compris la linguistique computationnelle.

Dans la littérature lexicographique, on trouve beaucoup d'exemples de classifications et de descriptions de données lexicographiques. Certains d'entre eux seront soumis à des analyses comparatives dans la partie suivante; nous avons choisi des exemples qui nous permettent à la fois d'illustrer la diversité de ces descriptions et de discuter des causes de cette diversité:

Dictionnaires sémasiologiques:

BONNLEX / MDW (Brustkern/Hess 1982; Hess/Brustkern/Lenders 1983), une structure de base de données, qui résume plusieurs dictionnaires/glossaires allemands, monolingues, synchrones et détectables par une machine;

L'essai de Schaeder (1981) d'une microstructure lexicale, destinée à la production électronique d'un dictionnaire monolingue, synchrone, mais contenant aussi des renseignements de linguistique historique;

The Longman Dictionary of Contemporary English (LDOCE):
a) introduction informelle et détaillée pour utilisateurs de dictionnaires inexpérimentés (LDOCE 1978);
b) introduction formelle et sommaire pour utilisateurs de dictionnaires expérimentés (LDOCE 1978);
c) structure de base de données (Michiels/Noël 1984);

The (New) Collins Concise English Dictionary (1982) (Michiels/Noël 1984), structure de base de données;

The Canadian Dictionary (Wilton 1978), description de données lexicographiques bilingues (anglais/ français) par le biais de l'informatique.

Dictionnaires onomasiologiques:

La fiche DANTERM, la structure des données de la Dansk Termbank (Banque des termes Danoise);

Roget's Thesaurus of English Words and Phrases:
a) mode d'emploi (Roget 1974);
b) description formelle (Dixon 1983);

Thesaurus sur Rabelais, assisté par ordinateur (Dixon 1983).

L'étude révèle une très grande variation en ce qui concerne les détails donnés ainsi que la terminologie et la structure, même là où plusieurs descriptions sont données d'un seul produit, comme dans les cas de LDOCE et de Roget; ici les différences s'expliquent par les buts différents des descriptions. Nous avons surtout attaché de l'importance à la discussion des modèles de description informatiques, et nous constatons que, malgré leur diversité, ils ont ceci de commun: ils précisent dans un modèle unique le contenu du dictionnaire et la structure à donner à ce contenu.

Il faut avouer que les essais de généralisation de tels modèles en vue d'obtenir un format général pour l'échange de données lexicographiques (Sherman 1974, MATER 1980), ont échoués; il en est de même pour les versions ultérieures de MATER (1982, 1984, 1985), qui, dans l'ensemble, laissent à l'utilisateur de spécifier et de nommer lui-même ses catégories d'information.

Dans la présente étude, la description du contenu des dictionnaires est séparée de la description de leur structure. Pour la description du contenu nous avons élaboré une taxinomie qui s'adapte à la description de n'importe quel dictionnaire impliquant la langue danoise. De plus, c'est notre thèse que cette taxinomie sera assez générale pour répondre également aux exigences lexicographiques imposées par d'autres langues, au moins par les langues germaniques et romanes. Par contre, nous ne jugeons pas de la question de savoir s'il servira à aucun but pratique ou théorique de proposer une classification assez générale pour être appliquée à toute langue et à toute combinaison de langues.

Le 3ᵉ chapitre (pp. 29-51) présente, explique et exemplifie la taxinomie générale. Une taxinomie est un système hiérarchique de classification. La visée de cette taxinomie est de décrire l'univers lexicographique en désignant une seule étiquette type à chaque renseignement qu'on trouve dans les oeuvres lexicographiques. Les unités lexicales sur lesquelles portent ces renseignements seront définies comme "des unités de signification jusqu'au niveau de la phrase ainsi que les concepts auxquels celles-ci renvoient", et "oeuvre lexicographique" est à prendre au sens large du mot, renvoyant ainsi non seulement aux oeuvres sémasiologiques ou onomasiologiques, mais également aux collections de données lexicographiques à l'usage de systèmes informatiques.

Les outils descriptifs que nous présentons sont indépendants de la signification qu'on attache aux expressions "mot", "lexème", "terme", "unité lexicale". En effet, la signification précise de celles-ci peut varier d'une discipline à l'autre: elle dépend de l'emploi anticipé des données lexicographiques. Pour chaque oeuvre ou projet on choisit son point de départ: on sélectionne les unités dont on désire fournir des renseignements. Dans la lexicographie technique ou spécialisée, qui est étroitement liée à la théorie terminologique, on part normalement des notions pour les décrire ensuite à l'aide des mots et des expressions qui renvoient à ces notions. C'est là l'approche onomasiologique, qui caractérise également les dictionnaires non spécialisés portant sur les concepts. Par contre, dans toute autre lexicographie non spécialisée, ce sont les mots et les expressions qui constituent le point de départ de la description, de la signification, par exemple. C'est là l'approche sémasiologique. L'approche adoptée est donc caractéristique de l'oeuvre ou du projet dans son ensemble, et non pas de l'unité isolée d'information. Le même vaut pour les renseignements apportés sur le choix de langue(s) traitée(s) dans l'oeuvre, ainsi que pour les renseignements sur ses modes de présentation. Aussi la première division de la taxinomie s'établie-t-elle entre les types de renseignements spécifiques de l'oeuvre en question et les types de renseignements généraux.

<u>Les types de renseignements spécifiques</u> portant sur la langue, l'approche adoptée et le moyen d'expression caractérisent l'oeuvre dans son ensemble, la tradition ou la culture lexicographique dont elle fait partie, et par ce fait ses unités lexicales. Dans les dictionnaires imprimés traditionnels, l'approche sera ou bien onomasiologique ou bien sémasiologique; mais en stockant dans les systèmes informatiques, où les différents types de renseignements sont reliés dans une structure multidimensionelle, on pourra adopter plusieurs approches pour les mêmes données. Le moyen d'expression pourra être la parole, l'écriture, l'image, ou n'importe quelle combinaison.

<u>Les types de renseignements généraux</u> servent à caractériser chaque unité d'information particulière de l'oeuvre. Ils comprennent une gamme de catégories de renseignements définies et cernées de manière indépendante. Ainsi, pour chaque renseignement lexical, il est possible de déterminer son appartenance à une catégorie de manière univoque. Les catégories sont au centre de cette partie de la taxinomie. Afin de faciliter la vue d'ensemble, nous nous sommes fondés sur leurs traits saillants pour les rassembler dans des groupes principaux qui correspondent aux différentes disciplines linguistiques: l'étymologie, la grammaire, l'orthographie, la phonétique, la pragmatique, la sémantique.

Les catégories sont caractérisées et illustrées à l'aide d'exemples tirés d'une diversité d'oeuvres lexicographiques. Les catégories particulières sont assez larges, et susceptibles de subdivisions. La nature de la division, ainsi que la quantité de détails donnés, dépendent de la spécialisation en types distincts des renseignements qui a été effectuée dans l'oeuvre particulière; toutefois, on exige que la subdivision aboutisse à des catégories indépendantes. Dans le tableau synoptique présenté ci-dessous, nous avons opéré une division en sous-catégories qui suffira pour la grande majorité de dictionnaires, mais qui n'est pas à considérer comme exhaustive:

<u>Groupes principaux</u>	<u>Catégories</u>	<u>Sous-catégories</u>
Renseignements étymologiques	- parallèle(s)	
	- origine	
Renseignements graphiques	- orthographie	
	- symbole graphique	
Renseignements de grammaire	- classe de mot	
	- flexion	* paradigme(s) * forme de la flexion
	- formation des mots	
	- renseignements syntaxiques	* valence * fonction syntaxique
Renseignements phonétiques	- traits prosodiques	
	- traits segmentaux	

Groupes principaux	Catégories	Sous-catégories
Renseignements pragmatiques	- renseignements textuels	* citation * contexte possible
	- utilisation	* dimension temporelle * d. spatiale * d. sociale * fréquence
	- référence externe	* référence bibliographique * indication des sources
	- renseignements d'évaluation	
	- renseignements administratifs	* renseignements sur la collection et le remaniement des données * référence interne * numéro d'homographe * renseignements techniques
Renseignements sémantiques	- classification selon le sujet	
	- relations sémantiques	* relation générique d'hypéronomie et d'hyponomie * rel. partitive * rel. de succession * rel. causale * antonymie
	- renseignements détaillant le contenu	* paraphrase lexicale * définition analytique * df. synthétique * df. dénotative * df. ostensive
	- renseignements sur les équivalences	* équivalence dans une seule langue * équivalence entre deux ou plusieurs langues

Dans le 4ᵉ chapitre (pp. 52-117) nous expliquons et explicitons la taxinomie en l'appliquant à diverses oeuvres lexicographiques et dans des buts différents. Il faut qu'il soit possible de faire un diagnostique qui amène chaque type de renseignement contenu dans une oeuvre à un seul endroit de la taxinomie. Ce travail est entravé par le fait que la pratique traditionnelle du lexicographe est de condenser les renseignements autant que possible, et il s'avère souvent qu'une abréviation ou une citation, par exemple, fournit plusieurs renseignements différents. Mentionnons à titre d'exemple l'abréviation fréquente <u>vt</u>: 'verbum transitivum', qui renseigne à la fois sur la classe de mots et sur les possibilités syntaxiques. Qui plus est, beaucoup de renseignements sont donnés uniquement d'une manière implicite: ainsi la flexion régulière est indiquée par l'absence de renseignements sur la flexion. Lorsqu'on désire faire une description univoque des renseignements contenus dans un dictionnaire à l'usage d'un système informatique, il est nécessaire d'étaler les renseignements condensés et d'expliciter ceux qui sont implicites. C'est une nécessité si les renseignements sont censés être utilisés dans un système informatique; mais c'est également utile si l'on désire avoir une image nette du contenu d'un dictionnaire et des conditions que celui-ci impose à ses utilisateurs.

L'application de la taxinomie au développement du format d'un dictionnaire nouveau est l'idée essentielle sous-jacente au dépouillement du Gammeldansk Ordbog (GLDO; Dictionnaire du vieux Danois). C'est un projet lexicographique scientifique qui vise à donner une description linguistique de la langue danoise de la période 1100-1515; en même temps, il sera à la base de la mise au point d'un manuel philologique qui pourra servir à l'étude des textes datant de cette époque. Nous décrivons le développement du format comme un procédé itératif, lors duquel on confronte un format préliminaire avec la taxinomie, pour réviser celui-là en se rapportant à celle-ci; on poursuivit ce procédé jusqu'à ce que toutes les catégories et toutes les sous-catégories répondent aux contraintes spécifiques de la rédaction, par exemple les contraintes concernant le traitement des renseignements par les méthodes informatiques. Quant aux <u>renseignements textuels</u>, la division en sous-catégories sera beaucoup plus détaillée que celle de la taxinomie, alors que pour d'autres renseignements, tels ceux qui portent sur <u>l'utilisation</u>, la division sera moins détaillée.

Pour analyser un dictionnaire déjà existant, nous examinons Vinterberg & Bodelsen: Dansk-engelsk Ordbog 1-2, un dictionnaire danois-anglais, non-spécialisé et imprimé qui est destiné au travail de traduction. Notre objectif est double: d'une part la taxinomie constitue le <u>tertium comparationis</u> qui nous permet de comparer ce dictionnaire avec d'autres dictionnaires, d'autre part l'analyse prépare le traitement par les méthodes informatiques lors des révisions ultérieures du livre (cf. chapitre 5). Cette analyse fait notamment ressortir que beaucoup de renseignements importants ne figurent qu'entremêlés à d'autres renseignements, présentés de manière implicite ou même par un "marquage zero", c'est-à-dire par l'omission d'un tel type d'information. Ce fait n'aura pas seulement des conséquences pour le traitement informatique, dans bien des cas, il pourra aussi induire en erreur les utilisateurs du dictionnaire. Une explicitation réelle de l'oeuvre réclame d'importantes connaissances préalables, y compris des connaissances qu'on ne trouve pas dans l'introduction du dictionnaire. Cela n'est nullement une particularité du dictionnaire en question, et l'analyse taxinomique fait nettement ressortir combien le mode d'expression que l'on trouve dans les dictionnaires imprimés est parfois dense et exigeant. Notre analyse prépare les voies, non seulement au traitement informatique des renseignements lexicographiques, mais aussi à l'élaboration de dictionnaires dont la structure sera plus claire.

Notre troisième et dernier exemple, l'analyse de la DANTERM (Banque des termes Danoise), est censée montrer que la taxinomie s'adapte aussi à un outil détaillé et bien documenté, pour la description de la langue spécialisée. La fiche électronique DANTERM (voir aussi chapitre 2) est le format utilisé pour l'élaboration et l'enregistrement des données dans la banque des termes. Son contenu et sa structure reflètent à la fois la méthode de travail terminologique et les utilisations qu'on a anticipées de la banque des termes. Bien que la fiche électronique DANTERM ne se fonde donc pas sur la taxinomie, il s'avère que sa division en plages de saisie y correspond en substance. Comme c'est le cas du Gammeldansk Ordbog, le format DANTERM est beaucoup plus détaillé, sur certains points, que la division de la taxinomie faite au niveau des catégories: il s'agit notamment des <u>renseignements sémantiques</u> ou <u>pragmatiques</u>. Or, au niveau des sous-catégories, la correspondance est bonne, et nous concluons que l'échange automatique de renseignements est possible dans la mesure où la division en plages se conforme aux sous-catégories de la taxinomie.

Le 5• chapitre (pp. 118-160) introduit les outils destinés à la description de la structure des dictionnaires: leur format. Sont présentés trois formalismes empruntés à la theorie des langages formels dits indépendants du contexte: la notation Backus-Naur (BNF), la notation ETTO et les diagrammes-accolade de Warnier/Orr.

La notation ETTO exprime l'enchaînement hiérarchique des catégories terminales et les possibilités d'éliminer ou répéter celles-ci. Dans la notation ETTO, on utilise ( ) pour désigner une catégorie ou une structure facultative, [ ]⁺ pour désigner l'itération d'une catégorie ou d'une structure obligatoire et [ ]• pour désigner l'itération d'une catégorie ou d'une structure facultative.

Les diagrammes Warnier/Orr utilisent l'accolade { pour l'enchaînement des structures. On a réuni l'itérativité et la facultativité en indiquant pour chaque catégorie une paire de nombres (x,y), qui indique le nombre d'apparitions minimum (x) et le nombre d'apparitions maximum (y) de la catégorie. La facultativité sera donc désignée par (0,1), la catégorie obligatoire avec itération par (1,n). Dans cette notation, il est aussi possible d'indiquer un nombre constant d'apparitions, cinq par exemple; cela se note par (5). De plus, le diagramme-accolade permet l'enregistrement de la sélection exclusive: dans le cas des structures séparées par ⊕, une seule d'entre elles est à choisir.

Dans ce chapitre nous développons la description du dictionnaire danois-anglais (déjà abordée dans le 4• chapitre): un enregistrement minutieux de la structure des articles est ajouté. Nous comparons les formalismes mentionnés en les appliquant tous à la même fraction du dictionnaire. La description structurale se fonde sur des caractéristiques formellement registrables, comme par exemple changements de type de caractères et de l'interponction. Les catégories ainsi établies sont contrastées aux catégories de la taxinomie. Il apparaît que le mot d'entrée même est une unité très complexe: beaucoup de mots d'entrée sont présentés dans une forme qui donne en même temps des renseignements provenant de trois ou quatre catégories de la taxinomie. A l'usage du traitement informatique, ces renseignements doivent rester séparés. Les autres catégories terminales peuvent être ramenées, de manière univoque, aux catégories de la taxinomie. Cependant, une seule catégorie de la description structurale pourra renfermer des renseignements si variés qu'il serait peu convenable d'en catégoriser les contenus particuliers par rapport à la taxinomie.

Sur la base d'une description minutieuse du format à l'aide d'une notation formelle, il est possible de faire une 'parsing' (analyse grammaticale et automatique) des articles d'un dictionnaire. On peut garder les résultats d'un tel enregistrement de la structure en introduisant, dans les articles du dictionnaire, un marquage conforme au Standard Generalized Markup Language (SGML). Cette norme (ISO 8879) est expliquée et illustrée par un article de dictionnaire marqué conformément au SGML.

La structure du dictionnaire danois-français de Blinkenberg et Høybye a été enregistrée et les articles stockés dans une base de données, en vue de révision et de réédition. Ce dictionnaire permet un ordre différent des mêmes types de renseignements et donne des renseignements identiques de plusieurs manières différentes. Cela se reflète dans la description diagrammes-accolade, qui montre beaucoup de niveaux et fournit une quantité de choix par sélection exclusive. La description formelle a créé la base d'une analyse structurale automatique des articles. Comme résultat de cette analyse, on aura les différents types d'informations du dictionnaire, reconnaissables de manière formelle et marqués des noms de plages de saisie utilisés par le système de base de données DANSTATUS, une version danoise de STATUS II. La plupart des catégories établies par cette analyse se ramènent de manière univoque à des catégories de la taxinomie.

Dans le 6ᵉ chapitre (pp. 161-230), nous présentons des formats de deux dictionnaires danois: Supplement til Ordbog over det Danske Sprog (Supplément au Dictionnaire de la Langue Danoise), dont le format doit s'adapter parfaitement à un dictionnaire déjà imprimé, et Gammeldansk Ordbog (Dictionnaire du Vieux Danois), dont le format a été élaboré dans le but de profiter pleinement de la technologie informatique. Les formats sont décrits dans le formalisme ETTO et élaborés à partir d'une analyse minutieuse du contenu des dictionnaires, de son côté fondée sur la taxinomie. L'emploi des formats est présenté dans le système informatique d'édition lexicographique Compulexis, et nous montrons, à l'aide d'exemples détaillés, comment les dictionnaires peuvent profiter de l'enregistrement structuré offert par ce système. Les nombreux exemples munis de commentaires facilitent le travail du lexicographe qui est sans expérience dans l'informatique; celui-ci pourra se faire une idée de l'utilisation d'un système d'édition lexicographique et de l'avantage apporté par un tel système, qui permet le contrôle des renseignements définis préalablement, par exemple les abréviations des indications des sources et les dénominations spécialisées. Nous donnons aussi des exemples des possibilités qu'a ce système d'exécuter le traitement de textes. Ainsi il est possible d'imprimer les articles enregistrés, sur l'écran comme sur papier, où ils seront présentés ou bien sous la forme d'un article de dictionnaire ou bien en tableau. Les procédures de recherche permettent l'impression de parties sélectionnées des articles, par exemple tous les mots d'entrée et les citations à l'appui. Nous concluons qu'un tel système d'édition lexicographique s'applique parfaitement à la rédaction des dictionnaires dont le format a été définitivement établi.

Dans le 7ᵉ chapitre (pp. 231-252), la notion 'bases de données lexicographiques' est mise en relation avec les outils descriptifs proposés dans cet ouvrage. La structure d'une base relationnelle de données est souvent mise en évidence par un diagramme-entités/relations. Nous esquissons, pour le Gammeldansk Ordbog, la construction d'un tel diagramme, établi sur la base d'un diagramme-accolade, qui, lui, est l'explicitation de notre description du format, notation ETTO, déjà faite dans les chapitres 4 et 6. Le regroupement de sous-catégories de la taxinomie nous permet de suggérer des entités. Le classement en sous-catégories se reflète donc dans les relations mutuelles des entités.

L'étude se termine par une liste exhaustive, munie d'exemples, des conditions que le lexicographe doit imposer au logiciel destiné au traitement des données lexicographiques.

DEUTSCHE ZUSAMMENFASSUNG

Im ersten Kapitel (S. 1-3) wird dargelegt, welche neuen Möglichkeiten der Einsatz von Computern in der Wörterbucharbeit der lexikographischen Zusammenarbeit eröffnet hat - z.B der Datenaustausch zwischen Wörterbuchprojekten, zwischen Wörterbuchredaktionen und Verlagen und zwischen Wörterbuchherstellern und -benutzern. Es ist der Wunsch der Verfasser dieses Buchs, die der fächerübergreifenden und interinstitutionellen DANLEX-Gruppe angehören, diese Möglichkeiten zu verbessern. Die dargelegten generellen Beschreibungsinstrumente können zur Entwicklung eines flexiblen, generellen EDV-Systems für die lexikographische Arbeit beitragen.

Eine Voraussetzung für den maschinellen Austausch von Wörterbuchdaten ist ihre einheitliche Beschreibung. Dies erfordert ein Klassifikationssystem, eine Typologie, die die Einordnung aller Arten von Wörterbuchinformationen gestattet; ferner sind Methoden zur formalen Beschreibung der Struktur des jeweiligen lexikalischen Werkes erforderlich.

Eine Vielzahl von Autoren vor uns hat Wörterbücher im Hinblick auf die elektronische Datenverarbeitung beschrieben und klassifiziert. Die vorliegende Arbeit geht jedoch einen Schritt weiter und ist dementsprechend breiter und tiefschürfender angelegt. Wir generalisieren die Kategorien, so dass eine Taxonomie entsteht, die viele, sehr unterschiedliche Wörterbuchtypen abdeckt und wir erproben die Taxonomie als Beschreibungsinstrument an höchst unterschiedlichen Wörterbuchtypen. Desweiteren behandeln wir Methoden zur Beschreibung des Formats eines Wörterbuches, d.h. das Format zur Beschreibung ist der formale Teil der Wörterbuchredaktionsregeln dargestellt als eine strukturierte Teilmenge der Kategorien der Taxonomie. Solche Beschreibungen können u.a. bei der Umsetzung gedruckter Wörterbücher in Datenbankstrukturen und umgekehrt Anwendung finden. Schliesslich zeigen wir in zwei Kapiteln auf, wie beschriebene und strukturierte Wörterbuchdaten durch den Computer registriert und gespeichert werden können; ferner wird zu den Forderungen, die an die Software der Wörterbuchdatenverarbeitung gestellt werden müssen, kritisch Stellung genommen.

Das zweite Kapitel (S. 4-28) handelt von den metalexikographischen Beschreibungsinstrumenten. Die Metalexikographie (die Theorie und Methodik der Lexikographie) hat terminologische Schwächen. Für die Bezeichnung eines Begriffs werden in der Literatur verschiedene Termini benutzt und ein Terminus wird von verschiedenen Verfassern für Begriffe verwendet, die nicht oder nur teilweise äquivalent sind. Eine der Ursachen hierfür ist, dass die Lexikographie ihre Begriffe und Termini aus der ständig steigenden Anzahl linguistischer Schulen und Disziplinen, u.a. der datenlinguistischen, entlehnt.

Die lexikographische Literatur enthält viele Beispiele für die Klassifikation und Beschreibung von Wörterbuchdaten. In den folgenden Ausführungen wird eine Auswahl solcher Beschreibungen behandelt und verglichen. Bei der Auswahl der Beispiele wurde darauf Wert gelegt, dass sie einerseits illustrieren, wie verschieden solche Beschreibungen ausfallen und andererseits sollen sie die Grundlage für die Erörterung der Ursachen dieser Verschiedenartigkeit bilden.

Semasiologische Wörterbücher:

BONNLEX/MDW (Brustkern/Hess 1982; Hess/Brustkern/Lenders 1983), eine Datenbankstruktur, die mehrere unterschiedliche deutsche, einsprachige, synchronische, maschinenlesbare Wörterbücher/Wortsammlungen zusammenfasst;

Schaeders (1981) Vorschlag zur lexikalischen Mikrostruktur gedacht für die computerunterstützte Ausarbeitung eines einsprachigen, synchronischen, zugleich aber auch sprachgeschichtlich informierenden Wörterbuchs;

The Longman Dictionary of Contemporary English (LDOCE):

a) eine zwanglos beschreibende und detaillierte Anleitung für unerfahrene Wörterbuchbenutzer (LDOCE 1978);
b) eine prägnante und kurzgefasste Anleitung für erfahrene Benutzer (LDOCE 1978);
c) Datenbankstruktur (Michiels/Noël 1984);

The (New) Collins Concise English Dictionary (1982) (Michiels/ Noël 1984), Datenbankstruktur;

The Canadian Dictionary (Wilton 1978); computerorientierte Beschreibung zweisprachiger Wörterbuchdaten (Englisch/Französisch).

Onomasiologische Wörterbücher:

Der DANTERM-Eintrag, die Datenstruktur der "Dansk Termbank";

Roget's Thesaurus of English Words and Phrases:
a) Benutzeranleitung (Roget 1974);
b) formale Beschreibung (Dixon 1983);

Computerunterstützter Rabelaisthesaurus (Dixon 1983).

Die Behandlung lässt grosse Unterschiede sowohl im Detaillierungsgrad als auch in der Terminologie und Struktur sichtbar werden, selbst wo mehrere Beschreibungen wie im Falle von LDOCE und Roget sich auf dasselbe Werk beziehen; in diesen Fällen sind die Unterschiede u.a. auf die unterschiedlichen Zielsetzungen der Beschreibungen zurückzuführen. Der Schwerpunkt wurde auf die Erörterung der computerorientierten Beschreibungsmodelle gelegt und es wird festgestellt, dass diese trotz ihrer Verschiedenartigkeit eines gemeinsam haben: sie legen in ein - und demselben Modell zum einen fest, was das Wörterbuch enthalten, und zum anderen wie dieser Inhalt strukturiert werden soll.

Versuche, solche Modelle zu einem allgemeinen Austauschformat für Wörterbuchdaten zu generalisieren (Sherman 1974; MATER 1980) müssen als gescheitert betrachtet werden, gleiches gilt auch für die späteren MATER-Versionen (1982, 1984, 1985), die es im grossen ganzen dem Benutzer überlassen, seine Informationskategorien selber zu spezifizieren und zu benennen.

Im vorliegenden Buch wird die Beschreibung des Inhaltes der Wörterbücher von der ihrer Struktur getrennt. Für die Inhaltsbeschreibung ist eine Taxonomie entwickelt worden, die alle Arten von Wörterbüchern mit dänischen Einträgen hinreichend beschreibt. Wir stellen ferner die Behauptung auf, dass sie hinreichend generell ist, um zumindest den lexikographischen Ansprüchen der übrigen germanischen und der romanischen Sprachen zu genügen. Wir nehmen jedoch nicht zu der Frage Stellung, ob es praktisch oder theoretisch sinnvoll ist, den Versuch der Festlegung einer Klassifikation zu unternehmen, die so generell ist, dass sie jeder Sprache und jeder Sprachkombination genügt.

Im dritten Kapitel (S. 29-51) wird die generelle Taxonomie vorgelegt, begründet und exemplifiziert. Eine Taxonomie ist ein hierarchisches Klassifikationssystem. Der Zweck der lexikographischen Taxonomie ist die Beschreibung des lexikographischen Universums, in dem jeder einzelnen Informationseinheit in lexikographischen Werken eine und nur eben diese eine Typenbezeichnung zugeordnet wird.

Die Einheiten, zu denen in lexikographischen Werken Informationen gegeben werden, definieren wir als "bedeutungstragende Einheiten bis hinauf zur Satzebene, sowie die Bedeutungen, die diese Einheiten repräsentieren"; lexikographische Werke sind im weitesten Sinne aufzufassen; sie umfassen also nicht nur semasiologisch und onomasiologisch geordnete Werke, sondern auch z.B. lexikographische Datensammlungen für informationstechnologische Systeme.

Das von uns vorgelegte Beschreibungsinstrument ist unabhängig von der Definition von "Wort", "Lexem", "Benennung" oder "lexikalische Einheit". Die genaue Bedeutung dieser Bezeichnungen kann nämlich von Disziplin zu Disziplin schwanken und damit von der Absicht abhängen, die man mit dem lexikographischen Material verfolgt. Für jedes einzelne Werk oder Projekt ist der Ausgangspunkt zu bestimmen, d.h. man legt fest, zu welchen Einheiten Informationen gegeben werden sollen. In der fachsprachlichen Lexikographie, die eng an die Terminologielehre gebunden ist, wird normalerweise von den Begriffen ausgegangen und man beschreibt sie durch die sie bezeichnenden Wörter und Ausdrücke. Dieser onomasiologische Ansatz kennzeichnet auch die gemeinsprachlichen Begriffswörterbücher. In der übrigen gemeinsprachlichen Lexikographie sind dagegen die Wörter und Ausdrücke der Ausgangspunkt für die Beschreibung von u.a. der Bedeutung: mit anderen Worten, es liegt ein semasiologischer Ansatz vor. Er ist charakteristisch für ein Werk oder Projekt als Gesamtheit, nicht aber für die einzelne Informationseinheit. Gleiches gilt für die Angaben darüber, welche Sprache(n) im Werk behandelt werden und für die Angaben über die Darstellungsformen des Werkes. Die höchste Einteilungsebene der Taxonomie zerfällt daher in werkspezifische und generelle Informationstypen.

Die werkspezifischen Informationstypen, Sprache, Blickwinkel und Ausdrucksmedium, charakterisieren das Werk als Ganzes, die lexikographische Tradition oder Kultur, von der es ein Teil ist, und damit auch seine lexikalischen Einheiten. Der Blickwinkel der traditionellen, gedruckten Wörterbücher ist entweder onomasiologisch oder semasiologisch; bei der Speicherung in Computersystemen aber, wo die verschiedenen Informationstypen zu einer mehrdimensionalen Struktur verkettet werden, ist es möglich, dasselbe Material aus mehreren Blickwinkeln zu betrachten. Das Ausdrucksmedium kann gesprochene Sprache, Schrift, Bild oder eine Kombination sein.

Die generellen Informationstypen werden zur Charakterisierung jeder einzelnen Informationseinheit des Werks gebraucht. Sie umfassen eine Reihe von Informationskategorien, die unabhängig von einander definiert und bestimmt werden. Jede einzelne lexikalische Information kann daher genau einer Kategorie zugeordnet werden. Die Kategorien sind das zentrale Element in diesem Teil der Taxonomie. Des besseren Überblicks wegen sind sie nach ihren dominierendsten Merkmalen in Hauptgruppen zusammengefasst, die den verschiedenen sprachwissenschaftlichen Disziplinen entsprechen: Etymologie, Grammatik, Orthographie, Phonetik, Pragmatik und Semantik.

Die Kategorien werden näher bestimmt und durch Beispiele aus vielen verschiedenen lexikographischen Werken illustriert. Die einzelnen Kategorien sind recht umfassend und lassen sich unterteilen. Die Art und der Feinheitsgrad der Einteilung werden davon abhängen, auf welche besonderen Informationstypen in einem

Werk Gewicht gelegt werden soll, jedoch müssen sich aus der Unterteilung unabhängige Kategorien ergeben. In der nachstehenden Ubersicht ist eine Einteilung in Subkategorien vorgenommen worden, die für die allermeisten Wörterbücher ausreichen wird, die aber nicht als erschöpfend anzusehen ist:

Hauptgruppen	Kategorien	Subkategorien
etymologische Angaben	- Parallele	
	- Herkunft	
grammatische Angaben	- Wortklasse	
	- Flexion	. Paradigma . Flexionsform
	- Wortbildung	
	- syntaktische Informationen	. Valenz . syntaktische Funktion
graphische Angaben	- orthographische Angaben	
	- graphisches Symbol	
phonetische Angaben	- prosodische Merkmale	
	- segmentale Merkmale	
pragmatische Angaben	- textuelle Angaben	. Zitat/Beleg . denkbarer Kontext
	- Anwendung	. zeitliche Dimension . räumliche Dimension . soziale Dimension . Frequenz
	- externer Verweis	. Literaturhinweis . Quellenhinweis

	- wertende Angaben	
	- administrative Angaben	. Angaben zur Sammlung und Verarbeitung der Daten . interner Verweis . Homographnummer . technische Informationen
semantische Angaben	- Angaben zum Fachgebiet	
	- Angaben zu semantischen Beziehungen	. generische Über-/ Unterordnung . partitive Beziehung . zeitliche Abfolge . Kausalbeziehung . Antonymie
	- inhaltsspezifizierende Angaben	. lexikalische Paraphrase . analytische Definition . synthetische Definition . denotative Definition . ostentative Definition
	- Angaben zur Äquivalenz	. Äquivalenzbeziehung innerhalb einer Sprache . Äquivalenzbeziehung zwischen zwei oder mehr Sprachen

Im vierten Kapitel (S. 52-117) wird die Taxonomie anhand ihrer Anwendung auf verschiedene lexikographische Werke und mit unterschiedlicher Zielsetzung eingehender erläutert. Es sollte nun möglich sein, alle Informationstypen eines Werkes an nur einer Stelle der Taxonomie einzuordnen. An diesem Punkt wird man auf das Problem stossen, dass die lexikographische Praxis und Tradition bestrebt war, Informationen weitgehend zu verdichten; es zeigt sich dabei häufig, dass z.B. eine Abkürzung oder ein Beleg mehrere verschiedene Informationen enthält, die zu verschiedenen Kategorien gehören. Ein Beispiel ist die oft verwendete Abkürzung vt "verbum transitivum", die sowohl Aussagen zur Wortklasse (v) als auch zu den syntaktischen Möglichkeiten (t) beinhaltet. Darüberhinaus werden viele Angaben nur implizit gemacht, z.B. wird die regelmässige Flexion durch das Fehlen der Angabe gekennzeichnet.

Will man eine eindeutige Beschreibung der Wörterbuchinformationen für ein Computersystem vornehmen, so ist es erforderlich, die Informationsdichte aufzulockern und die impliziten Angaben zu explizieren. Sollen die Informationen in einem Computersystem verwendet werden, so ist dies unumgänglich; es erweist sich aber auch als nützlich, wenn man sich ein klares Bild vom Inhalt eines Wörterbuches verschaffen will und welche Ansprüche es an seine Benutzer stellt.

Die Anwendung der Taxonomie zur Festlegung eines Formats für ein neues Wörterbuch ist der Hauptgesichtspunkt bei der Behandlung des "Gammeldansk Ordbog" (GLDO). Das GLDO ist ein wissenschaftliches Wörterbuchprojekt, das einerseits eine linguistische Beschreibung der dänischen Sprache zwischen etwa 1100 und 1515 geben und andererseits die Grundlage für ein philologisches Handbuch für das Lesen der Texte aus dieser Periode bilden soll. Die Formatfestlegung wird als iterativer Prozess beschrieben, wo ein vorläufiges Format der Taxonomie gegenübergestellt und so oft revidiert wird, bis alle Kategorien und Subkategorien eindeutig sind und die Subkategorien ausserdem die spezifischen Forderungen der Redaktion an u.a. die elektronische Verarbeitung der Daten erfüllen. Die Unterteilung in Subkategorien ist z.B. bei den textuellen Angaben weitaus feiner als die in der Taxonomie angebotene, in anderen Fällen, u.a. bei den Anwendungsangaben, gröber.

Die Analyse eines existierenden Wörterbuchs ist der Gegenstand der Behandlung des "Dansk-engelsk Ordbog 1-2" von Vinterberg/Bodelsen, eines recht umfangreichen gedruckten, gemeinsprachlichen, dänisch-englischen Übersetzungswörterbuchs. Die Analyse hat eine doppelte Zielsetzung: zum einen ist die Taxonomie das Tertium comparationis, das den Vergleich dieses Wörterbuchs mit anderen ermöglicht, zum anderen ist die Analyse eine Vorbereitung für die Verwendung der EDV bei kommenden Überarbeitungen des Wörterbuchs (vgl. Kapitel 5). Die Analyse ergibt u.a., dass viele wichtige Informationen nur mit anderen vermischt, implizit oder gar durch 'Nullmarkierung', d.h. dass ein Informationstyp nicht angegeben ist, angeführt sind. Dieses wird nicht nur für die elektronische Datenverarbeitung Konsequenzen haben, sondern kann auch in vielen Fällen die Benutzer des Wörterbuchs irreleiten. Viele Vorkenntnisse, auch Kenntnisse, die in den Hinweisen für die Benutzung des Wörterbuchs nicht vermittelt werden, sind für das optimale Benutzungsergebnis erforderlich. Das ist nicht nur für dieses Wörterbuch kennzeichnend; die taxonomische Analyse lässt deutlich erkennen, wie komprimiert die Darstellungsform gedruckter Wörterbücher sein kann und welche hohen Anforderungen an den Benutzer gestellt werden. Die Analyse ebnet nicht nur den Weg für die elektronische Wörterbuchdatenverarbeitung, sondern auch für übersichtlichere Wörterbücher.

Das dritte und letzte Beispiel, DANTERM, die "Dansk Termbank", soll zeigen, dass die Taxonomie auch einen gutbeschriebenen und feinmaschigen fachsprachlichen Beschreibungsapparat abdeckt. Der DANTERM-Eintrag (bereits im zweiten Kapitel behandelt) ist das Format, das bei der Datenbearbeitung und -eingabe in die Terminologiebank verwendet wird; sein Inhalt und seine Struktur spiegeln teils die terminologische Arbeitsmethode, teils die vorgesehene Verwendung der Terminologiebank wider. Obwohl der DANTERM-Eintrag nicht die Taxonomie zur Grundlage hat, stellt es sich heraus, dass seine Datenelemente im wesentlichen mit der Taxonomie übereinstimmen. Wie das "Gammeldansk Ordbog"-Format ist das DANTERM-Format in gewissen Punkten weit feiner als die Unterteilung der Taxonomie auf der Kategorienebene; es handelt sich hier besonders um die semantischen und die pragmatischen Informationen. Auf der Subkategorienebene jedoch besteht gute

Übereinstimmung, und es wird zusammenfassend festgestellt, dass der automatische Austausch von Informationen mit anderen Terminologiebanken, deren Datenelementeinteilung den Subkategorien der Taxonomie entspricht, möglich ist.

Im fünften Kapitel (S. 118-160) werden die Beschreibungsinstrumente für die Struktur von Wörterbüchern, ihr Format, beschrieben. Drei verschiedene kontextfreie Formalismen werden behandelt: die Backus-Naur-Notation (BNF), die ETTO-Notation und Warnier-Orrs Klammerdiagramme.

Die BNF-Notation ist von der Beschreibung von Programmiersprachen bekannt. Die ETTO-Notation erlaubt die hierarchische Verkettung terminaler Kategorien und die Möglichkeiten, diese Kategorien wegzulassen oder zu wiederholen. In der ETTO-Notation bezeichnet () die Wahlfreiheit einer Kategorie oder Struktur, $[\,]^{+}$ bezeichnet die Wiederholbarkeit einer obligatorischen Kategorie oder Struktur und $[\,]^{*}$ bezeichnet die Wiederholbarkeit einer fakultativen Kategorie oder Struktur.

Warnier-Orrs Klammerdiagramme verwenden die Mengenparenthese $\{$ für die Verkettung von Strukturen. Wiederholbarkeit und Wahlfreiheit sind vereint, da für jede Kategorie durch ein Zahlenpaar (x,y) die Untergrenze x und die Obergrenze y die Häufigkeit ihres Auftretens angegeben wird. Wahlfreiheit wird mit (0,1) und obligatorische Kategorie mit Wiederholbarkeit wird mit (1,n) bezeichnet. In dieser Notation kann zum Ausdruck gebracht werden, dass eine Angabe eine bestimmte Anzahl Male, z.B. fünfmal, vorkommen soll; das wird als (5) notiert. Ausserdem ermöglicht der Klammerdiagrammformalismus das Registrieren von exklusiver Selektion: bei Strukturen, die mit $\oplus$ getrennt werden, muss genau eine von diesen gewählt werden.

In diesem Kapitel wird auch die in Kapitel 4 begonnene Beschreibung des "Dansk-engelsk Ordbog" durch eine minuziöse Registrierung der Artikelstruktur vertieft. Die oben erwähnten Formalismen werden kontrastiv behandelt, indem derselbe Ausschnitt aus dem "Dansk-engelsk Ordbog" durch alle drei beschrieben wird. Die Strukturbeschreibung gründet sich auf formal feststellbare

Merkmale wie Schrifttypen- und Interpunktionswechsel. Die Kategorien, die sich bei der Strukturregistrierung als zweckmässig erwiesen haben, werden mit den Kategorien der Taxonomie verglichen. Es stellt sich heraus, dass der Eingang eine sehr komplexe Grösse ist: viele Eingänge sind in einer Form angegeben, die gleichzeitig Informationen aus 3 - 4 Taxonomiekategorien enthält. Für die elektronische Datenverarbeitung sind diese Informationen zu trennen. Die übrigen terminalen Kategorien können den Kategorien der Taxonomie eindeutig zugeordnet werden; nur eine einzige Kategorie der Strukturbeschreibung kann so variierende Informationen enthalten, dass es unzweckmässig ist, ihre einzelnen Inhalte in Relation zur Taxonomie zu typisieren.

Auf der Grundlage einer sorgfältigen Formatbeschreibung in einer formalen Notation lässt sich ein Parsing der Artikel eines Wörterbuchs durchführen. Das Ergebnis einer solchen Strukturregistrierung kann durch die Einführung einer Strukturmarkierung in den Wörterbuchartikeln gemäss der "Standard Generalized Markup Language" (SGML) bewahrt werden. Diese Norm (ISO 8879) wird durch einen mit Strukturmarkierungen gemäss SGML versehenen Wörterbuchartikel erläutert und illustriert.

Im Hinblick auf eine Überarbeitung und die Herausgabe einer überarbeiteten Ausgabe ist die Struktur des "Dansk-fransk Ordbog" von Blinkenberg/Høybye registriert worden und die Artikel sind in einer Datenbank gespeichert. Dieses Wörterbuch lässt unterschiedliche Reihenfolgen derselben Informationstypen zu und enthält dieselben Informationen mehrfach in unterschiedlicher Form. Dieses wird in der Klammerdiagrammbeschreibung, die viele Ebenen ergibt und die viele durch exklusive Selektion verbundene Wahlmöglichkeiten hat, offenbar. Die formale Beschreibung ist die Grundlage für die automatische Strukturanalyse der Artikel. Das Ergebnis dieser Analyse ist die mit Datenelementbezeichnungen für die Speicherung im Datenbanksystem DANSTATUS versehenen formal erkennbaren Informationstypen des Wörterbuchs; DANSTATUS ist eine dänische Version von STATUS II. Die meisten der sich aus der Analyse ergebenden Kategorien können eindeutig Kategorien der Taxonomie zugeordnet werden.

Im sechsten Kapitel (S. 161-230) werden die Formate von zwei dänischen Wörterbüchern dargestellt; es handelt sich um das "Supplement til Ordbog over det Danske Sprog", dessen Format mit einem schon gedruckten Wörterbuch völlig übereinstimmen muss, und das "Gammeldansk Ordbog", dessen Format mit dem Ziel entwickelt wurde, die Möglichkeiten der Informationstechnologie voll auszuschöpfen. Die Formate sind im ETTO-Formalismus beschrieben und nach einer sorgfältigen Analyse des Inhalts der Wörterbücher unter Anwendung der Taxonomie erarbeitet. Die Anwendung der Formate wird im redaktionellen EDV-Wörterbuchsystem Compulexis gezeigt; ferner wird durch ausführliche Beispiele veranschaulicht, wie die strukturierte Dateneingabe, die das System anbietet, in Wörterbüchern genutzt werden kann. Die vielen erläuterten Beispiele der Darstellung erleichtern es den Lexikographen ohne Erfahrungen auf dem Gebiet der EDV-Systeme, sich ein Bild davon zu machen, wie ein redaktionelles Wörterbuchsystem verwendet wird und welche Hilfe in Form von Konsequenzkontrollen zu Informationen, die zu einem in sich geschlossenen Bezeichnungssystem wie z.B. Quellen- oder Fachsprachenabkürzungen gehören, zu erwarten ist. Es werden auch Beispiele für die hochentwickelten Textverarbeitungshilfsmittel des Systems angeführt. Es ist z.B. möglich, sowohl auf dem Bildschirm als auch durch den Drucker bereits registrierte Artikel ausgeben zu lassen, die entweder einem gedruckten Wörterbuchartikel gleichen oder in schematischer Form dargeboten sind. Die Suchmöglichkeiten lassen die Ausgabe ausgewählter Teile von Artikeln zu, z.B. aller Eingänge mit dazugehörigen Belegen. Es wird abschliessend festgestellt, dass sich ein redaktionelles Wörterbuchsystem wie das beschriebene für die Ausarbeitung von Wörterbüchern eignet, deren Format entgültig festgelegt worden ist.

Im siebten Kapitel (S. 231-252) wird der Begriff Wörterbuchdatenbanken auf die Beschreibungsinstrumente des Buchs bezogen. Es wird aufgezeigt, wie das ETTO-Notationsformat des "Gammeldansk Ordbog" durch eine Explizierung in der Form eines Klammerdiagramms als Ausgangspunkt für eine vorläufige Strukturierung der Daten des "Gammeldansk Ordbog" in einem Entitäts-Relationsdiagramm verwendet werden kann, das bei der Datenstrukturbeschreibung relationeller Datenbanksysteme Anwendung findet. Durch die Zusammenführung von Subkategorien aus der Taxonomie findet man Anwärter für die Entitäten. Die Subkategorisierung wird dann durch die Relationen der Entitäten zueinander widergespiegelt.

Das Buch schliesst mit einer ausführlichen, exemplifizierten Liste lexikographisch relevanter Forderungen die, an die Software für die elektronische Verarbeitung lexikographischer Daten zu stellen sind.

Bei Fragen zur Produktsicherheit wenden Sie sich bitte an:
If you have any questions regarding product safety,
please contact:

Walter de Gruyter GmbH
Genthiner Straße 13
10785 Berlin
productsafety@degruyterbrill.com